WHAT MAKES US TICK?

Other books by Hugh Mackay

Social Analysis

Reinventing Australia
Generations
Turning Point
Advance Australia . . . Where?

Communication

Why Don't People Listen?
(re-published as *The Good Listener*)

Media Mania

Ethics

Right & Wrong: How to decide for yourself

Novels

Little Lies

House Guest

The Spin

Winter Close

Ways of Escape

WHAT MAKES US TICK?

THE **TEN DESIRES** THAT DRIVE US

HUGH MACKAY

hachette
AUSTRALIA

Published in Australia and New Zealand in 2010
by Hachette Australia
(an imprint of Hachette Australia Pty Limited)
Level 17, 207 Kent Street, Sydney NSW 2000
www.hachette.com.au

10 9 8 7 6 5 4

National Library of Australia
Cataloguing-in-Publication data

Mackay, Hugh, 1938- .
What makes us tick? : The ten desires that drive us

978 0 7336 2507 7 (pbk.)

Includes index

Motivation (Psychology)–Popular works.

153.8

Cover and text design by Design by Committee
Typeset in 11.5/17 pt Electra LT Std by Bookhouse, Sydney
Author photograph by Lorrie Graham
Printed and bound in Australia by Griffin Press, Adelaide, an Accredited ISO AS/NZS 14001:2004
Environmental Management System printer

To Sheila

CONTENTS

'WHY DID I DO THAT?'

Homo sapiens? Perhaps we're wiser than our evolutionary forebears, but that doesn't mean we're always rational.

We say one thing and do another.

We do the very things we criticise other people for doing.

We often say we are propelled purely by self-interest, yet we perform acts of kindness for total strangers, sometimes putting our own safety at risk.

We pretend to have rational explanations for actions we know to have been reckless, impulsive or irresponsible. Even some of our apparently rational decisions – what job to do, whether to have children, where to live – often turn out to be more like accidents than considered conclusions.

We are often at a loss to explain, even to ourselves, why we've done things that seem on reflection to have been foolish or inappropriate.

We are driven by such powerful forces – ambition, sexual desire, jealousy, greed – that we sometimes do things we know will bring misery upon ourselves and others.

It's no wonder we are puzzled by our own behaviour. All of us are driven by an array of desires, passions, yearnings and needs that are difficult for us to reconcile, let alone control. We want many different things, sometimes all at once, which is why we so often seem like walking contradictions.

This constant interplay among our desires is the reason there is rarely a single explanation for the things we do. It's not as if we go to work to satisfy one desire, go out dancing to satisfy another, and renovate our kitchen or buy a car in response to other, quite separate desires. Our desires intersect and overlap with each other, often competing for our attention. In our personal relationships, for example, we may feel the contradictory tugs of the desire for love and the desire for control. We struggle to reconcile the desire for stability and certainty with the desire for something surprising or exciting to happen.

Think of these desires as being like the strands of a web: we can pull them apart to examine them – as we're about to do in this book – but in real life none of them exists in isolation; they are always part of the web. That's why the chapters of this book are not numbered. I want to avoid any suggestion of a hierarchy of desires, or a list presented in order of importance. (After 'The desire to be taken seriously', which I think *is* the most important, read the others in any order you wish.)

Our desires don't only interact and compete with each other; they also wax and wane. Who hasn't lain in bed, staring at the ceiling, wondering how yesterday's all-consuming passion could so suddenly have faded? Or felt embarrassed by the realisation that something we felt compelled to do, or to have, has brought us none of the satisfaction we had anticipated?

◆

What are these desires?

Some are abstract, ethereal yearnings for truth, beauty, justice or harmony – the ideals we glimpse when we are dreaming how life could be richer and more deeply satisfying, or how the world could be a better place. Some of us are driven by such passion for these ideals, our life's work is devoted to them: we become great humanitarians, leaders of social reform movements, architects, painters, composers or writers. Others of us satisfy these longings by listening to music that inspires us, visiting beautiful places, or perhaps engaging with great works of art and literature.

Some of our desires are more basic: insistent bodily urges that demand food and water, or sleep, or shelter from the elements.

And then there's a group of desires – let's call them our 'social' desires – that are linked to our sense of personal identity, our relationships with other people and our place in society. They influence our approach to love and friendship, family life, work, power and our connections with neighbourhoods and communities. These are the desires presented in the ten chapters of this book.

How many of them can we expect to satisfy at any one time? The US psychiatrist Gordon Livingston believes that if you have something useful to do, something to look forward to and someone to love, you're doing well.[1] You might want to include different items on your personal wish list but, at any given moment, three or four out of ten seems about as much as we can reasonably hope for.

WHY ISN'T THERE A CHAPTER ABOUT SEX?

Having grown up in the post-Freudian era, we have all been influenced by the idea that sex is at the heart of everything we do (though even Freud didn't go quite that far). The sex drive is obviously powerful and famously troublesome: its urgent stirrings can distract us from everything else, especially when we're young or facing a midlife crisis. It propels us into some of the most sublime moments in human experience and some of the bleakest. It sometimes induces bitter remorse, guilt and confusion, yet it also allows us to express our most intense feelings of love . . . and it creates babies, of course.

So why isn't the desire for sex one of the ten strands of this web? In the context of our social and emotional lives, sex is one of the ways we satisfy other desires, rather than being a desire in itself. Of course, considered purely as a basic quest for sexual release, it *is* a desire in itself, though some people would reject the word 'basic' and put their yearnings for sexual bliss in the ethereal category, right up there with truth and beauty.

The difficulty of trying to create neat, discrete categories – like 'basic' and 'higher' desires – is most obvious in the case of sex, given the powerful effect of sex hormones on our brains and the tortured history of the relationship between sex and love. There's often more to sex than sex, and it's that 'more' we'll be exploring here.

EVERY DESIRE CASTS A SHADOW

None of the ten desires explored in this book is inherently good or bad. Each of them has the power to bring out the best in us, and the worst, since we are all a volatile mixture of noble and base motives. That's why several chapters include a brief reflection on 'the dark side'.

The darkest shadow cast by each of our desires is the wish to see that same desire frustrated in someone else – a malevolent urge that's most likely to grip us if we ourselves lack a sense of fulfillment. Refusing to acknowledge another person, for instance, is usually a shadow cast by our own unfulfilled desire to be taken seriously. Mocking another person's beliefs is likely to be a shadow cast by our own unfulfilled desire for something to believe in. Wanting less for someone else is a shadow cast by our own unfulfilled desire for more. The withholding of affection is a shadow cast by our own unfulfilled desire for love.

Unrestrained desires can land us in plenty of trouble, but unfulfilled desires can be emotional time-bombs. When the desire to be taken seriously is frustrated, the frustration can itself become a dangerous weapon in the hands of individuals, communities or nations. And frustration of the desire for love can darken our entire world-view.

Each of these desires can be turned to good account or bad: those are the choices we all make, every day, and they are choices that shape the kind of society we are becoming.

◆

What makes us tick? draws on my work as a social researcher, my direct observations of human nature (in myself, my family, friends and everyone I meet) and my reading of other people's work – especially novelists, since I believe no one works harder than a novelist at trying to make sense of human behaviour.

One thing I've learned is that you don't find out why people do what they do by asking them. My research methods have always been indirect: my favourite technique has been to invite small groups of people – friends, neighbours, workmates – to talk to each other about some aspect of their lives while I listen carefully to what they say and how they say it, then try to line that up with what they actually do. 'Why?' is the question we always want to ask, but it is usually best avoided, because it creates the expectation that there should be a rational explanation for everything we do. Sometimes we act in ways we can't explain even to ourselves.

Many of the points in the book are illustrated by quotations in italics. These are drawn, more or less verbatim, from participants in my research projects and from personal conversations with family and friends. Some quotes have been modified to conceal a person's identity, to be more fluent than the original or to combine two quotes into one.

◆

Why have I called them 'desires'? We could call them motives, wishes, dreams, goals: I'd be happy with any of those labels. But I've settled on 'desires' to convey the idea that although these are things we want – sometimes quite passionately – they do not rule us in the same way as our more basic bodily needs. We can't survive without water, food or sleep: those are non-negotiable.

But the ten desires we explore in this book are highly negotiable. They are not about survival; they are about how we choose to live.

THE DESIRE TO BE TAKEN SERIOUSLY

All any author wants from a review is six thousand words of closely reasoned adulation.

The English writer Antony Jay at a booksellers' luncheon

A golfer on the professional circuit, watched by a worldwide television audience of millions, sinks a sensational putt and acknowledges the applause of the crowd with a wave.

In the dead of night, two graffiti artists spray their tags on a railway viaduct.

A playground bully confronts a little kid and threatens him with violence if he doesn't hand over his lunch.

These examples of human behaviour are about as different from each other as you could imagine. Each will have been the product of a tangled web of motivations, including some that might seem to contradict each other.

The golfer might be supremely talented and confident in her technical ability, yet unfulfilled and insecure in her personal life, hooked on public adulation as compensation for lack of private affection.

The graffiti artists might be both swaggeringly arrogant and painfully shy, wanting to blazon their messages on a publicly visible surface while remaining unidentifiable, except to the cognoscenti.

The bully sounds like a textbook case: hungrier for acceptance than for lunch, but lacking the social or emotional skills to satisfy his yearning and only able to attract the attention he craves when he picks on a vulnerable kid.

A streaker zigzags his way across a sportsground while a game is in progress. He's tackled by two policemen and dragged away.

A philanthropist who has donated generously to medical research agrees to have his gift publicly acknowledged.

A teacher joins in a street demonstration as part of a campaign for better wages and conditions.

Any list of things people do – including both conventional and unconventional things – will have one underlying theme: almost without exception, the things we do express our desire to be taken seriously.

Not seriously as in 'Oh, what a serious person!' but seriously as in 'Please recognise and acknowledge me as a unique individual.'

This is the desire for the respect of others.
The desire to be noticed.
The desire to matter.
The desire to be appreciated.
The desire to be understood.
The desire to be valued as a person.
The desire to be accepted.
The desire to be remembered.

We all want our voices to be heard as authentic, legitimate and worthy of attention. We can't bear to be overlooked, dismissed or belittled. Among the factors that explain why we do the things we do, this one is sovereign. When we know we are being taken seriously, we can relax into that assurance. When we fear we are not, our reactions can range from sadness, resignation or disappointment, through envy of those who receive the recognition we crave, to a burning fury of resentment.

> *He dumped me – just like that. No explanation, no discussion. Just a text. Can you blame me for wanting to confront him? I needed him to look me in the eye and tell me what this was all about. He didn't appreciate me storming into his office like that, but he was never going to agree to meet me.*

People searching for work say the toughest part of the process is dealing with the silence that follows many of their applications. *It was as if I didn't exist.* Failing to get the job is bad enough, but at least the applicant could do something about building up their skills, or improving the quality of their application, if only they had some feedback.

Patients left waiting in a doctor's reception area, well past the time of their appointment and without explanation, are understandably irritated by the inconvenience and waste of time. Even worse is the unspoken message: 'You're not as important as we are.'

We are in an era of increasing demands for 'official' apologies from governments, churches and other institutions accused of damaging people – especially children – through abuse, neglect or indifference to their plight. Whether they are made to indigenous people who may have been dispossessed or marginalised, people abused as children in church- or state-run institutions, people vilified for their ethnic origins or religious beliefs, or employees damaged by dangerous working conditions, such apologies are a response to the appeal for recognition, at least as much as for restitution. The impetus for such demands comes from that same persistent cry: *It was as if we didn't exist.*

However it's expressed, the desire to be taken seriously continues to drive us to the end of our lives. Helen Bamber, the British campaigner for the care of torture victims, has described the experience of holding a dying woman in her arms after the liberation of the Belsen concentration camp at the end of World War II.

As the woman rasped out the horrific account of her experiences in the camp, Bamber said to her: 'I am going to tell your story.' This seemed to calm the distressed woman. 'I think she knew she was going to die,' Bamber said. 'She didn't want to die and [her story] not be told – that nobody would know.'[1] This was a woman anxious, even at her death, not to be ignored or forgotten. When all other desires have left us or become irrelevant, we are left with the desire to be acknowledged, identified, appreciated, and remembered.

◆

No one likes the idea of being lumped in with everyone else, or of being dismissed as 'typical'. But there are some striking similarities between us. Watch us eat, make love, walk, drive a car or catch a train. Watch us think, smile or frown. Watch us cheat, flirt, grieve, shop, pray, vote, gossip. Watch us sit in front of a computer, TV or cinema screen. Watch us sing, laugh or cry. The recurring patterns of human behaviour are so well defined they stand out like features on a relief map.

Yet we yearn to be known for the ways in which we differ from each other. Even if we are mere specks in space, we need this one speck to be acknowledged as both unique and significant.

That's one reason why we react so badly to racism and sexism, to any prejudiced attitude that lumps us into a category, as if our uniqueness doesn't count. We can handle criticism of our personal behaviour, for which we know we're responsible, more easily than we can handle an attack based on assumptions about us because we happen to be Baby Boomers, Muslims, students, unmarried mothers, lawyers, asylum-seekers, Presbyterians or homosexuals.

WHAT HAPPENS WHEN WE FEEL WE ARE NOT BEING TAKEN SERIOUSLY ENOUGH?

Over the past ten years I've listened to a friend describe the disintegration of his marriage, his attempts at reconciliation, his ultimate resignation to the idea of a divorce and his difficulties with his children.

When his wife finally left – after sending him warning signals for years that he'd either ignored or misinterpreted – he was distraught and confused. He believed he had been a loving husband and a good father to their teenage children, supporting the principles of feminism and fully respecting his wife's independence. He claimed he had always tried to do whatever his wife had wanted: she decided where they would live, how many children they would have, which friends they would entertain.

Only recently, long after his wife had moved interstate and begun a new life, did he have an inkling of the real cause of the split. He remembered her saying, *I've lost my voice in this marriage.* At the time he didn't know what she meant. *He* didn't think she'd lost her voice, because he felt as if he'd been listening to her and doing whatever she wanted.

But he'd clearly been listening on the wrong wavelength, and had only recently come to realise that his wife must have felt as if her whole identity had been submerged in the marriage and the family, and she could no longer hear her own voice.

I've lost my voice in this marriage is the cry of many women – and some men – who appear to enjoy parenthood, who seem comfortable in their middle-class prosperity, who may even have spouses and children who adore them, but who, at the deepest level of their being, feel as if their identity has been merged with other people's or blurred beyond recognition: *I'm not the person everyone thinks I am.*

Such things are said by people who feel their relationships have diminished or distorted them. They hear themselves speaking with a voice that is not their own and it's only a matter of time before they will feel an urge to break out. They yearn to recover their own voice and their own identity: *I don't just want to be part of 'us' – I want to be 'me' as well.*

◆

When teenagers take to drugs, there's always going to be a complicated story: many factors will be operating and generalisations are likely to be simplistic. Sometimes it's compensation for not having been taken seriously enough or not having been listened to at home; sometimes it's sheer bravado; sometimes it's the desire to gain or maintain membership of a particular social group; sometimes it's a quest for a heightened sense of excitement; sometimes it's curiosity. But one of the key factors, according to research conducted by Professor Bruce Robinson, director of the Fatherhood Project and Professor of Medicine in the University of Western Australia, is the absence of an involved and concerned father. Indeed, Robinson's research shows that an uninvolved father doubles the risk of drug addiction in teenagers.[2]

What's that about? Simply that when the yearning for love, understanding, support and guidance from a father is unsatisfied, the temptation to behave recklessly is increased and the teenager searches for something that might compensate for the lack of a father's loving presence.

Why does the research place such emphasis on a father's influence rather than a mother's? Professor Robinson's explanation is that mothers typically tend to be actively engaged and involved in the lives of their teenage offspring, whereas fathers, though often worried sick that their teenagers may become involved with drugs, seem generally less adept or less comfortable about being with them and talking to them. Of course there are many exceptions to that generalisation, but the disturbing implication is that if a father appears more distant than a mother, their offspring might interpret this as meaning, 'My mother takes me seriously but my father doesn't.'

◆

Not being taken seriously feels like the ultimate insult, and insults tend to fester and seethe, waiting for a chance to counterattack. If you've ever been shocked by the vehemence of someone's outburst against you, it might turn out that you had failed to take them seriously at a time when they needed your sympathetic attention. Ignoring someone when they desperately need not to be ignored, or treating something they've said too lightly when it seemed to them worthy of more serious attention, can sow the seeds of bitter resentment that might take weeks or even years to germinate.

Anger is rarely unprovoked, but sometimes it's ignited from a very long fuse. When an unfulfilled yearning for recognition and respect finally explodes, the result is likely to be all-round misery: the person who has boiled over has probably made things worse for themselves (being even less likely to attract sympathetic attention from people who now see them as 'irrational' or 'erratic') and the person who is the object of the attack may simply be puzzled: 'What have I done to deserve this? What did I say?' Even the person who launched the attack mightn't know where the anger came from.

People who feel they are not being taken seriously enough may well be tempted to compensate by taking themselves too seriously, as if to say, 'Well, if you won't take me seriously, I'll do the job myself.' And there begins a vicious circle: as needy people become more self-obsessed they appear less attractive, and others become less interested in devoting time and attention to them.

Arrogant people, similarly, risk placing themselves beyond the reach of our compassion, interest or respect: 'He doesn't need my admiration, he's too busy admiring himself.' This is the classic Narcissus figure, so preoccupied with his own reflection that he is oblivious to others. Vanity, like arrogance, is a perversion of our need for recognition.

And so is hubris. An excess of pride or ambition is a sign that the desire for recognition and respect has run out of control. No amount of acknowledgement is ever enough for the person whose need to be taken seriously has gone into overdrive. Celebrities who are offended by *not* being recognised; politicians who have placed personal ambition above morality and have lost touch with the idea that they are in office for the good of the people; lovers who are consumed by jealousy when their partners speak in praise or admiration of someone else . . . these are people who have let their desire to be taken seriously run wild.

WHY ARE SOME PEOPLE HUNGRIER THAN OTHERS FOR RECOGNITION?

Our desire to be valued is universal, but its intensity varies between individuals and at different times of our lives. Some crave recognition in the form of constant praise or even formal awards and decorations; others are satisfied with the occasional loving touch or word of encouragement. When life is proceeding smoothly, most of us are content with a nod or smile of acknowledgement, though we all go through patches of needing a little more attention than that.

Adolescents can be super-sensitive to any sign that they are not being taken seriously. They know they are on a rocky road to adulthood; they feel insecure, vulnerable, often a bit stupid, so they are more than usually in need of reassurance – by our respectful listening to them, for a start, and by assuring them they are 'normal' in any way we can. More than at any other time of life, being mocked or belittled in adolescence can create wounds that may take years to heal.

By contrast, when we are deeply in love and have decided to commit ourselves to a partner, our need to be taken seriously is likely to be fully – even if fleetingly – satisfied. We feel terrific, and we assume everyone else thinks we're terrific, too.

Parents often wish their offspring would take them more seriously; the elderly sometimes complain of feeling marginalised in a youth-oriented society; many people with special needs – the disabled, carers, the chronically ill – feel understandably frustrated if they believe those needs are not being taken seriously.

What of those who seem to have all the acknowledgement they could wish for, but still want more? In extreme cases, the desire to be taken seriously can become an obsession.

Those in the grip of an insatiable appetite for recognition are usually either seeking compensation for deep personal insecurities (perhaps based on neglect, trauma or disappointment), or revenge for perceived slights or humiliations. The tragedy is that intimate relationships are often the casualties of this appetite. Such people want to be taken seriously on a big stage; they want big prizes; they want recognition on a big scale, which makes it hard for those who can only offer them the small-scale love of a single person.

The satisfaction of success is enough for some of us; for others, success is merely the pathway to recognition. While some of our highest achievers never seek the spotlight, others spend their entire careers demanding proof that they are valued as highly as they believe they should be.

Writing from Berlin in August 2009, after the Jamaican sprinter Usain Bolt had broken the world 100-metres record for the third time, sports journalist Dan Silkstone reported that 'although he seems to take few things seriously, Bolt is not flippant about his sport, nor his place in history. He has said this year that he hopes to be remembered as one of the immortals – a true great.'[3]

Professional sport has become another arm of show business: it's about celebrity, fame and the potential to earn stratospheric incomes. In spite of this, sporting heroes are as desperate as the rest of us for acknowledgement: the more extravagant the adulation they receive, the higher they tend to set the bar. Their will to win is as much about the drive for recognition as for a sense of superiority or supremacy. *Take me seriously!* is the real cry from their hearts.

It's the cry from the hearts of many of the world's great comedians, as well. Being taken seriously doesn't have to mean you'll be treated as a serious person: achieving recognition is a serious business, but there are a million pathways to that goal and humour is one of them. People who are constantly joking, punning, sending everything up, are pleading for the same thing as the rest of us: 'Look at me, appreciate me, acknowledge me.' But comedians – professional or amateur – are often on a knife edge: some of them deliberately use humour as a way of concealing their private wounds; some settle for the clown role because they sense they'll never attract attention any other way; some are caught in the dreadful bind of never being sure whether their audiences are laughing at them or with them. But all of them know that getting the attention they seek depends on the next joke, and the next. *Is it me they like, or only my jokes?* The sad clown is not a universal stereotype for nothing.

At a seminar about the arts, John Marsden, Australia's most successful children's author, with worldwide sales totalling more than five million copies, spoke with remarkable candour about his motivation for writing: 'One of the main reasons I write is from a desire to be admired. It's not an easy thing to admit, but I suspect that it's quite a common reason for people who choose careers in the creative arts. When I was in Grade Four, the admiration I got from other kids, and even adults, for the stories I wrote in our class newspaper was very powerful . . . quite intoxicating, actually.'[4]

In his autobiography, US playwright Neil Simon wrote that 'when an audience laughed . . . it was a sign of approval, of being accepted'.[5]

Most of us do what we do as part of the lifelong struggle to be heard, to be appreciated, to be understood as individuals with a unique identity and a unique contribution to make. Acknowledged or unacknowledged, we are all achievers of one kind or another. But it's not just our achievements we want recognised. We want them to stand as mere expressions of our worth – *we ourselves* are the ones to be taken seriously. Whoever heard of an anonymous champion? 'Oh, he's set a new world record, but he doesn't want you to know who he is – he just wants you to acknowledge the record.' Or a champion who only wanted to be identified by his or her nationality: 'You don't need to know anything about me except that I'm French.' I don't think so. Whoever heard of anonymous TV presenters or movie stars? Or academics who don't want to be identified as the authors of their work? Or economists who want to let the graphs speak for themselves? Or politicians who want recognition only for their legacy, not for their role in creating it?

No – we don't want anonymity, most of us, because an invisible person can't be taken seriously *as a person.* Occasionally an author will write anonymously, or under a nom de plume, but their real identity is usually 'discovered'. In the British legal system, judges were once supposed to be treated as if they didn't have individual identities, blurring their distinctive appearance through the use of judicial wigs. Now, celebrity judges are almost as common as celebrity bishops.

PUT-DOWNS ARE SOMETIMES A SPUR TO SUCCESS, BUT . . .

Some stars in business, the professions, the media, the church, academia, the arts and sport can recall a moment when they felt slighted, undervalued or ignored: that became the spur to action that would ensure they were taken seriously in the future. You could argue that their stellar careers were at least partly about trying to overcome that dreadful feeling of rejection or humiliation that comes with knowing you are not being valued as a person. A former New South Wales police commissioner, Ken Moroney, tells the story of being assessed, very early in his career, by a superior officer: 'You'll never amount to anything, Moroney,' was the bleak verdict on a man who rose to the highest office in the force.

The quest to regain lost or stolen self-respect can turn ugly. Some of our worst criminals have spent their entire lives trying, misguidedly, to gain the respect they were denied in childhood or early adulthood. If you're a notorious hit-man, you'll gain respect from those who hire you, fear from your potential victims, and even the attentions of a celebrity-hungry media pack. *Now they're taking me seriously!*

But not everyone who feels ignored or belittled manages to convert their hurt into a motivation to succeed, even at crime. Some children are so comprehensively humiliated by their parents that they grow up as diminished people, never feeling they are taken seriously, never feeling they are properly acknowledged, unsure of who they are or what they might become. Children who are abused, sexually and otherwise, generally feel themselves to have been exploited as mere commodities, stripped of their self-respect and left with a confused sense of their identity: *I don't really know who I am.* Many remain forever victimised, never expecting to be taken seriously.

Although some damaged children do manage to blossom into fully functioning adults, most of them carry secret scars, sometimes in the form of the proverbial chip on the shoulder, a painful shyness, or less obvious manifestations of childhood wounds and humiliations. In adulthood, some of them compensate by becoming more ruthlessly competitive than they might otherwise have been, more heartless, more ambitious than is healthy, more cynical, more thuggish behind a mask of charm, more inclined to hold grudges, to seek revenge or to do their rivals down.

It's a cliché of pop psychology that rings true, almost without exception: the bullies are the insecure ones; the thugs are trying to hide their aching lack of self-respect; the loudest self-promoters are the ones least sure of themselves. In other words, if people are not taken seriously enough at crucial times in their lives – especially childhood – they may well spend the rest of their lives trying to ensure that others will take them seriously, even if 'seriously' includes fear and loathing.

Human nature is ruled by a Law of Reciprocity that helps to explain why those who have been put down tend to do the same to others. At its noblest, we call it the Golden Rule: I'll treat others the way I would like them to treat me. But it usually operates less charitably than that: I'll treat others the way they treat me, or perhaps even the way I think they *might* treat me.

At its most grotesque, the Law of Reciprocity comes out like this: treat other people in the future the way you yourself have been treated in the past. This is not about exacting revenge on someone who has treated you badly; this is about treating someone badly because someone *else* treated you badly. That's how the cycle of child abuse is perpetuated between generations. It's why people who have been treated badly in war, or even in business, may act badly against others in an entirely different context. It's why ethnic or other minority groups who have been subjected to prejudice-driven harassment may harass other minority groups in the very same way in the future. It's why the persecuted often turn into ruthless persecutors. It's why institutionalised bullying continues in some schools and colleges, generation after generation (sometimes disguised as ritual or tradition).

The passion, the energy, the sheer power of the desire to be taken seriously is what drives the Law of Reciprocity. It operates with such relentless logic that the way we treat someone today will probably show up in their behaviour towards us, or someone else, tomorrow. This is how we build, or destroy, a civil society.

This desire runs so deep that it can lead to terrible conse-quences – for individuals or even for nations – when it is frustrated or ignored. History is filled with examples of nations that have reacted violently against the contempt or indifference of others. Eventually, we must learn to accept that if we won't take others seriously, they won't take us seriously either.

WHY MINORITIES THRIVE ON PERSECUTION

When our attitudes, values or beliefs are attacked, our instinctive response is to defend them. In the face of persecution or ridicule, you don't hear religious believers saying, 'Oops, we must have made a mistake. Let's drop this stuff. It's making us look silly.' Instead, their religious practices tend to be more faithfully observed – to seem more important – when their faith is challenged.

Defending our beliefs is the best way of strengthening them. Those who try to change our minds via a frontal attack usually produce the opposite effect from the one they intend: their attack drives us to stiffen our resolve, to become more entrenched in our beliefs, to dig in. It's almost another law of human nature: the more directly you attack someone's existing beliefs, the more likely you are to reinforce them.

Another factor helps to explain why minorities thrive on persecution: persecution is a dramatic demonstration of just how seriously they are being taken. Religious faith – or any other kind of belief-system – is far more likely to erode and wither if it is ignored. Indifference is the real enemy.

There's often an adrenalin rush associated with being on the receiving end of an attack on our belief-system or world-view, even if the attack stops short of full-on persecution. The fight reflex switches on; we are energised, excited; we feel fully alive. *We are the centre of someone's attention,* even if that attention is negative. The attack implies that we are worth attacking, that we are a serious target.

Sadly, there's a parallel here with the tragic cases of women (they're mainly women) caught in a relationship with a violent partner. From the outside, there seems to be no reason at all to stick with it. In places where refuges and shelters are available for the victims of domestic violence, and where compassionate societies offer the support of sophisticated social security systems, it's hard to fathom the motivations for staying within reach of violence.

'I still love him' sounds a bit hollow: what kind of love is that? But some women in that situation do report a strong sense of connection to their violent partners, and some have even managed to explain it to themselves: *At least he's not ignoring me.* It might sound silly and self-deluded, but that's the power of the desire for recognition. Being bashed is hardly a sign of affection or appreciation, but it is a grim reminder that you are indeed being taken seriously.

Many spouses in the throes of separation and divorce report the almost irresistible pull of conflict: 'I know if I ring her up, it will just degenerate into a shouting match, but I still pick up the phone.' Why? Part of the explanation of such a complex phenomenon is that if she's shouting at me, at least she's not ignoring me.

BEWARE: PRAISE AND REWARDS MAY BE THE WRONG KIND OF RECOGNITION

If people have such a deep need to be recognised and appreciated, surely the thing to do must be to praise them lavishly and reward them for doing well? Not necessarily.

The strategy of praising and rewarding people turns out to be more hazardous than you might think, and positively counter-productive in many cases. The problem is that if you offer people rewards for doing good work, the reward can easily become the purpose of the exercise, so their motivation shifts from the *intrinsic*, where the focus is on the work itself, to the *extrinsic*, where the focus is on the reward.

This is a particular problem in the case of children. Giving treats, out of the blue, is a harmless festivity, but converting treats into bribes and attaching them to particular behaviour changes the whole game. In *Punished by Rewards*, Alfie Kohn makes the point that 'it is no less controlling to offer goodies for a desired behaviour than to threaten sanctions for its absence (or for the presence of undesired behaviour)'.[6] Rewards and punishments are both about the same thing: controlling a child – or anyone, for that matter.

Rewards alter the nature of relationships. The offering of a reward gives the power to the rewarder, and shifts the focus of the other person both to the reward and to the need to please the one who is dispensing it.

The principle holds even in philanthropy: offer someone a reward for giving generously – their name on a plaque, for instance – and the act of giving is changed. Generosity comes to seem less significant in its own right: it has now been set up as a means to an end. So although we might seem to be taking philanthropists seriously by offering such recognition, we are also likely to distort their motivation and their focus.

We fall into this trap all the time, especially if we're parents: 'If you'll tidy your room, I'll give you a dollar.' Now the act is more about getting a dollar, and less about tidying the room.

Students who become obsessed by the marks they are getting tend to be less engaged learners – in the richest sense of 'learning' – than those who are not driven by the extrinsic reward of marks. Marks become the goal. Learning, questioning, exploring ideas, making mistakes – all the hallmarks of an engaged student – tend to diminish in the pursuit of rewards. In one secondary school famous for the high marks achieved by its students, teachers reported that the students' focus on marks was distorting their approach to learning: 'Will this be in the exam?' students would ask, whenever a teacher introduced a topic or mentioned a book worth reading. The clear implication was that if there were no marks in it, the students wouldn't bother paying attention to it.

When I was in primary school, I had a well-meaning aunt who believed I was capable of doing better at my schoolwork. She offered me an extraordinary reward: a crisp one-pound note if I topped the class. Boy, did I want that note! I never won it, though, because all I wanted was the money – I was a shy child who didn't particularly want to be top of the class; nor had I connected the idea of learning for its own sake with the acquiring of that small fortune.

The problem is even easier to identify in the case of praise. If we praise someone, we are making a judgement about them and that assumes we are in a position of power over them – a position that entitles us to judge them. Praise can work just like a reward: people start to do things in order to receive our praise, rather than doing them because they are inherently worth doing.

From an early age, children learn important lessons from the misuse of praise, by parents and teachers alike. Especially if they are being victimised by the apostles of self-esteem who believe praising children to the skies will boost their confidence, they soon discover that whatever they do, they'll get a gold star or an 'encouragement' certificate.

Modest, occasional praise can provide useful reinforcement of a child's process of exploration and discovery; inappropriate praise (too lavish, too frequent) is more likely to hinder than help that process.

In essence, the problem is this: if we put too much emphasis on praise and rewards, we hijack the crucial, quite complicated process through which people come to feel as if they are valued. When we listen attentively to what they are saying, watch what they are doing, offer them guidance and encouragement, and help them solve their difficulties – whether at home, at work or in the classroom – we are signalling, in a substantial way, that we respect them and acknowledge their importance to us. If we simply reward them, we are deflecting attention away from that process and on to the process of winning approval.

As a customer, I'd want to avoid the car dealer or the estate agent or any other sales person who trumpeted the awards they'd won. I'd prefer to deal with someone who believes in what they are doing, for its own sake, and who won't regard me as mere award fodder. I'd want a sales person to take *me* more seriously than their place in the league table of top sales performers.

'LET'S GO TO BED': SEX AS A SYMBOL OF RECOGNITION

When a sexual relationship is being established and nurtured, there are desires in play that transcend even our basic and primitive appetite for sex.

Sex is about many things. It's not always a demonstration of how seriously we take each other or how intimate our relationship is. Sometimes it's purely about the stimulation of the senses. Sometimes it's about reproduction; sometimes about recreation. Masturbation is about fantasy, self-indulgence and relief, and copulation can be about those things, too. Sometimes sex is about duty. Sometimes it's about power, control or exploitation. At its worst, it's a weapon of manipulation or even violence. At its best, it's a source of mutual pleasure for people who care deeply about each other.

Even in the context of a loving, committed relationship, where the partners are generally willing to satisfy each other's sexual needs, sexual behaviour sends many signals – some conscious and deliberate, some unconscious – that reveal just how seriously each partner takes the other *as a person*.

Take foreplay. Many women thrive on it and need extended foreplay to get in the mood for sexual activity. Many men, by contrast, would quite like to dispense with foreplay, or at least limit it to what's absolutely essential to get things moving.

In bed as in so many other places, women tend to be more interested in the process, whereas men tend to be more focused on the outcome. That's a huge generalisation and there are many exceptions, but it *tends* to be true, whether we're talking about management styles, politics, parenting, holidaying, meetings, conversation or making love. We're not likely to change the biological and cultural factors that drive such differences but, when it comes to sex, we need to recognise our partner's deep desire to be accepted as the person he or she truly is.

You're a man whose partner loves extended foreplay, and you find that a bit tedious? Perhaps you go along with it because you hope the payoff (for you) will be more exciting and satisfying sex? Wrong motive: exploiting someone else's need is very different from respecting it. If your partner loves extended foreplay, then engaging in it with her is a sign that you take her seriously as a person – not just a lover.

Signs that you take your sexual partner seriously are fundamental to a satisfactory sex life, and those signals can easily become faint with the passage of time if you don't keep consciously and deliberately resending them. In *The Book of Love*, Dr David Delvin quotes a woman who compared lovemaking with her husband before and after marriage: 'Before we were married, my husband was so neatly turned out. When he came to see me he looked lovely – all clean and nice and smelling of after-shave. No wonder he used to sweep me off my feet!' And now? 'He comes to bed all unshaven and smelling of beer and doesn't even bother to clean his teeth or take his vest off. Then he wonders why he can't get me worked up.'[7]

Delvin makes an equivalent point for women: 'My impression is that the sexual side of many marriages breaks down because the wife simply won't pay her husband the compliment of beautifying herself at bedtime.' He compares her before-and-after behaviour: before marriage, 'If they went to bed with each other she made sure she was wearing the kind of exotic lingerie that turned him on, but nowadays, it's cream all over her face . . . and a woolly vest instead of slinky undies.'

While acknowledging the practical difficulties of a busy life, Delvin urges sexual partners to take more care with their preparation for lovemaking. The goal is to reassure the partner that, even if other aspects of the relationship have changed, one thing hasn't: I still value you as a person.

What is a wife supposed to make of a husband who puts her down in public (a classic sign that she is not being respected as a person) and then expects her to be responsive when he feels like sex? Or what should a husband make of a wife who ridicules his passion for golf – or cars, current affairs, UFOs, Mahler or the stock market – yet expects him to take seriously her passion for yoga, literature, philosophy, fashion or travel? The lack of respect for another's passions is bound to be interpreted, however unconsciously, as a lack of respect for the person. We don't have to share each other's enthusiasms; we only have to acknowledge and respect them as an integral part of the other person.

WHY WE FALL FOR THE CULT OF CELEBRITY

The American comedian Fred Allen described a celebrity as 'one who works hard all his life to become well known and then goes through back streets wearing dark glasses so he won't be recognised'.

Ever since the advent of silent cinema, the celebrity film star has been with us. Even before that, we accorded celebrity status to actors, dancers and other entertainers, sporting champions, chariot drivers, heroic warriors, explorers and scientists. Today, the ranks of celebrities have swollen to include media presenters and newsreaders, YouTube performers, models, eccentrics, the mega-rich and, in the latest celebrity twist, those who are famous for being famous. Entire industries revolve around the cult of celebrity – the paparazzi, the glossy magazine market, the branded products (real or fake) that offer us ways to experience a 'celebrity lifestyle', the fashion business, professional sport and, of course, the movies.

We're not so naive as to believe that celebrities are rich and famous because of their deep personal integrity or their exemplary private lives. Indeed, we half-expect them to behave badly – to be sexually promiscuous, steal each other's partners, abuse drugs, spend excessively and self-indulgently.

So what's the appeal? Is it simply that people have always wanted someone to look up to – royalty, the aristocracy, the numbingly wealthy, sporting or other superheroes? Why, then, are we so transfixed by celebrities who are clearly not in any of those categories? What's the lure? Why the insatiable appetite for news of their lives (real or fabricated)? Do we just want to gloat over the possibility that although they are rich and famous, their lives are a bit of a shambles – perhaps *because* they're rich and famous?

I suspect the enduring appeal of celebrities is not that we want to be like them – look or live or love like them; stumble and fall like them – but that we envy the attention they receive and look to them for clues about how to attract attention. Our fantasies about them rarely involve sleeping with their lovers, sailing on their yachts, or abusing the drugs they allegedly abuse; we don't want the life of royalty, or stardom, or notoriety. What we want is to be important to *someone*, to be noticed by *someone*, and celebrities are a signpost to that possibility.

So we keep stargazing – buying the magazines, pressing against the barriers, watching the TV chat shows and the Oscars, basking in the reflected glitz and glamour – partly to satisfy our simple desire to be entertained and amused but also to feed the secret fantasy that we, too, could be the star of someone's life. The cult of celebrity is really an expression of our yearning for recognition, not in the media spotlight (which most of us would hate), but in the glow of loving and respectful relationships in our private lives.

The irony is that many celebrities are not recognised for who they are at all: their fans are responding to an image constructed by a movie studio, or a public relations company, or a manager who has carefully designed and controlled the star's public persona. It's no wonder so many stars suffer mental and emotional disorders of various kinds, seek refuge in drugs, or become pathetically addicted to adulation: when it's an artificial 'me' that's being recognised, deep tensions are bound to arise between the real me and the construct.

Most of us have long known and accepted that we can't be the centre of attention for long, and that it wouldn't be healthy for us if we were. But when little starbursts happen – a wedding, a birthday party, a graduation – they carry heavy emotional freight, reassuring us that we are valued.

WHY WE BECOME SO ATTACHED TO OUR DOGS

As a social researcher, I've made frequent use of a technique that involves groups of friends, neighbours, colleagues, or other natural social groups, sitting around and chatting to each other about whatever happens to be the subject of my research. It's a kind of 'unfocused' group discussion technique (very different from the so-called focus groups currently fashionable in political and commercial opinion research).

Over the years, one of the things I've enjoyed observing is the fluctuations in the energy level of these groups, according to the topics they discuss. Sometimes they almost seem to be talking out of a sense of duty (especially when the conversation turns to politics); sometimes they're animated; sometimes emotional to the point of tears; sometimes tense; sometimes morose.

But here's a recurring observation: whenever the conversation turns to pets, the energy level rises. Politicians might drive us to despair; our kids might amuse and infuriate us, by turns; our spouses might disappoint us. But our pets? Just listen to this:

You know, I sometimes think I prefer dogs to people. They're more reliable.

The thing about my dog is that he's always there to meet me when I come home. No matter what kind of day I've had, or what kind of mood I'm in, he'll wag his tail and lick my hand and trot along beside me.

I know it sounds silly, but he puts his head on one side when I talk to him, and I just know he's listening to me. No one else gives me that kind of attention.

Yes, dogs are funny, cute, loyal, loving (and cats are some of those things, too – though the general consensus among dog-owners is that if cats could talk, they wouldn't). Is that why we love our dogs so much? Partly. But the real reason is that they treat us as if we're special.

We *are* special to them, of course: we're the source of their food, comfort, warmth, companionship, grooming and exercise, so it's hardly surprising that our dogs would value us highly. But we don't respond to their devotion as rationally as that: we love our dogs with such blind devotion because they seem to love us in that way, too. We seem oblivious to the fact that, when given the chance, they clearly prefer the company of other dogs: it's enough to know that when they're at home with us, we are the centre of their world and most of us find that irresistibly charming.

It's often said that the love of a dog is a heavy burden to bear, but most dog-owners bear that burden cheerfully. Where else could they encounter such an uncomplicated emotional relationship: you pat the dog, the dog responds.

In the same way as many people fail to crack the code between lovers – *I can't imagine what she sees in him!* – the devotion of dog-owners to their pets is generally mysterious to non-dog-lovers.

We've just spent a thousand dollars on a vet's bill for a very old dog. People say, 'Why didn't you get him put down?' Couldn't do that – he's part of the family.

I hate the way dogs jump up on you and their owners say drippy things like 'Don't worry, he won't bite.' Won't bite? I wasn't worried about getting bitten – I just don't like a dog putting its dirty paws all over me, or burying its nose in my crotch. It's a mystery to me how people can love these creatures.

There's no mystery, of course. It's all about the desire for attention, respect and recognition. We want to be the star of someone's show, even a dog's.

STATUS SYMBOLS ARE ABOUT MORE
THAN STATUS

So-called status symbols are not merely symbols of the aspiration to be elevated to a certain status in society: they can be more accurately interpreted as expressions of an unsatisfied need to be taken seriously. Luxury cars, expensive jewellery, houses, watches, luggage, IT gizmos – even the honours and decorations conferred by the state – are commonly used to draw attention to ourselves and to position us as people worthy of admiration or respect.

Some people who display such symbols are indeed worthy of our admiration and respect – the symbol matches the reality. But the cult of celebrity has spawned the idea that, if you aspire to higher status, the symbols will get you there.

It depends what you mean by 'status', of course. In a society strictly layered by social class or caste distinctions, status is almost impossible to acquire: you're born into a class and there you stay. In societies that aspire to be more egalitarian, the very levelling of the class structure, ironically, guarantees that people will invent their own quite intricate systems of fine discriminations via wealth, education, cultural interests, housing aesthetics, support for particular sports or teams, inflections of language, dress, and so on. Inevitably, the accoutrements of a contrived or even imaginary class system will create the basis for status symbols sold to the mass market.

The most formal non-material status symbols are the official honours awarded by most governments for a wide variety of reasons, to all kinds of people. There are those who are properly acknowledged for remarkable, but unsung, achievements – especially in humble service to the community or on remote frontiers of scientific research or academic work. There are those who perform acts of extraordinary bravery, or who give a lifetime of service to the common good, with no thought of personal gain. There are those whose elevated positions in public life carry automatic honours, almost as a badge of rank. There are entertainers – actors, media personalities, sporting heroes – who are rewarded for having amused, distracted or inspired us. There are those who are so rich or powerful, it would seem churlish not to grant them this additional bauble. And then there are those who seek official honours as a sign of respectability, rather like a mask to hide the deviousness or ruthlessness of their pathways to power and wealth.

Whether it's medals, plaques or luxury cars, the theory is that these things will signify that here is a person to be taken seriously by the rest of us. You might argue that if they are worthy of being taken seriously, they wouldn't need the trappings to prove it, but the desire to be taken seriously says otherwise.

WHY LISTENING IS THE GREATEST GIFT OF ALL

Since all of us yearn to be taken seriously, we place a high value on the people who are prepared to listen attentively and sympathetically to us. Being truly, seriously listened to feels like a welcome and precious gift: *Someone cares what I think!*

Listening is a skill that doesn't come naturally or easily to most of us. It is not about mere hearing: it is about trying to enter into the thinking of the speaker; trying to imagine what it must be like to be him or her; practising the gentle art of *changing places*

29

in your imagination. Listening is about entertaining another person's ideas, a bit like trying on their coat. It's like saying to the other person: 'I might not agree with you, I might not like what you're saying, but I'm going to try to understand it from your point of view.'

This is hard work. It's easier to nurse our own fondly held beliefs and prejudices than to open our minds to the possibility of change under the influence of a different point of view. It's easier to close our emotional ears to contrary arguments and use the time while someone else is speaking to marshal our own thoughts. If conversations and debates are thought of as nothing more than verbal jousting, we'll never get anywhere. Listening is the breakthrough strategy; listening opens up the conversation; listening says we are actually going to *value* each other's contributions.

Ah, but what about boring people? How can we be expected to devote ourselves to the task of listening to them going on and on? What about the people who only talk about themselves and never show the slightest interest in us? What about people whose conversation seems turgid and, well, boring?

Has it never occurred to you that there's no such thing as a boring person, only a bored listener? Humans are endlessly fascinating if you know what to look for. Even in an unpromising conversation, there's so much to learn, so many nuances to pick up, so much to understand. Many people who come across as boring are simply shy, socially inept, or conditioned to expect disappointment in personal encounters. They might even have reached the conclusion that they *are* boring, because they have never managed to attract a serious listener.

Your gift of active, attentive listening might not be enough to break a cycle of learned, self-protective behaviour, but it might open a window of possibility for that person. If you are treating them with respect, it might just register that they could show a little more respect for themselves as well. People with a healthy self-respect know when to stop talking and start listening; people with self-respect deficit keep trying to compensate, and one of the signs is that they never know when to shut up – neither, of course, do those with a towering self-esteem.

Listening is a form of therapy we can all offer each other, if we choose to. In fact, if I had to identify one way to make the world a better place, I'd say: *Listen more attentively and sympathetically to each other.*

If we are not prepared to attend to what another person is saying, two consequences will follow. First, we won't be in a position to respond sensibly to what they've said, because we won't have grasped it properly. But the second consequence is even more serious: we will have conveyed, without needing to say a word, that we don't take that other person seriously *as a person,* and where do you go from there?

WHY COUNSELLING WORKS

In spite of the strong and sometimes vicious disagreements between various schools of psychotherapy – the Freudian psychoanalysts, the Jungians, the Kleinians, the narrative therapists, the psychodynamic psychotherapists, the non-directive Rogerian client-centred therapists, the cognitive behavioural therapists, etc. – the truth is that most forms of interactive therapy can be beneficial. This is because counselling involves a deep commitment on the part of the counsellor to acceptance and acknowledgement of the client as a unique person who is worthy of the therapist's undivided attention.

Friends can make that kind of commitment, too. So can family members. But in a world where everything is speeding up, where 'stress' is the bogey we all battle, and where busyness is frequently regarded as a sign of a fulfilling life, who has the time for prolonged, sensitive and active listening – the kind of listening that reassures and perhaps even heals?

Whatever their presenting symptoms, clients go to counsellors for one all-pervading reason: to be treated as a fully authentic human being – a person worthy of attention and respect – and the proof of that is in being listened to sympathetically.

The surface problem might be an addiction to gambling, the lingering effects of sexual abuse, relationship issues, a generalised anxiety or a debilitating phobia of some kind. While such issues need to be addressed specifically, the first bridge to cross is the bridge to acceptance and acknowledgement: 'Your problem is a real problem.' And then: 'Your situation is uniquely your own, even if your problem is shared by many others.' And then, finally, the music to any client's ears: 'You have my undivided attention.'

There's a famous study in the history of workplace psychology – one of the early 'time-and-motion' studies – in which an Australian management researcher, Elton Mayo, tested workers' reactions to changes in the level of illumination in the Hawthorne plants of Western Electric, in Illinois, US, during the Great Depression (1927–33). Mayo reported that when the lights were brightened, productivity went up. But when the lights were dimmed, productivity also rose. Mayo concluded that the workers were responding more to the interest being taken in them than to the lighting levels per se. Controversial stuff, which left many social scientists unconvinced, particularly as Mayo's study was never properly replicated or validated.

He was onto something, nevertheless. The so-called Hawthorne effect became an established part of management theory for many years. Like many of Sigmund Freud's 'unscientific' theories and much of the truth about human behaviour embedded in myths and legends, the Hawthorne effect alerts us to an important truth that has implications for every kind of human encounter: people are more likely to engage with us if we first take them seriously by engaging with them.

THE DESIRE FOR 'MY PLACE'

Home is the place where, when you have to go there,
they have to take you in.

Robert Frost, *The Death of the Hired Man*

Where do you come from?

Where do you live?

Where do you feel most at home?

How many places do you think of as 'home'? Your country of birth? Your adopted country? The house you grew up in? The house where you now live?

Is there a place – a space – you think of as your very own? Is it a private nook inside the house you live in, somewhere at your workplace, in your car, or somewhere else?

Could you ever feel a sense of being in your own place in an airport, a shopping mall, a hospital or a prison? Could you live out of a suitcase and never feel the need to put your roots down? *Home is where the heart is. Home is where I hang my hat.* Could you settle for that, and only that? Do you ever envy the nomad, the itinerant worker or the swagman?

Is the idea of 'my place' so attached to your childhood home that you've never been able to recapture it? Did you feel as if you'd lost something irreplaceable when your parents sold the family home? Did the idea of home change when you had children of your own?

Home may be a multilayered concept but, for most of us, the deepest layer is located in our desire for a place that is unambiguously ours; a place that seems in harmony with us; that welcomes and comforts us; that says things about us we're pleased to have said. The absence of such a place can be a source of anxiety, restlessness and unresolved tension.

'My place' is partly an anchor, partly a refuge, partly a stable reference point in a world that seems kaleidoscopic in the complexity of its shifting patterns. (Even the homeless like to claim their favourite spot as their own territory, and to be left in peace there.)

Most migrants experience an initial sense of insecurity and uncertainty – sometimes bordering on panic – when they arrive in a new country, and some never quite recover from the upheaval, never being sure where home is; where they belong; which place is truly theirs.

At the end of the Second World War, the world was awash with people known as 'displaced persons' or DPs. The term was peculiarly evocative: persons without a place to call their own; dispossessed; persons whose very sense of identity was threatened by a fractured, tilting sense of place.

That's how significant the sense of 'my place' is to most of us: it helps not only to locate us, but also to frame us, to define us, to contribute to our sense of who we are. I belong here; this is my place; I feel at home in this space. And if I can't be there for a while (perhaps for years), the sense of a place that will still be mine when I return burns like a beacon in the back of my mind.

Yes, people are also crucial to our sense of identity and emotional security: for some people, family is the central, defining feature of home: *I feel at home wherever my family is.* But the sense of place also has a powerful role to play: we need to know where we belong; we need to feel that some physical place stands as a symbol of our uniqueness and acceptance.

Where do you come from? is a question that carries more freight than mere idle curiosity about geography. It's a question about origin, status, culture, ethnicity, context. It's a question about the kind of place that defines you.

And, surprisingly often, it's a question we find hard to answer.

◆

It goes without saying that we need shelter to protect us from the elements, to have an uninterrupted night's sleep and, in the case of most Westerners, to keep our stuff secure. Shelter is so fundamental to our comfort and, indeed, our survival – almost but not quite on a par with our need for food and drink – that we can hardly categorise it as a desire.

But the desire for 'my place' is a different thing altogether. The houses we live in are not necessarily the places where we feel most at home. Many of us have special spaces and places that answer a deeper and more powerful emotional need in us than the need for somewhere to live. 'My place' is the physical symbol of my emotional comfort zone.

The place I feel most at home is sitting on a rock not far from here. I don't own it or anything – it's out in the bush, but it's become my favourite place. That's where I do all my thinking. No one else knows about it – not even my husband. Just going there settles me down.

Home is special, of course. But I never feel quite as comfortable at home as I do in the office. That's my domain. I love getting there early, before anyone else arrives. I even shave there.

Although open-plan and 'hotdesk' (sit-anywhere) offices cut costs and are still fashionable with architects and interior designers, it's hard to see how they encourage the sense of connection people like to feel with their workplace. 'You can put your family photos on your laptop screen,' say the designers. But that hardly compensates for frustrating our desire for a place to call our own.

Home? I feel more at home in the local coffee shop than anywhere else. I always sit in exactly the same spot. They know me there, they know my order – it's the one place I can relax and unwind and do a bit of thinking, without being interrupted. I guess it's my bolthole. Sometimes I'm a bit reluctant to go home.

When I was a kid, I used to climb a favourite tree and sit up there for hours. It was my secret hide-out. I can remember

what that felt like – totally secure, totally safe. That was my
space. Nothing quite matches it now. Maybe my shed does.

'The shed' has long been a way for men to satisfy the desire for
'my place', whether it happens to be a literal shed in the back
garden or a symbolic place – a den, a study, a media room, a
'man cave' – that serves the same social and emotional purpose.
For some, this is a place of solitude and retreat. For some, it's a
place of creativity, activity and work – making things, repairing
things, painting things, even writing things. It's hard to escape the
feeling that, for many men, the shed is a symbol of something quite
primitive: a sign of masculinity; a vestige of men's clearly defined
role in the hunter–gatherer culture; a strictly men-only kind of
place, reserved for uninhibited men's talk and the accoutrements
of 'men's work'.

It's sometimes a place of male bonding, as well. Sons love to
join their fathers in the shed (or the garage, or the workroom) and
some men like to congregate in each other's sheds, complete with
a bar fridge, easy chairs and perhaps a TV set. In many suburban
garages, corners are specially set up for this purpose.

My wife and I are looking to move from here, up the coast.
Last weekend, I went scouting and found the perfect shed.
It's huge. My wife said, 'What about the house?' and I said,
'Bugger the house, I want that shed.'

In rural and regional Australia, a community-based 'men's shed'
movement has been gathering momentum, ever since the first
such shed was established in South Australia by a group of
Vietnam veterans who were having trouble resettling into their

community. More than two hundred communal men's sheds are now in operation around Australia and the movement is spreading to other countries. The members of these shed-based groups are typically retired or unemployed men. These are men who would not normally dream of joining something called a 'men's group', but the shed creates an informal, accessible space where they feel comfortable and secure. Open and frank discussion becomes possible, while doing some useful projects as well – making or repairing toys for underprivileged kids, building or restoring furniture – whatever needs might emerge in the local area. The movement is credited with making a significant contribution to the mental health of the men involved: it provides comradeship and that all-important sense of place.

'MY PLACE' CAN BE SMALL AND TEMPORARY, OR EVEN MOBILE

At a conference centre in the countryside outside Bathurst, a regional city in the central west of New South Wales, I used to conduct four-day courses in the psychology of communication for business executives, public servants, teachers and others. The first part of the course was a two-day immersion in communication theory. Then there was a break, usually of two months, before the participants came back to present their own case studies at a second two-day session. I wasn't surprised when, in the first two-day program, people returning for Day 2 sat in the same seats they'd occupied on Day 1, but I confess I was surprised when, time after time, people returning after the two-month break would occupy the same seats on Day 3 that they'd sat in on Days 1 and 2.

A trivial example? I don't think so. Our emotional comfort (especially in a semi-stressful situation like an intensive, small-group tutorial) is aided by the claiming of a space – even a chair – as our own. In staff lunch-rooms, meeting rooms, office carparks, long-distance commuter trains, playgrounds and libraries all around the world, people like to stake their claim to their own space, and are offended by any threat to their occupation of it. There are some people who have sat in the same pew in church for so long that they'd not only be miffed but actually destabilised if someone else took 'their' spot and they were forced to sit elsewhere, to see the service from a different perspective, to find a new place. (Historically, some churches even had family pews labelled with a brass plate and a lockable door: how's that for a sense of 'my place'? *Keep out!*)

When we are living in a strange place, the need to carve out a space of our own becomes even more compelling. An Australian friend of mine lived in Venice for a year, sharing a house with a group of students. In a city that, however magical, was strange to her, in a house that was not her home in any but the most transient sense, she noticed she was devoting an extraordinary amount of attention to the state of her small desk – obsessively straightening her books, sharpening her pencils, keeping up a supply of stationery – and unerringly heading for that comfortable, familiar spot every time she returned to the house. She wondered if this was a way of exercising control over one tiny part of a wildly uncontrollable environment, and that might well have been part of the explanation. But I suspect another factor was that, in such a strange and unfamiliar setting, she needed a place of her very own; a symbol of stability and refuge; a place made secure by her emotional attachment to it.

◆

The Western world is characterised by speed, restlessness and motion (look at any major airport at almost any hour of the day or night), so it's hardly surprising that for many people in modern urban settings, 'my place' is neither a building nor a piece of the Earth's surface, but that ubiquitous mobile enclosure we call the car.

My very own space? I'll tell you where that is – behind the wheel of my car. It's the only place I ever have to myself and it's the only place where I seem to get any real peace.

I've lost count of the number of times I've heard people say their car is the most comfortable place they ever inhabit; the place where they feel totally in control (helped immeasurably by the symbolism of a steering wheel in their hands and an accelerator pedal under their foot); the place that feels more like a personal space than anywhere else they spend their time.

Furniture retailers are irritated by customers who ask, 'Why can't I find a chair that's as comfortable as the driver's seat in my car?' The answer is that regardless of the ergonomics, no chair that sits on a showroom floor is invested with the same emotional power as a driver's seat.

Some people become so attached to their cars that they give them names. Some find the experience of selling a car and buying a new one an emotional wrench, a bit like parting with an old friend. The space inside their car has acquired, over time, a killer combination of characteristics: familiarity, privacy and security. It has become their precious personal space, often augmented by the radio, that most intimate mass medium of all.

Cars are for escaping into, for meditation, for thinking, for praying, for singing, for courting, for sex, for conversation, for eating and drinking, for sleep, for letting off steam (even when stationary) and for generating unrivalled – and positively dangerous – feelings of power. Oh, and for driving, too: cars are our most flexible and efficient means of transport, though at enormous cost to life and limb – to say nothing of the cost to the quality of the air we breathe and the health of the planet.

Our cars are like soft-upholstered mobile cocoons. Locked and belted in, protected from the elements, lulled by the sound system, we feel far safer than we actually are; more private than we appear to passers-by; freer and more independent than at most other times of our lives, the rules of the road notwithstanding. Cars, rather like telephones, generate a feeling of intimacy that encourages the kind of frankness we often find difficult in face-to-face encounters: when we're sitting side by side gazing out the windscreen, especially at night, we seem able to say what we really think more easily than in many other circumstances. Here again, the place – even though it's a mobile place – is working its magic.

If I want to find out what's on my daughter's mind, I drive her to netball training. All sorts of things come out when we're driving together, not looking at each other.

The car is where my husband and I do most of our serious talking.

My car is my office. I have the phone, the laptop and complete privacy. I also have that can-do feeling I only get when I'm behind the wheel.

Advocates of public transport are up against the fact that the private car is valuable for much more than A-to-B transportation. It is 'my place' in a peculiarly modern way.

THE MYSTICAL SENSE OF PLACE

One of the silliest ways of putting cultural distance between indigenous and non-indigenous populations in places like Canada, the USA, New Zealand and Australia is by attributing to indigenous people a unique sense of place, a mystical relationship with the land that transcends anything urban or suburban dwellers could understand or appreciate.

This is nonsense. Not the idea that indigenous people have a special relationship with the land; that's obviously true. What's nonsense is the idea that the sense of place is unique to indigenous people, or even that it's more special, more 'spiritual' for them than for the rest of us. Yes, there's a special connection with the land felt by those who live close to it, like primitive tribes or modern farmers. And different cultures obviously have different ways of expressing their sense of place: we identify and revere our 'tribal grounds' in different ways. But connection to place is vital to our sense of identity – both personal and communal.

I suspect that much of the uneasiness, anxiety and even the moral uncertainty of modern urban societies can be traced to our loss of a strong sense of continuous connection with places that help to define us.

What kind of places?

For cricket lovers, I need only mention Lord's or the Melbourne Cricket Ground to make the general point that all urban communities have sports grounds of various kinds that, over time, acquire almost mystical significance – places that symbolise deeply embedded cultural values and mark the location of great struggles, triumphs, defeats and outpourings of human emotion.

Sport may not be your thing, and you might think I'm belittling indigenous culture by mentioning sporting venues in the same breath as more ancient sacred sites. But you'd have to be blind not to have noticed the profound, if not spiritual, significance of such places as settings for the acting out of tribal rituals of the battle and the hunt. As in so many other aspects of life (including religion), our emotional response to the symbols is almost as powerful as our response to the thing they represent: could ancient warriors have been more emotionally aroused than, say, New Zealand's All Blacks in full cry with their supporters packed into Eden Park?

Think of the war memorials and battlefields, the parks, plaques, obelisks and buildings scattered across every nation, marking the places where homage is regularly paid to those who made supreme sacrifices on behalf of their country. Think of the military camps – some still in use, some long since abandoned – that mark one of life's most significant rites of passage for those who lived in them. Those places matter, as markers of nationhood.

Revisit your primary school playground, or a classroom you once sat in. The powerful sense of that place – the look, the feel, the smell of it – will stir all kinds of emotions in you, positive and negative. Those emotions spring from deep wells of half-forgotten memories of an innocence, a simplicity, that makes many of us ache with nostalgia. The places remind us of the stage of life when we were full of potential but didn't know it, when we had no sense of a past and not much connection with the idea of a future either. Yet they are the places forever associated with the early formation of our attitudes, our values, and the unconscious shaping of our vision of what might be possible for us.

Go to the suburb where you grew up and revisit the footpaths, the shops where you strolled and loitered as a teenager, the place where you first appeared in public in high heels, the park where you learned to kick a football, fly a kite or train your dog to fetch, the backyard where you took your first catch or learned to skip, climb, hide or whistle. Not significant? Go and have a look. Feel the sense of place tug at your heart.

The rush of recognition and response when we hear songs that supplied the soundtrack to our adolescence and early adulthood is an evocation of place as much as of time: the places where we heard those songs were inextricably intertwined with the events that were shaping us.

Most couples have a private list of 'sacred sites' – the place where they met, the location of their first date, the place where they were wed, the first apartment they lived in together. The sense of place is absolutely integral to each of those memories and their recollection is forever tied to their location.

You can see how much the places matter when they're torn down or ripped apart. That cinema where you learned about good and evil writ large . . . now a Persian rug shop, forever closing down. And whatever happened to that milk bar on the corner? Why have they widened the road? Where is the . . . Where is the . . . *Hey!*

Where is the house I grew up in? Where is our neighbour's house? Shocking stuff, the removal or disruption of places that helped define us. This is why conservation of the built environment is as much about psychology as it is about architecture.

The place where you worked at your first job. The quad at your university. Your favourite beach. Your regular holiday destination with its river or its mountain tracks.

It doesn't have to be a primitive, unspoiled place. It doesn't have to be grass and rocks and trees and streams. Ask the people who live in those sprawling suburbs so characteristic of large cities – suburbs that often seem ill-defined and even nondescript to outsiders – ask the residents if those places mean something more than just spaces to sleep and walk and eat in.

What about the cathedrals, churches, chapels, courts and concert halls – places that have enclosed and inspired some of our most numinous, uplifting, heartbreaking or clarifying moments? Or the places where we stood and heard terrible news: we know where we were when we heard of US President John F. Kennedy's assassination, or the terrorist attack on the World Trade Center, because we were rooted to the spot. The spot – the place – was integral to the emotion, as it always is. (Where were you when you had your first kiss? I hope you can still remember the person, but I'm sure you can remember the place.)

There are also places we never want to go to again, because they contain demons we know will catch us if we venture too close. I know of one man who will never, under any circumstances, visit his old school again; another who refuses even to drive down the street where he grew up in a desperately unhappy family. Why would he? The place is the most powerful of all the symbols of his unhappiness.

Although it's obviously true that communities are made up of people, and it's the people we connect with, it's hard to hold onto a sense of community without anchoring it to places. (Funny how we so carefully choose the places where we'll live, but not the people we'll have as neighbours. Did you ever interview the people in the street before you bought a house? No; it was the place that spoke to you.) The places where we live, play, work . . . the places that stand for our sense of ourselves as people who belong somewhere, and don't belong somewhere else. The sense, as a child, of even the next street being alien, let alone the next suburb. The sense of a relative's house in a distant suburb being like an oasis of familiarity in a desert of strangeness. Tribal grounds? Stamping grounds? Of course; what else?

What's less mystical about any of that than the mystical status of place in indigenous cultures? It is neither to detract from those cultures, nor to honour them any less, to say that a sense of place is fundamental to the *human* sense of self. We have nothing to learn from indigenous people about the significance of place in the formation of our identity, but we have a great deal to learn from them about how to protect and preserve the places that have formed us. Our problem is not that we lack the yearning for a sense of place; that yearning is universal. Our problem is that, with reckless disregard for our natural and built heritage, we've often frustrated that desire.

HOW PLACES HELP SHAPE OUR MORALITY

When we complain, as so many people in Western societies do, that we are losing both our sense of community and our moral clarity, we don't always realise that the second complaint is an inevitable consequence of the first. Our moral sense is a social sense, derived from the experience of living in a community and learning to take the needs and the wellbeing of others into account, especially those who aren't inside our personal circle of family and friends. This is why local neighbourhoods – the actual places where we share the experience of living in communities – play such a crucial role in our moral formation. The local neighbourhood is the test-bed of our values.

If we were interested in restoring or raising the moral tone of a community, the best strategy would not be to pass more laws to make people act as if they are responsible members of a community, nor simply to teach 'values' or 'ethics' via explicit instruction. The best strategy would be to find ways of putting people back together, and a critical part of that process would be to create – and preserve – the places and spaces that encourage our interactions with each other as members of the same neighbourhood.

Cyberspace won't do it for us. The 'global village' was a clever name, coined in the 1960s by the Canadian media guru, Marshall McLuhan. But its incorporation into the vocabulary of the IT revolution represents something of a hoax perpetrated by the high priests of the digital age. Villages, whether urban, suburban or rural, need real places to foster the incidental connections – the smiles, the nods, the gossip, the mutual concern and support – that are the very essence of village life.

'Cyberspace' is another clever name, but we should resist the idea that it bears any relation to the other kind of space. All kinds of useful, convenient and efficient transfers of data can take place in cyberspace, and friendships that have been established in the real world can be nurtured and maintained in the virtual world.

But think of all the messages conveyed by *place* that contribute to an encounter between two people: an office, a living room, a kitchen, a bedroom, a cinema, a candlelit dining room, a cosy corner of a cafe, a swank restaurant, a car, a ferry, a busy street, a dimly lit bar, a park, the seaside. *Place* is integral to the sense of human presence, and therefore to our sense of morality. 'Flaming' and other extreme forms of cyber-abuse thrive on the internet precisely because their exponents are not in the same place and may even be banking on the fact that they will never encounter each other offline.

If I had to pick the kind of people most likely to restore our sense of community and therefore to help foster our sense of identity and moral responsibility, they would be urban planners, architects and those involved in community development projects: people such as librarians, coaches of local sporting teams, arts organisers who create opportunities for members of a local community to come together and do something creative – sing, dance, paint, write poetry, take photographs, discuss books or current affairs. I'd add to that list anyone interested in preserving the heritage – the places and spaces – the buildings, the parks and gardens, the streetscapes, lanes and alleys that have helped shape our sense of who we are.

THE MEANING OF HOME

My wife spent the first twenty-four years of her life in Ireland, though she has been a naturalised Australian for longer than that. If, as so many people claim, home is where the family is, then where was Sheila's home, since her whole family, like so many

Irish families, was now scattered around the world? As a migrant, she had embraced her new country and made that her home.

The first time she took me to see her birthplace, Kilkenny, I was struck not only by the rush of emotion she experienced but also by her surprise at the intensity of her own response. She had not expected to be so deeply affected by the place, because she had never held on to the idea of Kilkenny as 'home'.

On an unexpectedly warm and sunny day, we rushed through the city, devouring it together, with Sheila's sense of excitement palpably rising. We began with the building that had been her family home – still intact, and freshly painted the day we saw it, but no longer a home: it had become a warehouse for a nearby retailer. We ran up Dairy Slip – the stepped alleyway that was her route to and from primary school. We strolled along the main street and found many shops and pubs still familiar to her. We walked by the river where her father had taken his children for a postprandial walk every Sunday while her mother stayed at home, recovering from the weekly ritual of the family roast. We visited the school – now a men's hostel – where the nuns, largely untrained as teachers, had mystified Sheila by their institutionalised otherness. (She had once called an especially obnoxious teacher from a public phone and said, as menacingly as a child could, 'This is the voice of your conscience . . .', but to no avail.) We toured the castle, recently restored, that had dominated the skyline of Sheila's childhood. We visited the office where the accountancy practice founded by her late father was now housed, his name still included on the sign painted on the front of the building.

Tears were shed.

◆

I am third-generation Australian. My family came from Scotland, via Durham in England (where, no doubt, the original pronunciation of our surname had been anglicised from Mack*eye* to Mack*ay*). Two years after our trip to Kilkenny, Sheila and I took a train from London to Edinburgh. I thought it was time to visit the land of my forebears.

Our train trundled through the north of England – York, Durham, Newcastle – every bend in the track revealing fresh and thrilling vistas. And then, as we crossed the border into Scotland, I was gripped by an intense sense that I had come home; this was my country.

It was nonsense, of course: Australia is my country, and none of my family had lived in Scotland for five generations, so what was going on? Was I simply experiencing that rush of emotion we often feel when reality suddenly matches our dreams? Had I spent so long thinking of myself as Scottish that it was a shock finally to be in the place where I had located myself in my imagination? Possibly no more than that; but possibly, also, a deeply ingrained belief that Scotland was my genealogical home.

Whatever the explanation, the experience of finding 'home' in what was actually a foreign country surprised me even more than Sheila's reaction to her rediscovery of Kilkenny. I loved Edinburgh and felt perfectly at home there. We drove to the Cairngorms and I felt at home there. We stayed in Kincraig and stood on the banks of Loch Insh, and I felt at home there, too. I have no idea where my Scottish forebears lived; I don't need to know. There are Mackays all over Scotland, but when I was there, I had no desire to trace specific family connections. Scotland itself was the thing. It felt, and feels, like my second home, however absurdly sentimental that might seem.

◆

Almost no one says that the bricks and mortar are what home is really about: it's about people, they say; families, relationships, intimacy, hardship, and even objects – photographs, clothes or furniture – that evoke those things. Yet for most of us, home is also bound up with a vivid sense of place.

> *I loved living where I did as a kid. I'd like to move back there one day – sort of curl back into it.*

'Sort of curl back into it' is a line that has stayed with me ever since I heard a respondent say it in a 2004 study of the meaning of home.[1] Some people talk about home being an idea lodged more in memory than present reality, or an ideal they are still trying to realise. But 'sort of curl back into it' captures something quite fundamental: wherever or whatever we mean by it, home is mainly about security and comfort, both physical and emotional.

Security and comfort can be interpreted in many ways:

> *My kids call me a control freak, because I like everything to be the way I like it at home. What's wrong with that? If you can't be in charge of your own place, there's something wrong.*

> *When I was in prison, we'd be working in the prison laundry and the blokes would say, 'I can't wait to get out of here and go home.' They meant their cells, of course.*

> *I remember when I moved into my first flat. It was tiny. There was no guarantee I would even be able to afford the rent,*

but I remember that feeling of independence and freedom. I really felt I had found a home, at last, even though everyone was asking me, 'How does it feel to move out of home?'

Ideally, home is the place – perhaps the only place – where you can be yourself, where you can please yourself, where you can express yourself. It is a place where acceptance should go without saying. That's one reason why many people who live alone relish their freedom and independence:

If I want to stay in my PJs all weekend and eat baked beans out of a tin, who's going to object?

Now I'm on my own, I find home is the one place I can truly relax.

If that confidence is lost, home is lost:

When I realised my husband and I weren't going to make it, the place no longer felt like home – you were on tenterhooks the whole time, trying not to offend each other or say something that would start another argument.

Divorce and bereavement can disrupt our sense of 'my place':

When my wife left and the kids and I tried to pick up the pieces, I realised the worst thing was that our house didn't feel like home any more. We needed to move somewhere new – somewhere we could create our own space.

After my wife died, I never slept in our bed again. I got my daughter to clear out the wardrobe and I installed myself in the spare room.

For many of us, 'home' is forever attached to the place where we grew up, the place where we discovered the meaning of family and friendship, the place where, if we were lucky, we experienced the joy of unconditional love.

When urban planners and local government authorities speak of the need to take *housing* (especially public housing) more seriously as a social issue, they don't always appear to understand that that should also mean taking the meaning of *home* more seriously – paying more attention to the need for people to connect; the need to build infrastructure that facilitates the development of communities; the need to avoid the appalling errors of the past, where shiny new housing developments were built as if in ignorance of the meaning of home.

We know, from bitter experience, that housing developments without a heart, a focus, a centre, breed disconnectedness, vandalism and a lack of social obligation and civic pride. We know that new towns and suburbs without adequate commercial, medical, leisure and entertainment services feel to their inhabitants like wastelands. The research respondent who said she felt most at home in her local coffee shop was speaking an important truth: houses, alone, rarely satisfy the yearning for home.

Our houses stand in streets and those streets are part of neighbourhoods. To interpret the meaning of home too narrowly is to miss this crucial point: for most of us, the idea of home can't be separated from the idea of a stamping ground, a locality, a clearly defined neighbourhood where we feel we belong.

I wouldn't want to move from here because the neighbours are terrific. We're not in each other's pockets, but you know they would be there in a flash if you needed them. Frankly, the house leaves a lot to be desired, but we've struck it lucky with the street.

I can't imagine ever wanting to live anywhere but here. People wonder how we stand the aircraft noise, but they don't understand we've got a real little community here. It's safe. It's the neighbourhood.

If we lose our sense of being connected to a local community, we lose a significant part of our sense of home. 'We don't even know our neighbours' names' may be a cliché of big-city life, but we never say those words with pleasure or pride: we know we've described a symptom of fragmentation and loss.

It's hard to imagine anyone creating spaces for humans to live in that actually discourage human contact and make incidental encounters difficult – like new suburbs constructed without footpaths, and without any 'hub' of shops and other community services. It's hard to imagine creating high-density housing where carparks feel dangerous and people who catch the same lift, day after day, avoid eye contact. Such deficiencies rob home of its deepest meaning: home is about feeling secure in a locality, not just inside a house or apartment. As many European cities have long since demonstrated, medium-density housing can encourage a sense of community where the life of the street becomes important not only for eating but also for socialising. The best medium-density housing developments incorporate plenty of built-in spaces where incidental contacts occur naturally, as they used to on the footpaths of low-density suburbs before the car took over. All those spaces have the potential to become part of the meaning of home.

A HOME WITHIN A HOME

Even people who regard their home as 'my place' in the richest emotional sense of that term often refer to a special, more narrowly focused place they think of as their *home within a home*. It might be a shed, a kitchen, a den, a favourite chair, the bathroom or a nook in the garden that feels 'mine'.

For many people, bed is the ultimate symbol of home; 'sleeping in your own bed' is a way of alluding to the magical properties of that cocoon of physical and emotional comfort, restoration and retreat. Bed is a place of solitude and privacy for some; of intimacy and sharing for others. Our beds can console us, refresh us and soothe us. If we can't feel at home in our beds, we're unlikely to feel at home anywhere else, which is perhaps one reason why so many insomniacs report general feelings of restlessness and anxiety, as well as sleeplessness.

When we express the wish to 'die in my own bed', we are thinking of being at home, at peace, in a place that is securely, unambiguously our own.

For many of us, bed is for far more than sleep: it can also be a place where we eat, drink, read, think, listen to music, talk and nurture ourselves. If we choose to use it as a communications centre, bed can also be a place for making phone calls, sending text messages and even checking emails or shopping online. But for most of us it is predominantly a place of escape from the demands of life, including family life. Many teenagers go through periods of using their beds as insulators to protect them from the intensity of the parental spotlight. ('When is he ever going to get up?' 'Probably not until you have gone out, Mum.')

Bed is also a place of sensual pleasure: crisp cotton, smooth silk, soft blankets, feather pillows. For lovers, bed is central, 'sleeping together' a favourite euphemism for sexual intercourse. Sex in other locations may offer the spice of variety, risk or recklessness, but bed is the place most couples yearn for. For some men, copulation itself is the ultimate expression of the idea of 'my place', that intimate enclosure symbolising the sense of acceptance, comfort, tenderness and relief they associate with an idealised homecoming.

Who can't imagine the pleasure of a day spent luxuriating in bed? Even recollections of being sick in bed, especially as children, are often tinged with guilty pleasure: as long as we weren't too sick, illness was the perfect excuse for slipping between the sheets and surrendering ourselves to bed. Many people's recollections of childhood illness are powerfully connected to the place where they lay in bed, gazing at the ceiling or out the window, with no one demanding that they get up.

One of my favourite memories is being a child, tucked up in bed in my own home, listening to my parents having a party. I felt so safe, so secure.

A room of our own is a luxury many of us will never be able to afford, with bed the best available alternative. But the desire for *a home within a home* helps explain why, in many Western societies, houses are expanding while households are shrinking.

Households with parents and children are now typically smaller than a generation ago, due partly to the falling birthrate and partly to the high rate of marriage breakdown. The smaller the number of people in a two-generation household, the more emotionally charged the atmosphere is likely to become and the greater will be the need for some personal space to escape to. As households continue to shrink, houses are likely to remain bigger than rational planners might think they need to be, simply because privacy – 'my space' – becomes more of an issue.

I love the open-plan look, but you have to have somewhere you can scurry away to be by yourself. You need lots of doors you can shut yourself behind.

The only thing I'd like to change would be to add a room of my own – something that's purpose-built, just for me – something really high-tech.

Everyone wants to have a bigger family room and a bigger entertainment room because they want their kids to stay at home. And then we all want our private spaces as well.

THE DARK SIDE: TERRITORIALISM

Being so intense, the desire for 'my place' can bring out the worst in us as well as the best.

Wars are almost always fought over territory: the attempt by one nation to incorporate another's territory into its own space is as old as history, as is the corresponding desire to resist such attempts and to defend whatever territory we control. Look no further than the Middle East for current examples of the primacy of territory – especially the continuing tragedy of the Israeli–Palestinian conflict, which is about nothing but the sense of place: the hatreds on both sides might seem to be based on religion, culture or ethnicity, but none of that would matter if the place question had been settled. Even when a war is said to be ideological – such as Iraq or Vietnam, or the Crusades of old – the battles are always over place: the Crusades were launched with the specific aim of wresting control of Jerusalem and the Holy Land from the Muslims. 'Winning hearts and minds' is rhetoric as futile as it is misleading: the goal of aggressors is to increase their influence in the world, and nothing but territorial control will do it.

Contrary to popular perceptions at the time, even the 2003 invasion of Iraq by the US-led coalition was, according to the UN weapons inspector Hans Blix, driven by a combination of two factors, both attached to place: the desire to protect US access to Iraqi oil, and the need to find somewhere to relocate US land forces then based in Pakistan. Occupation of Iraqi territory was essential to the achievement of both objectives. (Notice that neither goal had anything to do with weapons of mass destruction, nor the brutality of Saddam Hussein's regime.)

Government policies about border protection and the treatment of asylum-seekers are frequently harsher than they need to be, simply because governments know that any appeal to territorialism is bound to be successful with the majority of voters. Tough talk about borders and 'illegal immigrants' is always a vote-winner, because we have a natural, in-bred concern about any violation of our space.

On a smaller scale, neighbours have been known to come to blows over the erection of a fence, or the sharing of a common driveway, or the abuse of access rights. As a species, we are not very good at sharing territory, let along yielding it: common spaces have to be well defined for us to agree that they are, indeed, common. Even then, some people are tempted to convert public space – such as a street – into private space:

We thought about trying to put a boom-gate at the end of our street, to keep the riff-raff out, but the council wouldn't let us.

It's funny how attached you get to your own street. As kids we used the road as a playground, and we really resented any cars that drove through that weren't our neighbours' cars. Even now, I tend to think of this street as ours.

Gated communities carry the desire for 'my place' to another level, by extending territorial rights to entire neighbourhoods. An infamous advertisement for one such community, on Australia's Gold Coast, included the rather explicit line: 'Keep the cockroaches out.' The rest of us knew who they meant.

Lower down the economic ladder, but driven by the same impulse, some gangs decide that a particular street, beach or other area is their territory and are prepared to fight anyone who tries to invade it. Such urges might be understandable, but they become both ugly and absurd when put into practice.

The desire for our own place, like all the desires that drive us, needs to be kept in perspective, and sometimes to be kept in check: left to run wild, it can lead to an obsession with privacy, exclusivity and security. How many people have invested in alarms, electric gates and security bars on their windows, only to find they feel less secure? Obsession has a way of defeating its own purposes.

Our desire for 'my place' is more vulnerable to the excesses of possessiveness and assertiveness than any of the other desires that drive us. But if we wish to contribute to a civilised society, our desire for 'my place' will sometimes need to be tempered with generosity and compassion. Yes, I can plant a tree or add an extension to my home that will block my neighbour's view of a harbour or mountain and I can argue, with the law on my side, that 'no one owns a view'. But if I plant that tree or build that extension as a defiant expression of my entitlement to act as I wish in my own space, what other desires might be frustrated? My desire to be respected and valued? My desire to be accepted in the local community?

If we let the desire for 'my place' overwhelm other, nobler desires, we may find that we pay a high emotional price. 'My place' will only ever feel emotionally as well as physically comfortable if I haven't trampled over other people's sensitivities to create it.

IS 'HOME' A THING YOU CAN OWN?

Why are so many Westerners obsessed by the idea of home ownership? Is it that, being such an acquisitive culture, we need to possess the *place*? Or is it that we yearn for a sense of security associated with home, and we think ownership will give us that? Or is it simply that we have been convinced that 'bricks and mortar' are a good investment and 'owning your own home' is a sign of your material success? As usual, it's all of the above.

Home ownership is increasing in some countries, declining in others. In the UK and Canada, for instance, the percentage of people owning or buying their own home has recently climbed above seventy percent, while the Australian level has fallen below that figure. New Zealand's rate of home ownership has been falling steadily since its peak in 1991, and is projected to drop below sixty-five percent by 2011. In both Australia and New Zealand, the biggest falls have occurred among 25–35-year-olds. The USA has maintained a home ownership level of about sixty-five percent, rising to a high of seventy-five percent for non-Hispanic white Americans. (The dream of home ownership can seduce us, making us vulnerable to mortgage debt: the aggressive marketing of unaffordable mortgages to low-income earners was one of the factors driving the USA's sub-prime mortgage meltdown and, in turn, the global financial crisis.)

The countries of Western Europe have diverse traditions of home ownership. Some have very high ownership rates: over eighty percent in Spain, Greece and Ireland (at least before the financial crisis of 2008–10 hit those economies hard), and about seventy percent in Belgium. Other European countries have favoured long-term rental over buying. Switzerland, for instance, has a home ownership rate of less than forty percent, Germany about forty-three percent and France about fifty-five percent. In such countries, the characteristics often thought to be associated with home ownership – stable housing arrangements, householders' sense of responsibility for the house they live in and a sense of attachment to their neighbourhood – are generally found among long-term renters as well.

But the culture of home ownership is changing even in some countries with higher rates of home ownership – partly because of tougher economic conditions and/or soaring house prices, but partly also because of an emerging generational ethos among young adults that says, 'Let's keep our options open'. The attitudes of the present and coming generations of young adults have been formed by the upheavals – social, cultural, economic, technological – of the past quarter-century. Flexibility is their thing. Transience is their way of life – at least for now. Change is the air they breathe. So it's no wonder they've adopted a wait-and-see approach to almost everything: jobs, courses of study, marriage, parenthood . . . and housing.

A generation committed to postponing commitment is likely to find the idea of renting inherently more appealing than their parents or grandparents might have. To the argument that 'rent is wasted money' they simply reply, 'I'm buying a roof over my head the same way I buy food or concert tickets – and they don't last forever either.'

◆

Home ownership is generally expected to promote wealth, stability, self-esteem and a host of other material and psychological benefits, which is why many governments regard rates of home ownership as a useful index of both prosperity and social stability. In fact, as some of the most affluent countries of Europe have shown, the real magic is not in home *ownership*, but in *secure* housing, whether owned or not. The Australian Housing and Urban

Research Institute has shown that among poor and otherwise disadvantaged families who struggle for a toehold in the housing market, even as renters, the provision of secure public housing yields significant improvements in health and wellbeing and in children's educational performance.[2] Stable housing can serve as a crucial fixed point in an unstable and often threatening world, and increases the chance that this house – wherever it is and whoever owns it – will come to feel like 'my place', with all the attendant social and emotional benefits.

Changes in household composition, levels of home ownership and styles of housing don't change the fundamental meaning of home. You can think of home as an investment, or as a canvas for your interior decorating skills, or as a symbol of your material wealth and success, but no one mentions any of that stuff when they recall their most precious memories of home. Once you look beyond the economics and the aesthetics, you realise that 'home' can't actually be owned at all. It's an idea too deeply lodged, too big, too rich, too complex, too subtle for ownership.

THE DESIRE FOR SOMETHING TO BELIEVE IN

*The less a thing is known, the more fervently
it is believed.*

Montaigne, *Essays* I

Life on earth is variously conceived of as a simple scientific fact, a deep mystery, a lucky accident, or the result of a deliberate act of creation that meshed with some vast eternal purpose. Some people believe we have been planted here by a god who chose this planet for us and expects our gratitude and worship in return. Some are struck by such awe in the face of Existence that they want to devote their lives to contemplation of its possible meanings. Others neither know nor care why we're here but simply want to get on with making the most of it.

When the biologists and geologists and physicists try to explain it to us, and the theologians add their layers of interpretation, it still seems mysterious. Even if we accept that we are here as the result of mindless cosmic forces producing circumstances conducive to life that ultimately evolved into millions of species including our own, our personal existence doesn't *feel* like that. We would prefer a more reassuring kind of explanation, one that fits with our intuitive sense that we are special, we are here for a reason, that there must be more to this life than meets the eye.

Why are we here? might well be a pointless question to ask – a bit like asking *What colour is eight?* or *When will I die?* – but we're still tempted to ask it, in the hope of finding a metaphysical answer that means more to us than a physical one. We still want to ask what is the *point* of this life of ours that seems so meaningful to us? Why does it all seem to matter so much? Why do we take it so seriously, and spend so much time thinking about it?

It's no wonder we look for explanations that go beyond the scientific, just as we look for explanations for falling in love that go beyond the hormonal. We love a bit of romance, a bit of mystery. And we love being at the centre of the story: 'cosmic accident' isn't as emotionally compelling as 'God made you and loves you.'

THE ENDURING QUEST FOR 'GOD'

The idea of a god of some kind has been part of the human story since the very beginning. Sometimes our forebears were simply looking for explanations of natural phenomena that no longer puzzle us – things like electrical storms, floods, fires, erupting volcanoes, falling stars, the eclipse of the sun or the moon. They assumed that someone all-powerful was making such things happen. Sometimes they were trying to conceive of a superior being they could put their faith in, someone to be on their side in the face of life's challenges – especially challenges from their enemies across the river. Sometimes they were trying to work out ways of placating gods who seemed, on the evidence of the natural world, to be angry with them.

Throughout the ancient world, religion was an ever-present feature of daily life. From the most primitive to the most sophisticated societies, myths and legends evolved that have persisted, to a remarkable extent, in current religious beliefs and practices. Virgin births and resurrections occur in many legends; creation myths abound; religious festivals in one time or place turn out to be adaptations of festivals from other times and places – the Christmas tree displayed in Christian homes is an adaptation of a Germanic pagan symbol, and Easter a variation on Eostre, the Saxon Goddess of the Dawn. Many Christian rituals – baptism's 'second birth', communion – have taken ancient rites and invested them with Christian meaning. Such rituals persist because, through their changing contexts, they continue to dispel our fears of mortality, while comforting us with messages – verbal, visual and musical – that address our deepest longings.

Far from resisting the idea that modern rituals, myths and legends are adapted from ancient ones, Joseph Campbell suggests that these recurring stories are universal precisely because they have the power to transcend the local and specific aspects of our lives and reveal 'the image of the man within'.[1] For Campbell, a scholar in the field of mythology and comparative religion, the specifics of religious faith and practice are less significant than the general role they play in helping us understand the essence of humanity and the experience of living.

Theologians argue endlessly about the nature of God and, indeed, the very existence of God: Don Cupitt, the founder of the so-called 'sea of faith' movement, goes so far as to suggest that God is not a being or an entity of any kind, but merely an idea, a spiritual ideal, 'an imaginary focus for the religious life'.[2] Some regard that as heresy, others as an unexceptionable statement of the obvious. Most mainline believers, whether Jewish, Muslim or Christian, would argue that their religious belief 'originates from and is focused on a God who is distinct from human persons'.[3]

Regardless of the debates about the possible meanings of 'God', and regardless of the ever-expanding range and variety of religious faith and practice, the underlying truth is inescapable: there is a powerful human desire to believe in *something* in the realm of the non-material. In *The Interpretation of Cultures*, Clifford Geertz concludes that 'the existence of bafflement, pain and moral paradox – the Problem of Meaning – is one of the things that drives men towards belief in gods, devils, spirits, totemic principles'.[4]

Even the most sceptical of us find we have to resist the desire to believe, as if we are believers by nature, whether that desire is satisfied by conventional religious faith and practice or in some other way entirely – for example, in fervent deification of science, or an almost mystical belief in the inherent integrity of the free market, or passionate atheism. As the English literary critic James Wood wrote in the *New Yorker*: 'Nothing more clearly shows that atheism belongs to religious belief, as the candlesnuffer does to the candle, than the rise of the so-called "new atheism".'[5] Referring to the work of such anti-theistic writers as Richard Dawkins[6], Sam

Harris[7] and Christopher Hitchens,[8] Wood sees the zeal of the new atheists as a direct response to the parallel rise of fundamentalism in religion: 'Atheism is structurally related to the belief it negates, and is necessarily a kind of rival belief.' In Wood's view, and in the view of many contemporary liberal theologians, Dawkins-style atheism is barking up quite the wrong tree, because its attack is focused on such a narrow band of theism.

Richard Eckersley, Visiting Fellow in the National Centre for Epidemiology and Population Health at the Australian National University, has pointed out that the 'fundamentalist' Dawkins pits the worst of religion against the best of science:

> The picture Dawkins painted would have been very different if he had compared the worst of science (for example, its development of weapons of mass destruction, its sometimes brutal and inhumane treatment of experimental subjects, or its contributions to corporate greed and consumer excess) with the best of religion (for example, its role in social justice and human welfare, and in giving deeper meaning to our lives).[9]

Whether it's a supernatural being, a mysterious life-force, Cupitt's 'imaginary focus for the religious life', science, money, wisdom, information, ritual, power or love, most of us assign the status of 'god' to something in our lives, whether we give it that name or not. Non-theistic gods abound in Western culture, often coexisting with theistic gods on the multiple thrones of a modern pantheon: plenty of religious believers also appear to worship material prosperity, for instance (though so-called prosperity theology argues that prosperity is simply a consequence of honouring God).

Cleanliness is a god for some; sex or sport for others. Obedience and conformity are gods for those who find their meaning and purpose in the conventions of religious or other communities.

Some religious believers create idols out of scripture – the Torah for Jews, the New Testament for Christians, the Qur'an for Muslims – or dogma, or rituals, or even the equipment used in rituals. They worship and find meaning in those things as much as in the ethereal idea of the god that is supposed to lie behind them. The instruments of worship can become the objects of worship, eventually being regarded as 'holy' in themselves – holy pictures, holy water, blessed sacraments and so on.

Our yearning for a supernatural god can be seen as the ultimate expression of our desire for something to believe in – something larger and grander than we; omniscient, omnipotent, omnipresent; beyond time and space; immortal; invisible. If such a concept is sometimes criticised as being itself idolatrous, in the sense of being a thing we have imagined or created so we can worship it, then that's a theological argument, rather than a psychological one. Psychologically, we humans seem destined to keep creating gods that serve as projections of ourselves, reflecting our values and purposes, meeting our emotional and spiritual needs, meshing with our world-view and sustaining our aspirations for 'the world to come', either in a better future on Earth or in some half-imagined afterlife.

THE POINT OF RELIGION

The desire for something to believe in is more widely satisfied by religion than by any other set of beliefs we humans embrace.

Religion has always existed in human societies as a source of comfort, consolation and inspiration for those people who might otherwise be numbed by grief, or crippled by confusion about their place in the cosmos or by anxiety about the fragility of their mortal existence. Sometimes the comfort, consolation and inspiration spring from religious faith itself; sometimes they are derived from the rituals and practices of organised religion: indeed, many people who, like Buddhists, reject the notion of a Supreme Being still find religious rituals and practices immensely satisfying.

Anti-theistic fundamentalists such as Dawkins and Hitchens either miss or choose to ignore the point of religion when they attack its irrationality. *Irrationality?* That's a straw man if ever there was one: whoever said religion was meant to be rational? (The Swiss theologian Hans Küng wrote that 'faith in God is not an irrational, blind, daring leap, but a trust that is responsible in the eyes of reason and grounded in reality itself',[10] but I daresay that depends on what you mean by 'faith in God'.)

In the contemporary world, when agnostic or even atheistic secularism might have been expected to replace theism, religion continues to occupy a central place in the lives of millions of people, and a less central but still significant place in the lives of millions more. Is that merely a testament to the cultural power of ritual, passed on through generations? Or the aesthetic power of sacred music and art? Or the rhetorical power of religious language?

All that and more: whether we love it, hate it or feel indifferent towards it, religion survives because of its continuing appeal to those who will always be dissatisfied with purely rational, scientific explanations of human existence. It survives because it provides such people with an explanation, a story, an overarching narrative designed to satisfy the human need for answers to big questions about the meaning and purpose of life – answers that either ignore, reinterpret or transcend the scientific. Even those who regard the founding stories of their faith as no more than myths and legends might still regard them as divinely inspired in their capacity to teach us important lessons about how to live and how to make sense of life itself.

Religious pilgrims are not only seeking answers. Many are responding to religion's sacred places and rituals, its uplifting music and art, simply as an aid to contemplation of life's unanswerable questions. When they pray, it is more an inner-directed, meditative activity than an outer-directed appeal to their god to respond to a shopping list of requests. While more activist, interventionist, fundamentalist believers might look for answers to prayer in terms of tangible results, from winning a war to healing the sick, the contemplatives seek no more 'outcome' than peace of mind. For them, going to a church, a mosque, a synagogue, a temple or a meeting-house is an opportunity for time out; for meditation; for resting with the mysteries rather than wrestling with them. For others, going to church is a matter of duty, the content of the occasion less significant than the act of routinely turning up.

Religion is not only about the desire for something to believe in; it's sometimes also about the desire for something to look forward to and the desire to belong. Most varieties of religious belief have been captured and dogmatised by institutions, and their tribes and communities are tightly knit. Many people who once believed and no longer do – or are no longer sure whether they do or not – continue to identify themselves with religious labels, shamelessly using religion as a source of tribal identity, sometimes even toughening up their prejudices against those of different tribes. Plenty of ex-Catholics, for instance, still identify strongly with the Roman Catholic tribe and are even more scathing about Protestants than they were as practising Catholics, and vice versa. Many people who are no more than nominally Christian in terms of their faith and practice are nevertheless fiercely resistant to the appearance of Muslims in their midst, or to an idea such as inter-faith dialogue.

Religion is a bundle of contradictions, just like every other aspect of human behaviour. It's easy to lay lethal charges against religion – especially primitive, simplistic and fundamentalist religion – as a source of delusional and irrational belief systems that blind people to the realities of life. It's easy to spot the prejudice, hypocrisy and intolerance that weaken the case of those who claim to be following a religion of love, such as Christians and Muslims. And it's easy to attack the organised, institutional versions of religion for their corruption, their arrogance or their lust for power, to say nothing of their involvement in wars and terrorism that have seen millions slaughtered in the name of one god or another.

Part of the problem with debates about religion is that 'religion' can mean very different things depending on whether we're talking about institutional religion or the heartfelt faith of an individual. All of us can point to the damage done by religion to the lives of countless individuals and to entire societies, but we should not overlook the countless others whose lives have been enriched by a religious faith that has emboldened them to attack slavery, torture, injustice, suffering and inequality, or inspired them to perform compassionate acts of selfless service to others, or to create beautiful music, art or literature. Set against the horrors of the Crusades, or the sacking of Constantinople, or the bitterness of sectarian prejudice and hatred in Northern Ireland and the Middle East, there is all the creativity inspired by religious passion: the music of J.S. Bach, the architectural splendour of the world's great cathedrals, and the poetry of such mystics as Donne, Milton, Blake and Hopkins.

◆

Quite apart from the institutional corruption and the internecine intrigues, quite apart from the delusions and prejudices that can seem ugly or plain silly to the non-believer, quite apart from the appalling record of organised religion in human history, religion continues to play an enduring role in our culture because so many people find relief from the ravages of anxiety, fear, distress and disappointment through their religious faith. Religion exists, above all, to ease cosmic panic – panic in the face of the unknowable – the thing once known as spiritual despair.

There are people who enter a place of worship feeling troubled, defeated or care-worn and leave, an hour or so later, feeling luminous, joyful and even immortal. However much we might deride the damaging and delusional aspects of religion, it's hard to argue with its intensely therapeutic effects on some believers – especially those who are more interested in the quality of their spiritual lives than the politics or dogma of the religious institution to which they happen to belong.

For many believers, religion and morality are closely linked: they see religion as providing a reason to behave well. To non-believers, this seems a flimsy and redundant basis for a moral code, partly because it overlooks the impressive moral strength and clarity of those with no religious faith at all. At its best, religion encourages people to live noble – rather than merely moral – lives and to hope for a better world. To the extent that it does that, it has probably saved the sanity of millions of people who might otherwise have been crushed by despair.

BRIDGING THE GAP BETWEEN THEISM AND ATHEISM

Let's assume there is no Answer with a capital A. Let's assume there is no Secret with a capital S. Let's assume the universe had no beginning and will have no end; that infinity and eternity mean what they say. Let's assume that science will never be able to explain exactly what happened before the Big Bang, nor answer all our questions about the end of time. Let's also accept that no one can know, for sure, whether there is or isn't an afterlife where a non-physical soul lives on in a disembodied state, or is reincarnated as someone else.

What, then, are we left with? For some, faith might plug these gaps in our knowledge. (After all, faith and doubt are inextricably linked: you wouldn't have to believe if you *knew*.) For others, hope might sustain us until more answers emerge. But almost all of us are left with one thing we hold in common: the idea that love – charity, compassion, kindness, concern for the other – is what prevents us from descending into chaos and is the most civilising force in the world. That kind of love is sometimes nurtured by religious faith and sometimes it isn't: ideas such as mutual obligation, caring for the sick and marginalised, taking each other's wellbeing into account are so self-evidently the basis of any civil society that they don't require a religious impulse to animate them.

Doesn't that suggest that theists and atheists might be playing a tribal game that blinds both sides to a huge area of common ground? Atheists dream of a world in which our behaviour, our morality, our social life and even our international relations are not complicated by the presence of religion. And religious believers dream of a world in which everyone embraces their particular variety of faith. Neither of those dreams will come true.

So what kind of dream could come true? Suppose we think about how we might want to live – how we can most nobly live – in the absence of any certainties. What's left for us *all* to believe in?

Most of us – theists and atheists – would agree on a list like this: a world at peace; a world consisting of societies and individuals who respect each other's differences and focus on their common goals; a world where we are motivated by compassion, where we resist hatred, prejudice and intolerance; a world where the strong accept their responsibility towards the weak, the rich towards the poor, the highly intelligent towards the less intelligent; a world where privilege and entitlement entail charity and generosity.

That world is not just around the corner. Some of our desires – religious and tribal, in particular – are too powerful to yield to such idealism. But the Christian and other believers who declare that 'God *is* love' and the atheists or agnostics who regard love – charity, compassion – as a powerful force for good might have trouble finding any serious point of disagreement about their practical goals for making the world a better place. (Are Médecins Sans Frontières, Red Cross/Crescent or Amnesty International less effective or admirable than religion-based charities?)

An ethos of concern for others brings out the best in us, encouraging all that is noble, compassionate, selfless and kind in our thoughts and actions. Such an ethos – or 'spirit' – makes us whole (and the religious word 'holy' is simply a derivation of that). Those on the side of wholeness may choose to call themselves believers or non-believers but, in terms of practical outcomes, does that distinction matter? Isn't how we live more important than what we believe?

It's not that simple, of course, because our desire to have something to believe in fuels our desire not to let go of whatever form of belief we've embraced. But my heart bleeds at the thought that this desire, of all our desires, should be the one that breeds so much enmity, strife, conflict and tension.

IF NOT RELIGION, THEN WHAT?

'When people stop believing in God, they don't believe in nothing; they believe in anything,' G.K. Chesterton is supposed to have said.[11]

In a 1928 essay, Bertrand Russell wrote: 'Man is a credulous animal, and must believe *something*; in the absence of good grounds for belief, he will be satisfied with bad ones.'[12] The range of beliefs we embrace runs broad and deep, though few people are prepared to concede that their beliefs are irrational. However untestable it might be, belief feels, to the believer, as powerful as knowledge. The source of that power resides in the conviction – observable among strong believers in *anything* – that we have attained superior insight and/or superior understanding of mysteries that lie beyond the reach of the rational and scientific, and certainly beyond the reach of non-believers.

The idea that there is 'something out there' drives many people to accept that there are supernatural forces at work in the world, perhaps even forces that are somehow locked up inside us, just waiting for the next '-ism' or '-ology' to release them.

Most of us have a vague interest in such matters, without much conviction, but some embrace the idea of the supernatural, the paranormal, the extrasensory and the extraterrestrial with a religious fervour. Such people *want* there to be ghosts; they believe all of us, not just magicians, should be able to harness mental telepathy; they want remarkable coincidences to be more than coincidences; they want to believe they have discovered The Secret (which is one reason why Rhonda Byrne's 2007 book of the same name was an international hit, inevitably spawning websites with titles like 'The secret behind The Secret').

◆

On average, about thirty percent of the adult population of Western societies claim to believe in astrology. What is meant precisely by 'believe in' is anyone's guess, but it's hard to find a person who can't tell you their star sign, or a mass-market newspaper or magazine that doesn't offer an astrology column. The extraordinary success of Linda Goodman's *Sun Signs* and *Star Signs*, and countless other works of astrology, old and new, are symptoms of our widespread willingness to take 'the stars' seriously, or half-seriously. Many who rubbish the notion of daily horoscopes can be heard exclaiming how someone is a 'typical Aries'.

Astrology has taken up permanent and ever-expanding residence on the internet. You can obtain 'Astro-Clairvoyant' readings at SeeYourFuture.com, and many astrologers will offer you daily horoscope readings that promise to show you what's in store for you and the roughly 570 million people on Earth who share your star sign.

Sceptics might be appalled, and so might many theists, but the continuing appeal of astrology shows how badly we need to believe in something that offers an explanation of why we are the way we are and, even better, a glimpse of what might happen to us in the future.

◆

Conspiracy theories, similarly, catch fire precisely because they induct us into the closed world of the cognoscenti by seeming to provide something to believe in that transcends or undermines official or rational explanations of extraordinary events, ranging from the assassination of US President John F. Kennedy to the presence of UFOs in our skies or 'crop circles' on the ground, or the 'faked' moon landings. There's even a widespread belief in America that Barack Obama's birth certificate, proving he was born on American soil, is a fake. Whether it's international Jewry, the CIA, Freemasons, the Roman Catholic Church, the Gnomes of Zurich or al-Qaeda, many people can't get enough stories about secret – and preferably evil – conspiracies that are responsible for some of the most dramatic events in our history, or in today's news. Once you *believe*, it's as if you *know* what's really going on. The 9/11 terrorist attack on the World Trade Center? 'Ah, the Jews had all left the building, you know' or 'President George W. Bush was in on it, together with a couple of Saudi princes.'

Dan Brown's remarkable international success with *The Da Vinci Code,* one of the most popular novels in history, can be directly attributed to the ability of the book to tap into our need to believe in something. Though never anything other than a work of fiction carefully aimed at the mass market, it was embraced by thousands of readers as a book of historical fact, offering shocking revelations of 'truth' about the origins of Christianity, the 'real' life of Jesus, the corruption and deceitfulness of the Roman Catholic Church, and more. *Da Vinci Code* tours began sweeping through Europe, stopping at locations referred to in the novel and irritating priests who found their churches the object of gawking attention from *Da Vinci*-obsessed tourists. Countless defensive sermons were preached by nervous clerics confronted by the *Da Vinci Code* phenomenon.

I first heard of *The Da Vinci Code* over lunch with a friend who was urging me to get hold of this new book she had just finished reading. It had changed her life, she said, and she knew it would change mine, too. The basis of her unbridled enthusiasm was her conviction that this book unlocked secrets, broke the code, gave an insider's account, explained so many things that were previously unknown (including some nasty things about Roman Catholicism that many ex-Catholics, like her, were very ready to accept). It was a revelation to her. It was not just another clever page-turner; it was *something to believe in*.

◆

Superstition permeates every culture, though most of us are more entertained than enmeshed by it. Superstition is nevertheless a tacit admission that there are mysterious forces – luck, fate, destiny, chance – at work in the world, and that we should respect them. Many superstitions are observed tongue-in-cheek, like little rituals that are no more than unthinking habits, but some people take their superstitions very seriously indeed.

Perhaps you believe that the number thirteen is unlucky. Even if you can't quite bring yourself to admit that you *believe* it's an unlucky number, you might nevertheless try to avoid living in a house or apartment with that number, or working on the thirteenth floor of an office building, 'just to be on the safe side'. When the Apollo 13 moon mission struck trouble, millions of people around the world were nodding sagely, as if to say, 'I knew that one would go wrong.'

Perhaps you find yourself saying 'fingers crossed', or actually crossing them, as if this will increase your chances of a good outcome. Perhaps you cross your heart, or touch wood, or have a Saint Christopher medal in your car. Even though you might, when pressed, say you don't believe in the power of such superstitions, it might be worth asking yourself why you keep playing the game.

Or perhaps you have responded to the Western fashion for adapting the ancient Chinese art of feng shui to the design of your home or garden ('Outside waterfalls are especially helpful in creating more cash flow,' says one item on a list of feng shui tips); to the redesign of your bedroom in the hope of enhancing your love life or curing insomnia; or to the layout of your office in the hope of increasing harmony among your employees and improving your commercial performance. If so, you will have noticed that proponents of feng shui emphasise the need to embrace the philosophy wholeheartedly and not to approach the project in a purely pragmatic spirit.

Do you feel a little prick of anxiety when a black cat crosses your path? In some cultures, that would mean good luck rather than bad, depending on whether the cat approached from your left or right. When your palm itches do you, almost as a reflex response, wonder whether a windfall is coming your way? Do you avoid walking under ladders for reasons that go beyond mere prudence? Perhaps you half-seriously fear that a broken mirror will bring you seven years of bad luck – or at least a bad day. Do you throw a pinch of salt over your shoulder if you spill some? Do you panic if someone opens an umbrella inside? Do you ever wish someone 'good luck'? At some level, any of these practices could be interpreted as signs of a belief – or at least the vestige of a belief – in something 'beyond ourselves'.

◆

It's a short step from religion, astrology and superstition to the modern personal growth movements that promise to transform us and heighten our 'awareness'. Typically based on repackaged and embellished versions of ancient wisdom, especially Buddhism, these movements shamelessly offer a commercial response to our desire to believe in something. A classic example of the modern quasi-mystical personal growth movement was California's est, founded by Werner Erhard (real name John Rosenberg) and based on his so-called technology of transformation. The est movement spread widely and spawned many 'transformational' imitators through the 1970s and 1980s. It was later relaunched as The Forum and, more recently, as Landmark. (One of my research colleagues threw herself into est for a while, finally reporting that 'the secret is there's no secret'.)

Some personal development programs are purely educational, being designed only to increase people's interpersonal skills at a technical level – rather like a course in communication or the psychology of relationships. But when such programs move beyond the educational to the inspirational or quasi-mystical, when they call on their adherents for an emotional commitment that amounts to faith, they appeal to precisely the same desire for belief as religion: they promise that, from deep within ourselves, we will discover a power and a set of insights that will accelerate our spiritual growth and personal development and unlock our understanding of Life. But we have to *believe*. (And we also have to pay.)

The commercial self-help system that has most explicitly repositioned itself as a religion is Scientology. Its founder, L. Ron Hubbard, developed a self-development program known as Dianetics that borrowed some of the ideas of Freud and was essentially concerned with the relief of the lingering effects, the 'pain', of psychological trauma. In 1953, Hubbard incorporated the Church of Scientology in New Jersey, USA, and claimed religious status for his project (though it would be another forty years before its status as a religion would be acknowledged by the US Inland Revenue Service).

Whether it is a 'religion' in the conventional sense remains a subject of debate, particularly because of the high fees charged for its services. The Australian High Court gave it that status in 1983, in a case that was mainly about the taxation benefits available to a religion rather than a commercial organisation. Spain, Portugal, Italy, Sweden and Hungary have similarly granted Scientology the tax status of a religion. Germany has decided it is not a religion, also because of taxation: if Scientology were to be declared a religion in Germany, it would become a beneficiary of the German 'church tax'. Many other countries, including the UK, Canada, France and Greece, have also refused to give Scientology the legal status of a religion.

Scientology doesn't appear to identify a god in the conventional religious sense, though its teachings – like those of Hinduism and Buddhism – include reincarnation. Its continuing existence, outlasting many other 'awareness' programs of the twentieth century, may be attributable to the fact that it offers its members a comprehensive set of spiritual beliefs about the nature of the universe.

Part of the folklore of personal growth movements – like the folklore of some religious sects – is that the beliefs of the group might well come between you and your family and friends. People who embrace extreme or hardline belief-systems sometimes find that they have unwittingly sown the seeds of destruction of their marriage or other relationships. They attend a weekend retreat to 'find themselves' and then discover that they have embarked on a longer and more demanding journey than their partner bargained for. Throughout the history of 'awareness' movements – whether religious, quasi-religious, mystical or flagrantly commercial – many people have come to the shocking, or simply sad, realisation that they have grown apart from their spouse or other loved ones.

◆

Most medical practitioners – and virtually all practitioners in the area of 'complementary' medicine – recognise that a patient's faith in a prescribed medication, whether chemical or 'natural', can be a major contributing factor to its efficacy. In fact, when drugs are subject to controlled clinical trials in which the performance of an active drug is compared with a neutral or benign placebo, there's typically a thirty percent placebo response – that is, thirty percent of patients taking the non-active 'fake' drug experience positive effects comparable to the effects of the active drug being tested. In the case of oestrogen therapy for menopausal women, the placebo response rate climbs as high as fifty percent, which is why some products with no clinically proven efficacy in the treatment of menopause symptoms can still appear to work.

The placebo effect turned up in a 1996 study of a drug designed to reduce stress incontinence associated with a weakness in women's pelvic floor muscles – a problem so physical and mechanical, you'd hardly imagine anything less than an efficacious drug, or even surgery, could produce a result. Yet the ever-reliable placebo effect kicked in once again: thirty percent of women taking a placebo experienced an improvement in their condition as significant as the improvement experienced by the women taking the drug. Call it the power of the mind; call it the power of belief; call it what you will. I'd say it's a sign of the strength of our desire to believe.

It can even happen with surgery. In 2002, *The New England Journal of Medicine* reported a study in which patients undergoing surgical arthroscopy for osteoarthritis of the knee were compared with a control group who simply received a knee incision, without any surgery. Result: no difference between the two groups in subsequent reduction of pain and improvement in knee function.

Here's a further twist: in a 1994 paper, Dr A.A. Mason, a US psychotherapist, described how he had successfully used hypnosis for treating what he thought were severe viral warts. He subsequently learned that the patient was in fact suffering from a congenital skin condition, which made the partial cure of the warts seem quite remarkable, even 'impossible'. Dr Mason attempted to replicate his success with a number of other patients who came to him for help with the same condition; none responded to hypnosis. Dr Mason's conclusion was that hypnosis is a *folie à deux* – which he explained as 'mutual projective identification between two people'.[13] For hypnosis to work, not only would the patient have to be a believer, but so would the therapist. Once he had learned what he was really up against, Dr Mason apparently lost faith in his own ability to help, and so his 'power' to help was diminished.

How do 'faith healers' produce the dramatic results sometimes attributed to them? If the placebo effect is so powerful in response to inert pills and potions, why not in response to other healing practices, especially if the 'healers' have faith in their own powers?

◆

We sometimes look like a species that's overly anxious to believe whatever we're told. That's because we humans are characterised by such curiosity, such a strong desire for understanding of the world around us – and worlds beyond this world – that we are disposed to accept any explanation that seems either plausible or satisfying. For many of us, that satisfaction need only be emotional, not rational: faith supplies its own proof.

BELIEFS NEED REINFORCEMENT

Once we've embraced a particular set of convictions – religious, astrological, political or scientific – we constantly seek reinforcement of them. We love to hear people saying things that confirm them. We even enjoy, in a limited way, being attacked, because the experience of defending ourselves against attack is itself a reinforcing, affirming experience.

You can see this phenomenon at work in the debate about climate change. Those who believe the most dire predictions about global warming sound like the prophets of old. Those who remain sceptical are derided, ridiculed and chastised for their non-belief. Those in the middle, who don't know which expert to believe, are seen as rather pathetic, lukewarm creatures; agnostics; fence-sitters. But those with a view – at any point on the spectrum – constantly seek reinforcement of it, hungrily devouring any fresh news that might confirm their fears of the worst or their scepticism about the whole thing.

At the most trivial level, you can observe the reinforcement effect in our relationships with the branded products we buy. The keenest readers of advertisements for luxury cars are the existing owners of those vehicles, who appreciate reinforcement of the idea that they did the right thing forking out so much money for a car. But it's not just the luxury car market where this phenomenon can be observed: most advertising works like that, most of the time. Advertising's vital role in the commercial marketplace is to reinforce the commitment – the faith – of the user. (Converting non-users to users takes a great deal more than advertising to achieve.)

No matter how strong a conviction may be, it's still belief rather than knowledge, and beliefs of any kind need reinforcement to survive. If our beliefs are religious, we'll tend to engage in regular religious activities – attending services of worship, praying, reading scripture and other books about our faith – that perform the vital function of strengthening our convictions, smothering our doubts and reinforcing our faith. No wonder religious leaders place such stress on the need for regular participation in religious exercises: without them, our faith might waver for lack of sustained reinforcement.

People caught up in any kind of non-religious movement – ranging from politics or civil liberties to schools of psychotherapy or personal growth movements – are similarly disposed to seek reinforcement of their beliefs. Attending meetings, classes, retreats and conferences, as well as reading widely within the canon of acceptable material, all help to stifle doubt and deepen commitment.

Reinforcement comes partly from exposure to the material itself, and partly from the sense of belonging to a tribe whose identity is based on a set of common beliefs. Many churches place strong emphasis on the idea of the 'faith community'; other varieties of faith generate their own mutually supportive communities.

Our need for reinforcement is so strong that it creates a filter that distorts our perception of the world. We see the world from our own point of view. Not surprisingly, such a selective process reinforces our existing point of view – our prejudices and precon-ceptions – because we are focusing on evidence that supports it. If that sounds rather circular, it's because it is: we see what we are looking for, what we expect to see. We bring all our experiences, learnings, convictions, attitudes, beliefs and prejudices – our 'baggage' – to the process of perceiving and interpreting the world, and our perceptions are coloured by what we already believe to be true. In other words, the viewer is part of the view.

This is not a function of any particular set of beliefs; it's just the way humans are. Selective perception is one of our most important and effective psychological mechanisms for defending our beliefs against unwelcome challenges; it even allows us to see what isn't there. In an experiment described by Jonathan Miller in his landmark television series, *The Body in Question*,[14] staff in a mental hospital in London saw evidence of various kinds of mental disorders in a series of perfectly normal people who had been 'admitted' as patients, simply because each of those patients was identified on admission as suffering from those particular illnesses. Conversely, dozens of scientists might miss a particular piece of apparently obvious evidence until one person – perhaps coming fresh to the field – spots what they had all missed, because they were looking at the evidence through the filter of their preconceptions. 'Professional deformity' is a hazard for any highly educated person: it refers to the tendency to be blinkered by your specialised knowledge.[15]

So our desire for something to believe in, while understandable, carries the risk that once we've settled on a particular set of beliefs, we might be blind to other possibilities. This is the sense in which love, too, is blind. Even our most irrational prejudices, if we can manage to cling to them, provide the comfort of certainty. The certainty might be an illusion, but it still feels like certainty.

THE LURE OF CERTAINTY

Emotionally, we prefer conviction to doubt. Most of us have a low tolerance for ambiguity. When we are confronted with a complex idea, we like to simplify it because that makes it easier not only to grasp but also to believe in.

This tendency helps explain the continuing appeal of so-called fundamentalism. Whether in religion, politics, economics, environmentalism, feminism or science, the appeal of black-and-white certainty lies in its offer of a simplicity we can understand and embrace.

Fundamentalism is inherently appealing to those who seek a stable reference point in a world of kaleidoscopic change. The past thirty years have been a time of sociocultural upheaval in many countries, so it's almost inevitable that we should have seen a corresponding surge of fundamentalism in all three of the Abrahamic religions – Judaism, Christianity and Islam.

In its religious context, fundamentalism refers to the tradition that places 'holy writ' (Bible, Torah, Qur'an) at the centre of its theology, is suspicious of modern (let alone postmodern) interpretations of religious stories, and believes that God has a personal interest in each individual, rewarding the faithful and punishing the unfaithful here and/or in the afterlife.

The word 'fundamentalist' arose from a formal movement, launched after World War I by a group of US Baptists who published a series of leaflets under the title *The Fundamentals*. Their purpose was to impose a hardline literalism on biblical interpretation as a form of protest against modern liberalism. The early fundamentalists were convinced that the idea of America as a Christian civilisation was an illusion: in their view, the apparent decline of religious observance was paralleled by social decline as well. The same linkage typically occurs today, where religious fundamentalists are often at the forefront of hardline movements against social liberalism: indeed, fundamentalism could almost be regarded as a form of ultra-conservative social protest movement.

Fundamentalists, of whatever stamp, typically fall in love with the idea of certainty: when unwelcome doubts flit ghost-like across their consciousness, they are simply banished.

If some of the doctrines of the church seem a bit hard to reconcile with your world-view, put 'em in the deep freeze and get on with it.

Don't play with dangerous notions like continuing revelation – just hold fast to your Bible-based faith.

To non-fundamentalists, rigid dogmatic positions appear incompatible with modern scholarship in theology and the sciences, yet fundamentalism remains a popular demonstration of the appeal of certainty.

Though religious in its origins, the word 'fundamentalism' is now widely applied to other non-religious beliefs. The hardline feminists of the 1970s and 1980s, for instance, embraced a set of simplistic slogans as part of their campaign to awaken men – and many women – to the injustices of sexual inequality, and to ignite a gender revolution: A woman needs an independent income to be truly liberated. Women can be anything they want to be; do anything they want to do; have anything they want to have. If relationships with men are diminished or destroyed in the process, that's just collateral damage.

Not all feminists thought – or think – like that, but there was a generous measure of fundamentalism in the dogma of the pioneers (as there usually is in the rhetoric of revolutionaries), still evident when some of them criticise the rising generation of young women for becoming too liberal in their interpretation of the meaning of liberation. Today's young women still want to have it all but, having seen what 'liberation' did to their often-conflicted and exhausted mothers, they don't necessarily want it all at once.

◆

The medical controversy over hormone replacement therapy (HRT) is a dramatic example of how the quest for simple certainty can even get in the way of good medical practice. HRT has had a chequered history marked by controversy, apparently contradictory research and wild swings in the attitudes and behaviour of medical professionals and menopausal women.

The 1960s and early 1970s saw a burst of enthusiasm for HRT that gave it almost mythical status – 'the elixir of youth' – and propelled it to unprecedented levels of uncritical acceptance among doctors and patients.[16] Simple certainty ruled; pro-HRT dogma prevailed: 'Everyone should be on this!' Then in 2002, early results from a major US research project called the Women's Health Initiative (WHI) suggested an association between HRT and breast cancer.

In fact, there were many flaws in the WHI project, and clear grounds remained for recommending HRT for certain women under certain conditions where the therapy would be likely to be beneficial. But the game was up. HRT became, almost overnight, 'not worth the risk' and usage dropped dramatically. Even among highly trained professionals, the quest for simple certainty overwhelmed the evidence pointing to the need for a more nuanced, case-by-case assessment of the risk and benefits of HRT.

The Australian social analyst Richard Eckersley has noted the lure of certainty as a hazard for scientists: 'From my own work, I've become very aware of the role of dogma and prejudice in science, and the tendency for scientific disciplines to develop a false consensus about things.'[17]

THE LEADER VIRUS

The wildly irrational faith we sometimes place in political leaders reminds us how vulnerable we are to our desire for something to believe in. From the Children of Israel's faith in Moses as the man to lead them out of Egypt, to Germany's unbridled passion for Hitler or America's hysterical Obamania, human history is littered with sobering examples of a psychological 'virus' that regularly infects us when we turn too eagerly to a leader to deal with our own sense of powerlessness, uncertainty or insecurity. 'We need a strong leader,' the cry goes up, and then we cast around for a suitable candidate onto whom we can project our aspirations.

Inevitably, the euphoria surrounding the election of leaders at such times ends in disappointment and disenchantment. It happened swiftly and terminally with Kevin Rudd in Australia. It happens whenever we make a euphoric investment in a new leader who comes to power at a time of crisis, or at a turning point in a nation's mood. The greater the euphoria, fuelled by the marketing methods that convert politicians into brands, the more likely the crash.

The disappointment is a direct result of our misplaced desire to *believe in* a leader. How easily we forget that leaders are human, and therefore frail, flawed, conflicted and corruptible (by power, if nothing else). They may even possess a particular type of frailty that propels them into the kind of role where they feel obliged to appear stronger, wiser and more unflinchingly confident than any one person could reasonably be expected to be.

But we continue to hope, to invest, to fall victim to the epidemic of leader worship. Believing in the power and authority of a new leader, charmed by their aura, it is tempting for citizens to leave it to the magic of the leader to achieve the assorted legislative, economic or social miracles promised in an election campaign. Paradoxically, the leader virus may actually weaken our own engagement with the political process. Reflecting on the popular error of portraying the African-American freedom struggle as 'Martin Luther King's movement', Diane Nash, a founder of the Student Nonviolent Coordinating Committee, said: 'If people understood that it was ordinary people who did everything that needed to be done in the movement, instead of thinking, I wish we had a Martin Luther King now, they would ask, "What can I do?" Idolising just one person undermines the struggle.'[18]

The disappointment and disillusionment that follow outbreaks of 'leader virus' do us no harm: we need correctives like this. The danger is that when we elect the kind of leader we believe in with a quasi-religious fervour, we may feel that everything will go the way we want it to, and we can 'leave it to the leader'. Germany in the 1930s was a classic case of how leader-based euphoria can lead to a widespread abdication of the citizens' sense of responsibility for what is happening.

Charismatic leaders can inspire us, albeit briefly. We like them to appear strong, because we feel that might make us feel stronger, too. We want leaders with integrity, because we keep hoping for someone to restore our faith in the integrity of government. We admire leaders with courage and passion, because they radiate the kind of confidence and the kind of commitment we wish we had. But political charisma usually has a use-by date. Gradually, we come to recognise the frailty, perhaps the folly and even the weakness of the leaders from whom we had expected too much. And then we feel worse, not better. Realpolitik being what it is, our disenchantment will be compounded as we are forced to accept – all over again – that no leader is a magician when it comes to withstanding the influence of powerful lobbies and institutions, whether big business, religious lobby groups, the military–industrial complex, manufacturing and resource industries, or the parliamentary institutions themselves.

In the face of the evidence that our leader-heroes are neither invincible nor omnipotent, we might fleetingly wonder if we could have done better with someone who was less exciting in the beginning. But politics, like sport, has gone the way of celebrity-based entertainment (a politician's five-second grab has more in common with a TV commercial than a political manifesto) and so we keep looking for the next rising star. In this quest, we are encouraged by the politicians themselves: after all, simple certainty is precisely what most candidates want us to feel about them, and once elected, they want us to remain true believers, through thick and thin.

Unlike religious faith, faith in leaders can neither console nor comfort us in our disappointment, let alone in our struggles to make sense of our own lives. We are always left, in the end, with ourselves, and no leader can insulate us from the private pain of that encounter.

EVERYONE'S BELIEFS LOOK WEIRD TO THE NON-BELIEVER

'You believe in reincarnation? You can't be serious!'

'But you believe in the physical resurrection of the dead. Not just Jesus, but all his followers as well. What could be weirder than that?'

'But that's documented in scripture.'

'Documented? What about all the documentary evidence for reincarnation? Have you never read Ian Stevenson's case studies?'[19]

'I can't believe you really think Neil Armstrong never landed on the moon. I saw it on television, with my very own eyes.'

'Ah, you saw it on television. You believe everything you see on TV? This was just a very clever piece of NASA propaganda.'

'But you believe in aliens and UFOs.'

'That's not a question of belief. That's fact. If you'd seen what one of my friends saw . . .'

'How can you possibly say that the world would be a better place if the free market was allowed to run riot? What about the poor and disadvantaged? They would just be trampled underfoot! You need government intervention, government controls and safeguards. You need regulation.'

'You've just listed all the reasons why a true free market would work better. It's all those regulations and interventions that interfere with it. We've never been allowed to see a true free market – governments always get in the way.'

'If you kill any of these wild donkeys, you'll be punished by drought.'

'How can you believe that in this day and age?'

'Well, you believe God controls the weather. What's the difference?'

'But, but . . . why donkeys?

'Donkeys are special to us, just like cows in India. Jesus rode into Jerusalem on a donkey, don't forget.'

Find me a believer – in anything – and I'll find you ten sceptics on that topic, each of whom will have a set of their own beliefs, equally puzzling to another group of sceptics. The world is as full of sceptics as it is of believers, and they are mostly the same people: it all depends on which set of beliefs is in the frame. No one is as sceptical of fundamentalism as a liberal; no one is as sceptical of agnosticism or of humanism as the ardent religious fundamentalist. There are plenty of apparently rational humanists who still say things like, 'It was meant to be' (meant by whom?), or who sneak a peek at the astrology columns in their newspapers and magazines.

I don't really believe all that stuff – not the day-to-day predictions, but I sometimes wonder if there could be something in the basic idea. For instance, my wife is a classic Scorpio. Classic.

In politics, the leader who inspires starry-eyed faith in some people will look like a phony, a fraud, or even a monster to others. We might all desire the same thing – something or someone to believe in – but our ways of satisfying that desire will always be subject to the individual differences in our personalities, preferences and prejudices.

Because our particular beliefs are such an intimate, personal response to the general desire to believe in something, it's hardly surprising that other people, from the perspective of *their* personal beliefs, should find ours bewildering, threatening or simply ridiculous.

But they need theirs, just as we need ours.

THE DESIRE TO CONNECT

A vast similitude interlocks all . . .

Walt Whitman, 'On the Beach at Night Alone', *Leaves of Grass*

I love going to the movies, and I enjoy reading film reviews. Movies, like novels and plays, are like a conduit to other lives, other ways of being, other ways of seeing the world. I feel *connected* when I'm at the movies – maybe it's an illusion, but that's how I feel. Even if I dislike the characters, I enter into their lives in much the same way as I imagine, when I look in the window of a real estate agent's office, what it would be like to live *there*, or *there*.

I also feel connected when I read a review because I'm catching a glimpse of someone else's experience of a film, someone else's frame of reference. I enjoy reading reviews even more after I've seen the film because then I can explore both connections at once.

When I'm fully engaged with a movie, the sense of connection goes deeper than mere empathy: I also reflect on *who I am*.

Most of us find that kind of reflection therapeutic. If the experience of living through a story played out on stage or screen – or in a novel – really grips us and excites our imagination, we can't help testing ourselves against what is going on, imagining how we might have acted in that situation compared with the heroes and villains of the piece. Being moved to laughter or tears is an obvious sign of engagement, but sometimes it's also a symptom of self-recognition: we are laughing or crying *for ourselves*.

The desire to connect, to engage, is one of our deepest yearnings. But connect with what? With whom? This is actually a trio of desires that vary in strength from person to person and from time to time:

the desire to connect with ourselves – to know ourselves better

the desire to connect with each other – to communicate

the desire to connect with the natural world.

GETTING TO KNOW YOURSELF

'There is only one problem.' That's what the American psychotherapist Carl Rogers concluded after many years in clinical practice. Although his clients brought a wide variety of troubles and complaints to his consulting room – difficulties with relationships, work or studies, concerns about their own bizarre behaviour or their disabling phobias – the fundamental issue was always the same: 'Who am I, *really*? How can I get in touch with this real self?'[1]

J.D. Salinger described the process of getting in touch with his real self before he could settle to the task of writing: 'It takes me at least an hour to warm up when I sit down to work . . . Just taking off my own disguises takes an hour or more.'2

There's a long and rich philosophical tradition that encourages our desire to connect with ourselves. *Know thyself* is the headline. (Here's Oscar Wilde's version: '"Know thyself" was written over the portal of the ancient world. Over the portal of the new world, "Be yourself" shall be written.') Attributed to Socrates among others, 'Know thyself' was inscribed in the forecourt of the Temple of Apollo at Delphi. Quoting it in *The Republic*, Plato mused on how absurd it would be to be curious about other matters 'while I am still in ignorance of my own self'.

The novelist E.M. Forster's famous dictum, 'Only connect!', was a plea from a character in *Howard's End* to connect 'the prose and the passion, so both will be exalted', the implication being that we are at our best when we act in ways that are consistent with who we really are.

So how do we find out 'who we really are'?

For some people, the most effective way to connect with ourselves is through disciplined meditation. They believe that when we are deeply relaxed, unencumbered by stress and distraction, we experience a heightened sense of self-awareness and are more closely in touch with our 'inner being'. (Some people use prayer in the same way.) But meditation doesn't appeal to everyone: many people say they simply can't submit to its disciplines, or they find the process unhelpful.

The Buddhist concept of 'mindfulness' takes the meditative process one step further. Mindfulness describes a way of thinking, a way of being, that can be incorporated into daily living. Lama Surya Das describes mindfulness as 'relaxed, open, lucid, moment-to-moment present awareness. It is like a bright mirror . . . mindfulness implies an understanding of what we are doing and saying'.[3] In the Buddhist tradition, the art of mindfulness is acquired through meditation that 'explores, investigates, unveils, and illumines what is hidden within and around us'.

Some will claim the best pathway to self-awareness is psycho-therapy – perhaps psychoanalysis (Freudian, Jungian, Kleinian or otherwise), or Carl Rogers's client-centred approach, based on the therapist's active and reflective listening, or any other form of therapy designed to create an atmosphere of freedom in which clients feel able to drop what Rogers described as 'the false fronts, or the masks, or the roles' which have concealed them, even from themselves. But not everyone feels psychotherapy is the right pathway for them: many regard therapy as appropriate only for people grappling with particular problems or unresolved issues, rather than for those who simply want to explore and clarify their own stories.

◆

There's another pathway to connection with your 'inner' self that makes a deeply satisfying contribution to the lives of those who follow it: it's valued by many counsellors as way of gaining access to the emotional lives of their clients or even as a healing therapy in its own right. It's also embraced by educationalists, who have traditionally assigned it an important role in the education and development of young children.

I'm talking about creative self-expression; participation in the creative and performing arts.

When you are engrossed in the artistic process – writing, taking photographs, composing, playing or singing music, dancing, painting, sculpting, drawing or creating any kind of art or design – you are lost to your surroundings. The intensity of your concentration allows your innermost thoughts and feelings to be expressed in what you are doing.

The therapeutic and 'connective' benefits of the creative process seem so powerful to those who engage in it that it's a wonder any of us hold back. 'I'm not the arty type' is hardly a defence: the creative spark is in all of us, and if you doubt it, take a look at some of the things you did when you were a child.

When I'm painting, I'm in another world. I lose track of the time. And when I look at what I've done, I sometimes ask myself, 'Where did that come from?'

The Russian literary critic, Viktor Shklovsky, wrote that 'art exists that one might recover the sensations of life; it exists to make one feel things, to make the stone stony'.[4] His point was that, through the creative process, whether in the written word or on canvas or film or any other art form, we are challenged to see the world in a new, more intense way.

Recent research into responses to music among sufferers from autism suggests that 'emotions in music are accessible when other forms of expression are difficult to decipher. It also seems that music can be especially enriching and life-enhancing when everyday existence is hard.'[5]

Reading or viewing or listening to other people's artistic output can be a great source both of emotional release and of connection: watching films, listening to music, standing in awe before a work of art, or being deeply immersed in a novel. At its luminous best, exposure to the work of creative artists in any field opens us up to a new sense of our own nature and our own potential.

But if we really want to learn more about who we are and where our minds can take us, we need to get hold of a camera and explore for ourselves new ways of seeing the world; open our mouths and sing; take up a pen or a laptop and start writing a journal or jotting down ideas for stories; pick up a brush and start painting a picture or creating a design; throw off our inhibitions and do some free-form dancing; join with friends and start a poetry-writing group or create and stage a play for the amusement of friends and family; plant a garden of our own; refurnish a room to reflect our tastes and preferences more accurately; find a recorder, a ukulele, a piano or a guitar and learn to play it.

It doesn't seem to matter what medium, what art form, we choose: some are drawn to writing or painting or music; some will experiment with several until they find something that works for them.

When we lack any outlet for creative self-expression, we miss out on one of the great adventures, one of the great pleasures of life. We also deny ourselves one means of access to our own souls. 'A book must be the axe for the frozen sea within us,' Franz Kafka once wrote to a friend. He was talking about reading, but the metaphor can be extended to our experience of any art form, and works even better when we apply it to our own creative output. Once we embark on the creative process, we may find we are connecting with ourselves in ways that surprise us: 'Where did that come from?' might well be a sign that we've cracked the frozen sea within us.

If we only consume and never create, there's every chance we'll become jaded in our responses to the arts, increasingly hard to please, too worried about the 'meaning' and 'value' of the work. Create something yourself and such questions either dissolve or evolve into a more sympathetic appreciation of the power of the arts to connect us to ourselves.

Those who make time for regular creative activity in their lives report a tranquillity of mind that is otherwise hard to achieve: the narrow focus of the creative process admits no distractions, and that's therapeutic in itself.

Do we have to do it well? Not at all, though it becomes more satisfying as we get better at it, which is why starting off with a teacher is a good idea. But we only have to *do it* for the therapeutic benefits to flow. Other people don't have to listen to us sing or play. No one else ever has to read what we've written. The pictures we paint never have to be hung: plenty of artists just keep painting over their old stuff.

Richard Gill, the Australian music educator, musical director of the Victorian Opera and artistic director of the Sydney Symphony's education program, insists not only that listening attentively to music develops areas of the brain that other forms of activity don't, but that *making* music, and especially *creating* music, are proven breakthrough experiences in our cognitive and emotional development.

Just as the teaching of literacy involves creative writing and the teaching of art involves pupils in painting and drawing, so, according to Gill, 'a serious music education includes composition of music'.[6]

Why all this emphasis on the practice of the creative arts? Simply because creativity is all about exploring the self; it's about the therapeutic benefit of learning how to express yourself, and that, in turn, is all about connecting with your own thoughts and feelings. (It can also turn out to be about connecting with others, but that's a bonus.) If 'Know thyself' is your goal, this may be the most reliable of all the pathways to it.

We don't need to limit our creativity to traditional, conventional meanings of 'the arts'. In *The Mud House,* the Sydney radio presenter and newspaper columnist Richard Glover chronicles the 25-year process of designing and building a mud-brick house in the Australian bush. Writing about the intense satisfaction he obtained from completing the project, Glover quotes the psychoanalyst Carl Jung, who had himself built his own house outside Zurich. Jung described his house as a 'representation in stone of my innermost thoughts' and Glover clearly feels the same way about his. 'I made the house and it made me,' he writes.[7]

◆

What makes us tick? One of the things that does it is our creative spark. Creative self-expression does more than help to satisfy the desire to connect; it also equips us to function more confidently in other aspects of our lives.

Does this mean that professional artists, being so closely in touch with their own feelings, are better adjusted and better balanced than the rest of us? Not necessarily; in fact, their very absorption in their art creates the risk of becoming lopsided. I have described this as a three-fold desire – connection with our inner selves, with others, and with nature – and if we indulge any one of those at the expense of the others, we're unlikely to be well-rounded, balanced people. There are plenty of neurotic, self-obsessed, uncommunicative and generally unpleasant professional artists, writers and musicians, just as there are plenty of neurotic, self-obsessed, uncommunicative and generally unpleasant lawyers, accountants, plumbers and nurses.

It's all about balance.

SELF-EXAMINATION IS A NECESSARY PART OF SELF-KNOWLEDGE

A good place to begin the process of getting to know ourselves is by examining any gaps that exist between our professed attitudes and our behaviour – what we say and what we do. Are there things we do that create tension in us because we know we are sending false signals about our real attitudes or values? Are we saying what we really think? Are we frank with ourselves about our beliefs, our fears and even our uncertainties and insecurities?

Are we conforming to other people's behaviour in ways that, if we were being true to ourselves, we would not copy? Are we persisting with relationships that make us feel uncomfortable and seem to distort our sense of who we are?

Do we spend too much time doing things we later come to resent or feel ashamed of? How often do we find ourselves regretting we haven't spent more time doing other things, or spent more time with people we claim are important to us? Do we have a sense of obligations not fulfilled? Creative impulses not yet expressed? Ambitions not yet achieved? Potential not yet realised?

Constructive self-examination involves being open to all such questions about ourselves, our motives, our values, our goals. This does not have to be a grand inquisition: it is more likely to consist of a continuous series of small investigations as we become accustomed to the process of listening to ourselves.

The challenge of accepting the truth about ourselves is not always an easy one. For a start, we are bound to come across some unexpected inconsistencies, ambiguities and contradictions in our attitudes and even in our values. (That's part of what being human means: we are *all* a walking bundle of contradictions, partly because the desires that drive us are so often in competition with each other.)

We may believe in the idea of free will, for example, yet also believe we are sometimes driven by desires that seem beyond our control. Our attitudes to religion may be shot through with contradictions: even if we desire a simple faith in a god or an afterlife, we are constantly stricken by doubt. In our intimate personal relationships, we marvel at how someone we love with intense passion can sometimes irritate us so much, or how one of our children can seem much more attractive than another, even though we love them equally.

How can we feel so unsure of ourselves at forty when we were so sure of ourselves at thirty? How can we seem to want something so badly, then, as soon as we have it, wonder why it ever seemed so important to us?

Connecting with ourselves often involves facing up to unre-solved inner tensions and conflicts. It's a safe assumption that some of our most deep-seated and debilitating conflicts are not between us and others but within ourselves, and inner conflicts often affect our ability to connect with others. If we are permanently in an adversarial frame of mind because we are 'at war with ourselves', this is bound to affect our relationships: we will be inclined to be argumentative and perhaps even aggressive for reasons that may have little or nothing to do with the person we're talking to, or even the topic we're discussing.

Self-examination often leads to the conclusion that we need to do some work on ourselves – either alone or with the help of a close friend, or perhaps a counsellor. But there are many things about ourselves we are not going to change, and sooner or later we will have to accept that we are this kind of person and not that; we have these strengths and not those; our lives are like this, and not like that . . . so we might as well get on with it.

Connecting with ourselves is both harder and more rewarding than we imagine. After all, we have been living with this person all our lives – what more is there to know? The answer, almost always, is: much, much more.

CONNECTING WITH EACH OTHER

A ten-year-old rushes home from school and bursts through the back door shouting, 'Mum! Mum! I won!' Winning isn't enough; he needs to communicate his excitement.

A young woman gazes at a spectacular mountain view. She is alone, but turns to look for someone to share the moment with. A middle-aged couple is standing near her at the lookout. 'Isn't it sublime? Doesn't it make you feel small?' They smile at her and nod their agreement.

A baby, lying in her cot, makes repetitive sounds that are almost words, practising for the moment when verbal communication with her parents will become possible. In the meantime, she will make do with cooing, gurgling and crying, and her parents will hang on each sound as if it were as eloquent as a sonnet: *I think she said 'Da-da'.*

◆

Communication is the lifeblood of human society. Apart from life itself, it's our most precious gift from the gods – or, if you prefer, from the glacial process of human evolution that led us to become such fluent and sophisticated communicators. With few exceptions – hermits, isolates, surly adolescents – we love to share with each other whatever we are thinking and feeling, via the full range of signs and symbols available to us: words (sometimes the least effective of all the signals we send each other), facial expressions, postures, gestures, tones of voice, rates of speech . . . all the ways we try to convey meaning. We communicate to connect, by establishing common ground or mutual understanding.

We neglect the communication process at our peril. 'Know thyself' is a wise exhortation, but 'Communicate!' should be uttered in the next breath, because the establishment and main-tenance of social connections is fundamental to our social and emotional health and wellbeing. As herd animals, we rely on communication to survive and prosper. I don't know whether moose, geese, chimpanzees or dolphins are into self-knowledge, but they are all into communication in a big way. And so are we.

Most children are wonderfully impulsive communicators, capable of sharing whatever's on their minds with anyone who will attend to them. We become a little less spontaneous, a little more inhibited, as we grow older, but the desire to communicate stays with us. It's how relationships form and mature; it's integral to our mating rituals; it sustains family and community life; it makes a crucial contribution to our sense of who we are.

Most of us define the meaning of our lives in terms of our relationships, and our relationships in turn define us. We are someone's parent or someone's child, someone's spouse, neighbour, friend or colleague. Unless we nurture those connections through communication, they lose their significance for us – which is another way of saying we lose something of ourselves.

You can see the disappointment in the eyes of people who were once close but have lost the art of communicating with each other, or the will to stick at it. If they live in the same house, the silences between them become even more deathly and destructive than furious arguments. To come into their presence is to understand how vital it is either to keep the lines of communication open, or else to go away entirely. Never seeing you is more sensible – and healthier – than seeing you and failing to communicate with you.

I once heard a woman who had been married for decades explain to a friend how she coped with her husband's incessant chatter combined with his failure to attend to her: 'Oh, I stopped listening years ago.' They lived separate lives, devoid of mutual respect, and his insensitive talking was like a wall of sound between them.

There are many reasons why we might fail to communicate, even when we want to do it or, more tragically, when we think we're doing it because we talk a lot.

Here are seven classic barriers to communication:

If I'm not a good listener myself, other people are unlikely to listen to me (the Law of Reciprocity again).

If I've said it before, I probably don't need to say it again. Repetition, especially in the form of nagging, is one of the quickest ways of losing an audience. (And don't say, 'Stop me if I've already told you this,' unless you mean it. A friendship between two women I knew foundered over just such an exchange: the listener said, 'Stop!' and her friend never forgave her.)

If the message in our words is contradicted or modified by our tone of voice, rate or volume of speech, gestures, facial expression or body language, the words will be swamped by those other messages. If you say 'I'm not angry' with a red face and a trembling chin, your audience will get the clear message that you are angry (plus another message: that you're trying to pretend not to be). In face-to-face conversation, the words are only a small part of the total message people receive from us, which is why we can feel as if we're being misinterpreted without knowing why. We rarely take each other's words at face value, and most of us are good at reading meanings into the full set of messages we exchange in our face-to-face encounters. When we're feeling defensive – *I didn't say that!* – we might need to acknowledge that even if our words weren't saying it, the look on our face might have been expressing it with great clarity.

If we are only talking to clarify what we really think about something, the other person will come to feel redundant and switch off. Hearing yourself say something – just like the experience of writing something down – can be very illuminating but you shouldn't assume that talkers always need listeners, or that writers always need readers.

If someone feels insecure in their relationship with us – intimidated, anxious, frightened or mistrustful – communication between us will be difficult. They will be unlikely to listen attentively and unable to respond honestly and openly.

If we're always talking about ourselves, it's hard for the other person to find a way into the conversation or a way of seeing its relevance to them. Narcissism is hard to listen to; so is arrogance. (Advertisers know this. One of the most fundamental principles of effective advertising is this: always talk to the consumer about the consumer; always spell out the benefit *to them*.)

If we lack self-knowledge and are unable to resolve our own internal conflicts, we're less likely to be able to express ourselves clearly. If we're not in touch with ourselves, it will be harder for other people to get in touch with us.

◆

The greatest barriers to connection are within us. We'll never communicate successfully with another person unless we're prepared to take their point of view seriously. And we'll never reach that stage if we let our own prejudices or expectations limit our capacity to listen attentively.

In an essay on communication breakdown, Carl Rogers identified the main challenge we face when we try to connect: 'If you really understand another person . . . if you are willing to enter his private world and see the way life appears to him, without any attempt to make evaluative judgements, you run the risk of being changed yourself.'[8]

Connecting with others takes courage. Relationships have a way of changing us, and the risk of being changed can be a daunting, even frightening prospect. But good listeners are prepared to run that risk.

That kind of connection doesn't imply agreement with everything another person thinks or believes. We can connect with people who have very different points of view from our own: many friendships and many marriages thrive on just such differences. The key to connection is acceptance of the other person and respect for their point of view.

CONNECTING ONLINE

Even in the era of digital devices that allow us to transfer data at astonishing speed and with blithe disregard for our physical absence from each other, it's tempting to cling to the idea that face-to-face contact is the form of communication most likely to satisfy our desire to connect. Other contacts inevitably lack some of the subtleties and nuances inherent in face-to-face encounters and it's those very nuances that play such a big part in illuminating our understanding of each other. No matter how closely connected we may feel online, I suspect the desire to connect can't be fully satisfied without a small network of relationships that are maintained through regular in-person contact.

On the other hand, a thirty-year-old friend recently told me a story that challenged me to rethink the many meanings of 'connected'. My friend had committed 'Facebook suicide' (by deleting her Facebook profile) because she felt she was becoming a lazy friend:

I was putting everything I was doing on Facebook. All my friends knew what I was up to, and there was nothing left to talk about when we met. So we stopped seeing as much of each other. After a while, I realised we were not phoning each other and not meeting for coffee, so I cancelled my Facebook account.

What happened next? She soon found that by abandoning Facebook, she had effectively cut herself off from her friends – they were all too busy to meet regularly in the ways they might once have done, so Facebook had become their preferred medium of 'maintenance' communication. My friend was forced to acknowledge that it was Facebook or nothing. But at least she knew what risks she was taking; at least she knew what she was losing in the process.

The extraordinary advances in communications technology have opened up new meanings of 'connected'. In many ways, online networks like Facebook and Twitter operate like offline networks, often with far more frequent and spontaneous contact than most of us manage offline. Yet, like all 'mediated' exchanges, from the handwritten note to the telephone, they have their limitations.

In our early experience of them, online networks encourage reckless personal revelations that seem to be more about self-expression than communication. Tapping away on the keyboard and only seeing our message on our own screen can easily tempt us into forgetting that this is the equivalent of exposing ourselves to a very large roomful of people, with messages that are capable of being stored forever and retransmitted. Over time, we tend to adapt to the online phenomenon and begin imposing some self-censorship on the messages we exchange.

We've all had to learn a similar lesson about the telephone: that disembodied voice in your ear can encourage a particular kind of intimacy that sometimes leaves us wondering if we went too far. Many teenage romances have taken huge leaps forward on the phone, sometimes to the embarrassment of the people concerned when they've had their next face-to-face encounter, almost as if there were two dimensions to the relationship: the real one and the 'phone-y' one.

Digital exchanges are mostly reliant on words, whereas traditional interpersonal communication relies on many of the nonverbal – especially visual – cues that simply don't survive the transfer into cyberspace (as they didn't survive the transfer into the written word for previous generations). Even when a video clip is put on YouTube, or a series of photos posted on Facebook, there is none of the ebb and flow of continuous interaction that characterises face-to-face exchanges.

Of course text messages, emails, Facebook and other electronic links – to say nothing of old-fashioned media such as letters and postcards – are brilliant ways of maintaining established relationships. But more than that? Digital data-transfer is becoming so sophisticated that it has already blurred the traditional distinction between real presence and virtual presence. Even in the case of mourning, online connections are proving beneficial to many people. The US culture critic Meghan O'Rourke reports that, in the era of the internet, 'some mourners have returned grief to a social space, creating online grieving communities, establishing virtual cemeteries, commemorative pages, and chat rooms where loss can be described and shared'.[9]

For people who are unable or unwilling to mix socially in their neighbourhood or other communities, for those who find the telephone intimidating or stressful, or who simply prefer non-face-to-face communication, the online revolution has offered a sense of easy, low-stress, controllable connection that feels like a new lease on life.

> *I can think what I want to say before I say it. I can edit. I can ignore messages if I don't want to respond to them. And I'm in touch with all kinds of interesting people I would never have met at the local bus stop, I can tell you.*

In spite of its seductive appeal, the IT revolution might paradoxically be destined to frustrate our desire for connection. Communications technology, no matter how swift and convenient, no matter how clever, is creating the illusion of bringing us together while actually keeping us apart. That's what had rattled my friend who committed 'Facebook suicide'. We thrive on social interaction and feel the loss of it when all we have is the screen-based alternative, no matter how well we adapt to the technology. At work, we need to wander around the office, chatting; we need to 'waste time' together over a bit of tearoom gossip. When our working environment is dominated by non-personal activity – being locked onto a screen, for instance – the need for personal relief is correspondingly acute.

This helps explain why workplace boredom is common among people whose working lives are dominated by electronic stimulation. It's simply the wrong kind of stimulation. Not only is it impersonal, but it contributes to a sense of frustration that springs from our perceived lack of control over our working environment.

Some observers of the online scene fear that as we become saturated in the new technologies, sending and receiving more messages than ever before in history, the desire for connection may itself be sated.

Sometimes I have to turn my mobile phone off, just to get some relief.

How did we ever manage before email? It's terrific, but it does tend to take over. I'm trying to limit myself to just checking emails once an hour, otherwise you can spend half your life handling emails.

Others dismiss all such concerns, embracing these new modes of connection as an enrichment of our capacity to connect, and arguing that the traditional condition for interpersonal connection – being 'present' – is simply no longer a prerequisite. However this part of the story unfolds, the underlying desire to connect, one way or another, shows no sign of abating.

FROM THE GARDEN TO THE COSMOS: CONNECTING WITH THE NATURAL WORLD

When I'm out there on my surfboard, I sometimes get this huge charge. I don't just feel as if I'm part of the ocean – I feel as if I'm part of the universe.

It doesn't matter what's going on, which member of the family is playing up, or who's going to win the next election. When I'm out in the garden I can put it all behind me. If I didn't get my hands in the soil on a regular basis, I think I'd need to see a psychiatrist.

You can see why the ancient psalmist was inspired by mountains – 'I will lift up mine eyes unto the hills, from whence

*cometh my help.' I sometimes feel the same way myself.
I'm not a believer, but I do feel that sort of awe when I get
close to nature. I love gazing at the night sky, too – sort of
communing with it, in a way.*

Some of the most evocative photos in your family album are
likely to be those that record time spent 'getting back to nature' –
camping, caravanning, swimming, sailing, skiing, fishing, hiking,
horse-riding, picnicking.

Not everyone gets dewy-eyed about nature. I once worked with
a woman who said she felt uneasy whenever she left the city, and
couldn't wait to get the pavement back under her feet. Her family
owned a farm, and she dreaded being asked to visit. But hers was
an unusual case of disconnection from the natural world: most
city-dwellers hanker after a rural or coastal escape. In Australia,
the rural fantasy is often based on a rather romanticised vision of
the joys of country life, which doesn't include dust, flies, drought,
snakes or plagues of mice or locusts, but does include the idea of
being close to the land.

In urbanised Western societies, most of us don't live close to
the land, but there are many signs of our desire to retain some
connection with it. The resurgence of interest in gardening is
perhaps the most obvious – from traditional suburban lawns and
flower gardens to vegetable plots, hydroponics, potted gardens on
apartment balconies, or community gardens.

*'Back to nature' sounds so hokey, but that's exactly what the
garden is for me – especially the vegetable patch. Nothing
says organic like organic.*

Why do the residents of high-rise apartment blocks so lovingly tend the pot-plants on their balconies; even one solitary pot-plant? Why is that tiny 'plot' of earth so symbolically important to them? For the beauty of the plants and flowers? Perhaps; but also, surely, because it is part of the natural world. Why do an increasing number of the residents of inner-urban areas become involved in community gardening, often including vegetables? To save money and have access to fresher food than is available in the supermarket? No doubt. To participate in a communal activity that recaptures some of the imagined camaraderie of village life? Very likely. But it's also an expression of the desire among people who live highly urbanised lives to reconnect with nature. The 'guerilla gardeners' movement now catching on in some cities has the same object: planting unauthorised gardens in neglected public places both beautifies and adds a natural element to the overbuilt environment.

Why do so many people keep pets – dogs, cats, goldfish, birds, even snakes – in their houses and apartments? For companionship, certainly, but might it also be because animals are a link with our primitive urge to be part of the natural world – perhaps symbolising the farm animals from a real or imaginary rural heritage, or even the animals we hunted or took with us on the hunt?

The pet rock craze of the 1970s, complete with owners' manuals for sale, might have been conceived as a joke or as a clever marketing opportunity by its originator Gary Dahl, a Californian advertising executive, but its widespread appeal looked like yet another sign of our desire to connect with the natural world, via that most undemanding of pets.

Why are bush-walking and mountain-climbing such popular activities, qualitatively different in the minds of their devotees from walking the streets of a suburb or town? A healthier place to walk, certainly; a welcome and even therapeutic contrast with the sights and sounds of the city. But serious walkers are devoted to the sense of being connected with nature via their exposure to fresh air, native flora and fauna, and perhaps grand vistas as well.

From Beethoven's *Pastoral Symphony* to Monet's haystacks and waterlilies, artists and composers have long drawn inspiration from nature. The Impressionist revolution in art was partly driven by the fact that painters moved their easels outside, *en plein air,* to make a closer connection with the natural world they were trying to represent. Poets, too, consistently turn to the natural world: John Masefield wrote of the compelling urge to go 'down to the seas again, to the lonely sea and the sky … for the call of the running tide/Is a wild call and a clear call that may not be denied'. And here is Walt Whitman in 'Song of Myself': 'I think I could turn and live with animals, they are so placid and self-contained,/I stand and look at them long and long.'

The popularity of recreational or sports utility vehicles (SUVs) might not be a reliable sign of our urge to get in touch with nature: some buyers simply revel in the feelings of power and safety SUVs imbue. But others are clearly indulging the rural fantasy: even if their vehicles never leave the sealed roads of the city, the image of the coast or the countryside is projected by SUVs, whose 'soul' is off-road.

Zoos, parks and gardens in cities and towns, and nature documentaries on TV, all help to satisfy our desire to connect with the natural world. Even the Green political movement reflects a growing awareness of our dependence on the physical environment and the need to protect air, land, vegetation, rivers and oceans from the impact of overpopulation and the relentless march of industrialisation.

The controversy raging about climate change and global warming has heightened our interest in our connection to the natural world. Catastrophes like the 2010 earthquake in Haiti, Hurricane Katrina's devastation of New Orleans in 2005, the Boxing Day tsunami of 2004 in the Indian Ocean, or the prolonged bushfires in California and southern Australia, all add to our fears of an upset to 'the natural order' and therefore to our very way of life.

The growing demand for organic food, like the 'slow cooking' movement, is another sign of our wish to close the gap between urban life and the natural world.

> *It's such a pity the market gardens have gone from the city fringe. We used to be so conscious of where our food came from – now all that farming land is wall-to-wall McMansions. I sometimes wonder if kids even understand that milk comes from cows.*

New Zealand's successful international marketing of dairy, meat and other food products is partly based on a perception of its unspoilt rural environment and an urban population that has remained 'closer to nature' than those in many other developed countries. Its well-conceived tourism slogan, 'Stay where you are, New Zealand – I'm coming over', ran successfully in Australia for five years, evoking the idea of a modern society that had somehow managed to retain its traditional, rural-based values. Its current slogan, '100 percent pure New Zealand', further reinforces the image of NZ produce – and the country itself – as 'natural'.

◆

'No man is an island, entire of itself . . . Each man's death diminishes me/For I am involved in mankind,' wrote John Donne in *Meditation 17*. This is a grand and noble vision of connectedness, implying something more than digging in the garden, playing music, writing poetry, nurturing our friendships or, for that matter, sending a donation to an international aid charity, valuable though all those things are as pathways to connection.

Echoing Donne, some of us speak rather mystically of 'the Unity of all Being' or 'the sense that everything's connected'. Erich Fromm, in *The Art of Loving*, saw love as the great unifying influence: 'If I truly love one person, I love all persons, I love the world, I love life.' For Fromm, love is the way we overcome our sense of separateness and satisfy what he called our 'universal, existential' craving for union.[10]

But what do we mean when we speak of the vast interconnectedness of life or the Unity of Being? Are we making a simple ecological point – that all forms of life on Earth are interdependent – or are we implying more?

To be connected with ourselves, with each other and with the natural world involves an unflinching acceptance of the nature of life on Earth. Being connected to the natural world means we won't settle for abstractions or media representations of it; we'll seek direct, first-hand experience of how the world is and how it works – its beauty, its grandeur, its ugliness, its life-giving richness and life-sapping desolation, its seasonal decay and renewal, its capacity for both nurture and brutality.

It also involves accepting the whole truth about the human condition as integral to the natural world. That includes the good news that we are creatures who experience love, joy, satisfaction, triumph; we are fuelled by faith and hope; we strive for 'personal growth'; we thrive on self-fulfillment and the realisation of our potential. We are also heirs to sadness and despair; we disappoint ourselves and each other; we are flawed, frail and conflicted; our plans go awry; not all our dreams come true; we die.

Being richly connected to life means taking death into account: internalising it and accepting it as not just inevitable but as the natural end-point – not a tragedy, but a completion. Martin Amis has described death as 'the dark backing a mirror needs before it can show us ourselves'.[11] If we haven't connected with the idea of our own death, we may be missing out on the richest connection of all: the full realisation of what it means to say that life is fleeting. As the English nature writer Richard Jefferies put it: 'It is eternity now, I am in the midst of it.'[12]

AND IF WE DON'T CONNECT?

If the desire to connect – with ourselves, with each other, with nature – is frustrated or neglected, my impression is that two other desires expand unhealthily to fill the vacuum: the desire for control and the desire to be taken seriously. Pomposity generally goes with a lack of self-awareness; control freaks are rarely good communicators; people with an unquenchable yearning for recognition are generally not yet in touch with who they really are. And those who won't have a bar of 'nature' may not admit it, but they are probably reluctant to engage with a world that is inherently unpredictable and therefore beyond their control. As goals, power and money are much easier to grasp than the notion that planting a garden, or walking along a beach, or gazing at the stars, might actually save your sanity.

On the other hand, if we are so devoted to skiing, astronomy or nature walks that we neglect our creative lives and ignore the people who wish we would communicate with them, we're in trouble. If our inward journey has preoccupied us to the extent that we're neither staying in touch with nature nor with the people close to us, then that balance isn't right, either. If we're such incessant communicators that we neglect our own inward journey, we might be socially popular but unaware of how seriously out of touch we are becoming with ourselves, or how difficult it is for us to spend time alone.

◆

Ultimately, to be connected is to be free – free from the prejudice that blocks our contact with others; free from the delusions that limit our vision of what we could become; free from the preoccupations that blind us to who we are and how we might best live in this world; free from the burden of pretending we are here for more than a brief appearance.

To be connected is to acknowledge that my life is a link in the infinite chain of existence – nothing more, but certainly nothing less.

THE DESIRE TO BE USEFUL

You've a lot to learn about trucks, little Thomas. They are silly things and must be kept in their place. After pushing them about here for a few weeks you'll know almost as much about them as Edward. Then you'll be a Really Useful Engine.

The Rev. W.V. Awdry, *Thomas the Tank Engine*

Useful. What a gratifying word. 'She's a useful person to have on your team.' 'He's very useful with his hands.' 'This is a really useful implement.'

But *useless?* Ugh. What a miserable fate. 'She's useless in a crisis.' 'He's been a pretty useless father.' 'This is a useless patch of ground.'

Not surprising, is it, that we desire to be useful; not surprising that even the laziest of us tend to rise to the occasion when there's an opportunity to prove ourselves useful; not surprising that the legacy most of us would like to leave is the memory of someone who 'pitched in', made a contribution and left the world a better place than we found it.

◆

In the northern suburbs of Sydney, Carolyn Stedman is trying to answer my question about the number of babies and children she has fostered. She thinks it's about sixty. These are not ordinary children whose mothers simply don't want them or can't care for them: these are children suffering severe deprivations and disadvantages – sexual or physical abuse, neglect, drug addiction (via an addicted mother) and abandonment.

Carolyn emphasises that fostering (now officially known as 'Out of Home Care') is a whole-family affair that has involved her husband and their six children, now all grown up and married. She began fostering in 1976, when her first child was six years old, so this has not been a brief episode in the life of the Stedman family. Carolyn and her husband heard on the radio about the need for foster parents, did a six-week training course, and have been fostering ever since.

When I contacted her, Carolyn was looking after 'a sweet little five-month-old'. Over the years, she has cared for children ranging in age up to thirteen. Keen on kids? You can say that again: 'I am sixty-three and still run a home-based childcare service [in addition to our fostering]. There is nothing nicer than a small child running towards you with arms outstretched! David and I now have sixteen grandchildren, so our lives are very child focused.'

Carolyn Stedman might seem like an extreme case because her desire to be useful – augmented, she says, by her religious faith – manifests itself in such a remarkable way. But the desire itself is almost universal: most of us want to play a useful part in society; most of us want to be good neighbours, good parents, good partners, reliable employees, responsible citizens. These desires are not usually expressed in particularly noble or dramatic ways: offering to take in the neighbours' garbage bin or look after their mail while they're on holidays might seem routine acts of neighbourliness, but they are small symbols of the much larger desire to make a useful contribution to the life of a fully functioning, civil society.

Most of us, when asked, act helpfully; some of us don't even wait to be asked. In fact, the more you look at us, the more our desire to be useful becomes apparent. It shows up at work, at home, in the neighbourhood, and especially in an emergency.

When our house was devastated by a storm, people came from everywhere to help. Some of them were neighbours from our own street – people we'd never met before.

Floods, bushfires, storms . . . it's funny how they bring out the best in people. And they often bring communities closer together. Everyone pitches in.

Disasters can bring out the worst in us, too: looting is a common phenomenon after devastations wrought by floods, fire, earthquakes or war. There are opportunists in every society, but they are far outnumbered by those who want to do the right thing.

I'd only been living here six months when my husband died. People were marvellous – people I'd never met before. They were so helpful with food and offers of help around the house. People were mowing the lawn, cleaning the gutters, offering to do the shopping. I just hope I get a chance to repay all this kindness.

Though cynics might argue differently, altruism is one of the most attractive characteristics of humans. We often do things for others with no thought of a reward or even recognition for ourselves. Yet those who believe we do *everything* in pursuit of happiness want to interpret altruism as nothing more than another way of getting a charge – a bliss-burst. That suggests a degree of calculation that doesn't stack up when you think of the spontaneity of many altruistic actions, especially those performed in a crisis.

Evolutionary psychologists are now wondering whether altruism might be another form of 'mate attraction' and that a possible explanation for acts of kindness and generosity may be found in Darwin's theory of sexual selection: 'Altruism signals many positive qualities such as being kind, resourceful and generous, which are important partner qualities likely to attract potential mates.'[1] In other words, altruism is sexy. While this might explain the tendency for a man to respond more generously to an appeal for a charity donation when he is out on a date with a potential partner, I'm not sure it accounts for secret altruism, or for acts of kindness performed by men when no women are present, or vice versa. Still, it's perfectly possible that a tendency towards altruism is implanted in us as part of the evolutionary process: kindness is certainly valued as a desirable quality in a partner.

The desire to be useful is not just a pragmatic thing, as in 'Here's something that needs to be done – I'd better do it'; it's also an expression of something deeper and more charitable in our nature. We desire to be helpful as well as useful.

SOMEONE TO HELP

It's a curious fact that we are often more easily galvanised by someone else's need than by our own.

> *If I ask my son to load the dishwasher for me, he completely ignores me. When the chap next door asked if someone could give him a hand cleaning out his gutters, Jeremy was up the ladder in a flash.*

Helpfulness in the family doesn't always come as readily as parents wish it would – especially if the parents have spent most of their children's lives picking up after them, cooking their meals, ironing their clothes and generally acting like their servants. Why would kids think their parents need help under those conditions? By the time they're eighteen, it's a bit late to be expecting much cooperation, let alone spontaneous offers of help. The evidence, built up over many years, is that help is not needed.

But when we encounter someone in obvious need of help, the desire to be useful propels us into action.

> *There was this elderly woman trying to cross the road at our local shopping centre. She was stranded on the median strip, cars whizzing past in both directions. She looked really*

frightened, so I pulled over and went and helped her over to the footpath, then drove her home. She seemed amazed, but what else would you do? What if it was your own mother?

So what are we to make of the oft-repeated claim that, in urban societies, people are becoming less responsive to calls for help; that people can die in their homes with no one even noticing they've been missing; that people who collapse in the street, or are attacked in a public place, often have trouble getting assistance from passers-by?

The desire to be useful doesn't exist in a vacuum. Being part of the web of desire, it can be subdued by other competing desires. For instance, our desire for control can inhibit us from doing something that might turn out to be messy or dangerous, and our desire to be taken seriously can discourage us from doing anything that might make us look foolish or foolhardy.

Research has shown that if you're the one needing help in an emergency – in a crowded city street, for instance – the best way to get it is to make yourself the focus of an individual's desire to be useful by selecting one person out of the crowd and addressing your appeal for help directly to that person. A more general cry for help is less likely to get a response because it is more easily ignored. US psychologist Robert Cialdini suggests that the most effective strategy is to look directly at someone, point at them and say, 'You, sir, in the blue jacket, I need help. Call an ambulance.'[2]

Cialdini is drawing on evidence that suggests we need 'social proof' – that is, evidence from other people's behaviour that indicates our help is required – before we will act, even if we are disposed to be helpful. If we see someone lying on the footpath and people are walking past looking unconcerned, we are likely to assume that there is no cause for concern: perhaps the person is drunk or under the influence of some other drug, or just 'acting', or perhaps someone has already summoned help. Examples of such incidents occasionally appear in the media, usually accompanied by a general tut-tutting about the insensitivity and heartlessness of city-dwellers. In fact, the problem is usually one of social proof: where is the proof that this person needs help, and that I am the right person to give it?

The media also report cases of heroic assistance being offered, often at personal risk to the helper, when it's been clear that someone was in difficulty and there was no one else around to help. 'Anyone would have done it' is the typically modest claim made by people who have just rescued someone from drowning, or from a burning building, or from the attentions of a would-be assailant and, in a way, they are right: anyone *might* have done it, simply because the desire to be useful runs so deeply in us.

Most of us doubt we have the capacity to act heroically; on the other hand, who wants to be tagged as useless? The desire to be useful sounds modest enough, but it can make heroes of any of us.

SOMETHING TO DO: THE MEANING OF WORK

Common sense might lead us to think that being paid to do not very much would appeal to us. The truth is otherwise. When people are underutilised on the job, the most likely outcome is a lowering of their morale. Since paid work is one of the main ways we satisfy the desire to be useful, that desire is frustrated when we are not working as hard as we know we could.

Two of the girls at work are taking longer and longer lunch breaks because there isn't enough work to keep them busy. But they are both looking for other jobs. They'd rather be busy.

One of the places I worked, it was outrageous. Blokes would spend hours playing cards in the crib-room and you'd knock off as soon as there were a few drops of rain. It was a rort. But morale was rock-bottom. It was a cushy life, but you got no satisfaction from it.

Work is a complicated phenomenon. Social scientists have probably devoted more time and effort to the study of why we work and how we work than to any other area of our lives. Our attitudes to work are an inextricable mixture of deeply embedded evolutionary imperatives – vestiges of the hunter–gatherer in us – and motivations specific to our desire to earn a certain amount of money, or to live in a certain way, or to do something we regard as 'worthwhile'.

Work can be a significant focus for many of the desires that drive us: our desire to be taken seriously, our desire to belong, our desire to connect, our desire for control, our desire for something to happen and to have something to look forward to. Even our desire for 'my place' is sometimes satisfied more completely by a personal nook in the workplace than at home.

We are all familiar with the psychological benefits employment can bestow on us. Work gives us a strong sense of identity and a welcome sense of purpose: *I'd better get on with it.* It also supplies us with the gratification – the pleasure – that can only come from the completion of specific tasks: however much we might mock the term, most of us need the regular experience of 'closure'. In most jobs, we also enjoy the feeling of being part of a group, even if we don't particularly like the content of the job itself. And the fact that we are being paid for what we do at work gives tangible expression to the idea of being valued.

Work provides many people with a ready-made escape from a domestic situation that might be demanding, troubling or stressful. How often have you heard working mothers say that paid work is the easy part of their lives, being more structured and more predictable than the management of a busy household with children? And how often, even on holiday, have you felt you'd like to return to the routines, the structures, the familiarity of work?

Work can be ennobling. Work can be therapeutic, stimulating and deeply satisfying. But let's not get carried away: mindless and unsatisfying work can be tedious, stressful, frustrating and debilitating. Some workplaces are demeaning and dehumanising. Some employers are exploitative, ruthless and unfair. Bullying in the workplace can sap the human spirit.

For most of us, work is a necessity: we are obliged to work to earn a living and we envy those fortunate few who claim they are being paid to enjoy themselves. But the idea of work as being anything more than a duty is a relatively modern one that is not always helpful: the growing emphasis on work as a source of fulfillment is bound to be counter-productive for many people whose jobs seem to them to be anything but fulfilling, even if they manage to extract some satisfaction from features of the workplace other than the work itself. In a world where we are constantly being urged to obtain more qualifications through higher levels of education, there is also a risk of expectations about job satisfaction being raised unrealistically: being over-qualified for a job can be just as frustrating as being under-qualified.

Apart from those who work because they have no choice, there are people who work when they don't need to – either because they could be financially supported by a partner's income, or because they've accumulated enough wealth to live on. Why would they bother? And why do some people continue to do work they don't like when other jobs are available?

Answers to those questions will depend upon the interplay of many different factors, but perhaps the primary desire satisfied by work – apart from an income – is the most simple and obvious one. In our attempts to explain why we work as long or as hard as we do, it's easy to overlook the most basic explanation of all: the desire to be useful. Work gives us something to do, something that *proves* we are useful.

Even a simple and relatively unrewarding job stands as a symbol that I am a useful person. The mere fact of being employed is a powerful source of recognition and acknowledgement of our usefulness, and the satisfaction flowing from that can ease the frustration of never quite finding the 'right' job.

A good test of this proposition is to listen to people who have retired from the workforce or been retrenched:

It was such a hollow feeling. Most of your life was bound up with the job and then, suddenly, that wasn't you anymore. Where I come from, if you haven't got a job, you're a bit of a non-person – a bit useless.

My husband was painful to be with when he first retired. He moped around the house, looking for jobs to do. He even started coming shopping with me, trying to tell me what to buy. Eventually I said to him, 'Why don't you make

*yourself useful?' We started asking around and now he's
doing voluntary work up at the local school, helping the kids
with reading and even doing a bit of gardening, which I can
never get him to do here.*

That was partly about identity, no doubt, but it was also about
a particular anxiety many new retirees feel: will I be regarded
as being as 'useful' as I was when I wore an occupational label?

Here's another case, typical of middle-class retirees everywhere:

*When I first retired, I thought I'd have trouble filling in
the time. I painted the house – doesn't everyone? – and we
thought about a caravan trip but we couldn't see ourselves
as Grey Nomads. The thing was, you felt as if you didn't
count so much. You wondered who you were. People would
say, 'What do you do?' and you could hardly say, 'Nothing'.
Anyway, I ended up taking on so much, I now wonder how
I ever found the time to go to work.*

He wasn't doing it for the money: this was a retired man well taken
care of by his superannuation, and none of the jobs he took on in
retirement carried any remuneration. 'Taking on so much' may
well have been a symptom of a wish to offer some community
service: joining local clubs and committees connects us to local
networks, gives us a focus, a sense of purpose, and adds a new
dimension to our identity. But it's also likely to have been born
of the unquenchable desire to be useful.

Usefulness comes in many different forms, and they change as
we move through the life cycle: a useful authority on which band is
playing at which pub; useful at work; a useful medium-pace bowler

in the local cricket team; a useful soprano in the church choir; a supportive spouse and an involved parent; a reliable employee; a willing participant in the community; perhaps, eventually, a source of useful wisdom based on a lifetime's experience. What doesn't change through the course of our lives is that our self-respect is closely tied to our confidence in our own usefulness.

> *I sold my business when I turned fifty. Made a motza. Then I spent the next ten years trying to figure out what to do with myself. Being rich and useless isn't a healthy combination.*

WHERE'S THE EVIDENCE OF MY USEFULNESS?

The need for *something to do* as a way of satisfying our desire to be useful can lead us in unexpected directions. The British author and playwright Alan Bennett once wrote of his welcome discovery of a way to spend up to ten minutes away from his desk: cleaning the lint filter in his washing machine.

It's easy to dismiss such behaviour as the mere search for a distraction from the task at hand – like a student who suddenly decides to paint his room when an essay is waiting to be written. And it's true: we're all good at working out strategies for putting off things that need to be done. But I suspect that in the case of people whose main work is cerebral, the lure of some practical work is particularly seductive. If Bennett cleans the lint filter on his washing machine, there is tangible evidence of his usefulness. If, on the other hand, he sits at his writing desk and manages no more than a few words before lunch, it rather looks like an unproductive morning.

Thinking is useful work, of course; it just doesn't look like it until it's been converted into something audible, visible or tangible. 'Publish or perish' says the academic slogan – no amount of theorising is enough; we need to see the evidence. Even teaching, that notoriously ephemeral process, is increasingly being subjected to political pressure to be assessed against objective criteria – students' exam marks are the obvious one, but in some tertiary institutions students' evaluations of their teachers are also being taken into account.

Tradespeople and manual workers have a great psychological advantage over those who work in less practical, less structured areas: the nature of their work means that, at regular intervals, they complete something. They see the evidence of their usefulness: the frame is up; the room is painted; the pile of bricks has been turned into a wall; the trench is dug; the roof is on; the leak is fixed. A writer who has been toiling for years on a novel is bound to be frustrated by the lack of such evidence. When friends say, 'How's the book going?' what they really mean is, 'When can you show us some evidence of your usefulness, your productivity? Let's see a pile of pages, at least.'

People who work in administrative jobs often feel as if they are on an endless conveyor belt of unfinished business and the lack of evidence of 'completion' can be a major source of frustration.

In the days before the gender revolution, a popular slogan was 'a woman's work is never done': 'I tidy the place in the morning, and it's messy again by night.' 'I slave over a meal, and they've wolfed it in no time, with not a word of appreciation.' 'I wash their clothes and after one wearing, they're back in the laundry basket.' In other words, the evidence of my usefulness keeps disappearing.

No wonder so many housewives of that era created small, symbolic compensations: 'I love to see a pile of ironing done. In fact, I let people put their own things away after I've ironed them, so it might register.' 'When the beds are made and I can sit down with a cup of coffee, I feel as if I'm ready to face the day.' 'A line full of washing is a real joy.' All of us need the evidence of our usefulness, and in the domestic environment, there's usually precious little reward for effort in the form of praise or recognition.

As men have gradually and reluctantly taken over some of the housework, they have begun to understand the issue, often dealing with it by making loud announcements and demanding praise for the tiniest domestic task: 'I've done the washing up!' or 'I pegged out the clothes that were in the machine!' or 'The school lunches are ready!' as if expecting a vote of thanks. In the words of one English journalist, fed up with her husband's expectation of praise and gratitude: 'He acts as if he deserves the Queen's Award for Enterprise.'

An empty in-box, another chapter of a book read, a garden weeded, a lawn mown, a house built, a file closed, a meal prepared and served, a suitcase unpacked, a crossword completed, a contract signed, a musical composition performed . . . all of us need some hard evidence of our usefulness. That's why modest, short-term goals are a good idea: at regular intervals we can say, 'At least *that* much has been achieved.'

SOMETHING TO BE GOOD AT

Part of the desire to be useful is the wish to achieve some particular competence, recognised as 'my special subject'. Whether it's the ability to hammer in a nail, balance the books, sew a straight hem, make people laugh, remove a diseased appendix or write a poem, our skills are our passport to usefulness. Most of us get a kick out of being asked to do something we are well equipped to do: we like to be helpful anyway, but there's a particular gratification associated with being able to offer specialised help.

I was asked to help out with a charity that needed some accounting skills. I was glad to be asked.

Being a builder, I get roped into all sorts of jobs down at the local school.

Everyone's good at something – you just have to ask around if you need help. I find people are very willing to help if it's something they're good at.

Throughout her adult life, my mother was in demand to perform at concerts and friends' dinner parties, reciting the poems she had been taught as a young woman by her elocution teacher. Others decorated cakes, arranged flowers, wrote witty sketches, sang or played musical instruments, but my mother's particular skill was recitation. She had had limited education and always felt her attainments were modest, but this was something she was good at, and she received constant encouragement from that.

'I'm paid to enjoy myself' is something we'd all like to be able to say. The truth is that as we develop experience in any area of paid or unpaid work, we tend to become good at it and there is some satisfaction to be gained from that, even if it might not be the thing we most enjoy doing.

In the army, we did a lot of things we didn't particularly want to do – who wants to drill for an hour every morning, or polish their boots to a mirror finish? Or learn to handle weapons, for that matter. But you get bloody good at all these things, and you find yourself becoming proud of what you've achieved, and then you find you start to enjoy it. No one in the army ever feels useless – the training sees to that.

When the paid job isn't about doing the thing we love best, hobbies, pastimes and recreational activity soon make up for that. We become proficient tennis players or golfers; we learn how to fish, sing or paint; we become expert in a particular area of history or astronomy, an authority on stock-car racing or vintage steam trains, or a cook with specialties admired and acknowledged by our friends. We might study art history, learn a foreign language or take up Latin dancing. We might become a walking encyclopedia of sports statistics or an expert on camellias.

We all need to be proficient at something and the good news is that, generally speaking, we are. Most of us are competent in many areas of our lives, and particularly skilful in some of them. These might be unsung skills. They might include things like being kind, being willing to listen to other people's woes, being able to brew a decent cup of tea (a rarer skill than you might think), or being the family's 'rock' – calm in a crisis and always ready to mend broken hearts.

Sometimes people say, 'I'm no good at anything.' That would be a tragedy if it were true. What is more likely – and equally tragic – is that the rest of us have failed to recognise their talents or acknowledge the value of their contribution.

THE DARK SIDE: 'I KNOW WHAT'S BEST FOR YOU'

It's hard to see how the desire to be useful could have a dark side, but of course it does; all our desires do. Like most of the others, this one turns dark when it gets out of hand – when an urge to be a helpful person turns into a desire to control someone else by 'helpfully' telling them what to do, or when we are so convinced we know what's best for another person, we just can't stop ourselves from sharing this helpful insight with them. Sometimes it's a case of bossiness thinly disguised as helpfulness.

We mostly mean well when we fall into these traps. Our motives are sometimes so pure, we don't even realise the error we're making.

When we find ourselves tempted to be *too* helpful, it's a good idea to remember that no one has the right to control another person's behaviour, no one has the right to take charge of another person's agenda (unless asked – and that's a worry in itself), and no one has the right to judge – let alone alter – another person's way of being. People must be left free to make their own mistakes.

Okay, so I don't prune my roses the way you would. Tough. Perhaps I'm wrong; perhaps I will furtively watch how you do it and copy that next time. Or perhaps my roses will respond just as well to my incompetent mutilation as yours will to your finely honed skills. If, out of the depths of my ignorance, I ask you how I should prune my roses, feel free to advise me. If I don't ask, don't tell me. Unsolicited advice – like unsolicited reminiscences – can be both unwelcome and irritating. As for roses, so for investments, car purchases, political opinions, choice of children's schools, hairstyles or home furnishings.

Pruning roses is one thing; raising children is another. How tiresome it is for parents to receive 'helpful' corrective advice about their child-rearing practices, especially from non-parents, or strangers. If a child's health or wellbeing is at risk, or the parent seems all at sea, by all means approach the topic gently and sensitively (especially if you're the grandparent), perhaps by describing what you did in similar circumstances. But full-on criticism or too many explicit suggestions usually breach the acceptable boundaries of helpfulness.

One of the biggest sources of stress in our lives is the almost irresistible urge to change the way other people think and act, so they'll conform more closely to the way we'd like them to think and act. While it can be deeply frustrating to stand by while someone does something you regard as unwise, inefficient, unproductive or plain stupid, it is even more frustrating to find that your attempts at being helpful have not only failed to convince the other person they were wrong, but probably made them defensive and angry into the bargain.

Helpfulness carried to excess turns our relationships into a contest of wills, and where's the charity or good nature in that? Excessive helpfulness is almost always perceived as a put-down. It's as if we're saying, 'I can see you're a bit out of your depth here, but – *lucky you!* – I can set you straight.' (Thanks, but no thanks.)

You want to make the world a better place? Go easy on the helpful advice.

MAKING THE WORLD A BETTER PLACE

In his fifteenth-century classic *The Imitation of Christ*, Thomas à Kempis wrote: 'Never be idle, but either reading, or writing, or praying, or meditating, or at some useful work for the common good.'[3]

Most of us would find that agenda a bit relentless for our taste. Those gripped too tightly by the work ethic are more likely to envy that man in the cartoon: 'Sometimes I sits and thinks, and sometimes I just sits.'

'In Praise of Idleness' remains one of Bertrand Russell's most popular essays, especially among students looking for an excuse to postpone an assignment. Yet Russell was strongly in favour of making the world a better place and he was a passionate advocate for the common good. This was his big argument in favour of shorter working hours (in 1935, he was proposing a maximum of four hours work per day in the looming 'machine age'):

> Good nature is, of all moral qualities, the one that the world needs most, and good nature is the result of ease and security, not of a life of arduous struggle.[4]

Earlier in the essay, Russell had suggested that because workers 'will not be tired in their spare time, they will not demand only such amusements as are passive and vapid' and predicted that 'at least one percent will probably devote the time not spent in professional work to pursuits of public importance'. Russell himself, for all his irony and cynicism, was energetically devoted to 'pursuits of public importance'. After his glittering academic career as a mathematician and philosopher, he spent the later years of his life as a tireless and controversial educator, anti-war protester and nuclear disarmament campaigner. An atheist whose sexual attitudes and behaviour offended many of his contemporaries,

Russell would certainly not have supported Thomas à Kempis's call for time to be spent praying, but he was as idealistic as any mystic about the goal of a better life for all people and more widespread 'good nature' was part of his dream.

Whether we're atheists, theists, mystics, contemplatives, cynics or harsh pragmatists, doesn't the final phrase in that Thomas à Kempis quote ring true for us? Though we want to be able to enjoy life to the full – and we appreciate the value of time off – we instinctively acknowledge the importance of 'useful work for the common good'.

This is a motivational minefield. It's easy to be cynical about things done ostensibly for the common good that also seem to advance the cause of those doing them. Some people who act in ways that appear altruistic are no doubt exploiting their 'public service' as a platform for personal ambition or public recognition. Some wealthy individuals who speak of 'giving something back to the community' may well be giving back a whole lot less than they owe.

We don't have to examine the hidden motivations involved to recognise the desire to be useful when it surfaces. We might think philanthropy more convincing if it were undertaken in secret, but philanthropists' money is still useful, so let's not be too squeamish if they also seek recognition.

However it manifests itself, the desire to be useful *is* the desire to make the world a better place. The smallest acts of kindness or helpfulness do make the world a better place, sometimes in more intense, personal ways than grand gestures. The efficient discharge of our duties at work makes the world a better place (unless we're engaged in work that is exploitative or harmful).

Creating music, words or pictures that give people pleasure and illuminate their sense of themselves makes the world a better place, and so does changing a light bulb for a frail person who can't manage it themselves. Conscientious parenting makes the world a better place, and so do the moments we spend chatting over the front gate to the lonely old man at the end of the street, or helping a lost child find its parents.

Anything we do to make the world a better place is useful; anything useful makes the world a better place. Civil societies don't just happen: they are the sum of countless useful acts by well-meaning people.

'He never did anything by halves.' 'Her heart was in everything she did.' 'She always did her best' . . . we've heard these things said at farewell parties, funerals and other occasions to honour someone's life and work. They are among the highest compliments we can pay each other because they imply that, in great or small ways, someone has left the world in noticeably better shape by the contribution they have made to it.

The biggest influence we are likely to have on the world around us isn't directly related to the kind of paid work we do, important though that may be. Most jobs don't shape the character of a society, but here's what does: the way we handle our personal relationships. Whatever job we choose, it's the goodwill, care and sensitivity we bring to our encounters with our customers, clients, colleagues or employees that will be our most influential contribution to making the world a better place. It goes without saying that the same applies to the quality of our relationships with our families, friends, neighbours and, especially, the strangers we meet in the course of our daily lives. The way we deal with strangers in our midst is perhaps the most revealing indicator of our commitment to a truly civil society.

Kindness, courtesy and respect: these are the great bulwarks against a society's disintegration.

THE DESIRE TO BELONG

All the Norwegians were Lutherans, of course –
even the atheists

Garrison Keillor, *Wobegon Boy*

If ever you're tempted by the thought that contemporary Western culture is more individualistic than in the past, just take a look around you. From the family to the workplace, from the school gate to the local coffee shop or pub, and from religious, political or sporting affiliations to friendship circles, both online and offline, we are as socially interdependent as ever. Our default position, as humans, is *together,* even for those of us who also cherish time alone.

We love to meet to talk, to work, to eat and drink, to socialise. We love to go to concerts, movies, sporting events, or the theatre *with* someone. Courtesy of the information technology revolution, we're in constant contact with each other: the rising generation of young people has redefined and enriched the meaning of 'networks'. We're joiners. We cohere. We hunt in packs (in the stock market and elsewhere). We swarm. We hang out together. We congregate. We cooperate. We thrive on the intimacy of small groups of friends and colleagues, and on the thrill of being part of a crowd. We still believe there's 'safety in numbers'. We need to belong.

Yet there's a popular view of human psychology that we're a dark, murderous lot who have trouble keeping our violent urges on a leash; that we're ruthlessly competitive by nature and would do each other down as soon as look at each other; that 'anti-social' is our default position and we need years of training and discipline to be socialised.

It's true that as a species we have an ugly history of selfishness, greed and violence. But we have other histories as well. We're generally kind to each other: we care about our families and friends, of course, but we also show kindness to strangers. Not universally: there are ruthless, pushy and self-serving individuals in our midst; there are thugs and bullies – you encounter them in the school playground, in a queue at the sandwich shop, on the road, in the boardroom – but they are in a small minority.

Through fifty years of social research, much of it spent sitting in people's homes listening to them talk about their attitudes, values and aspirations, I have been repeatedly struck by the attachment most people feel to their families, their neighbourhoods and communities, and their loyalty to the various organisations they are associated with. The sense of belonging is palpable, and the lack of it is distressing – to those experiencing loneliness or social exclusion, for instance, or to recent arrivals who haven't yet made the sort of connections that help us feel we belong to a neighbourhood, a city or even a country. It's no wonder immigrants and refugees tend to gravitate towards their fellow expatriates when they arrive. Even years later, some of them report the desolate feeling that 'I don't belong anywhere.'

I've also been moved by people's attentiveness to each other's needs; by their willingness to help and to show consideration to each other. I'd say we're an extraordinarily social species in our behaviour, and extraordinarily sociable in our dispositions.

Students often prefer to study in groups – at the library or in a common room. Gardeners form clubs; so do book-readers, sports-car enthusiasts, stamp collectors, chess players, trainspotters and motorbike riders. Work groups often become friendship groups. Neighbours – total strangers when they first move into the same street – are generally disposed to chat to each other and keep an eye out for each other, and sometimes become friends. We need companionship, human presence, a social context.

Here's a weird sign of it. The producers of American TV sitcoms long ago realised that when people are watching television, it's not like being in a cinema, with an audience around us. We are likely to be alone or with just one or two other people – hence the 'laugh track', designed to create the illusion of an audience being present, and us being members of it. They're laughing, why aren't I? You might hate laugh tracks, but you have to admire the ingenuity of the people who dreamed them up: they know we are social creatures, and that our response to any form of entertainment – movies, plays, sports events, sitcoms – is likely to be heightened when we're in the midst of others who are reacting.

Carl Rogers acknowledged that clinical psychologists are at a disadvantage in trying to generalise about the human condition because the people they see are all grappling with unresolved issues, problems, neuroses and phobias (a bit like the bleak impression of a society you might receive if you only attended to its news and current affairs programs). He wrote that 'untamed and unsocial feelings are neither the deepest nor the strongest . . . the inner core of man's personality is the organism itself, which is essentially both self-preserving and social'.[1]

Yes, we do appalling things to each other – from engaging in malicious gossip to unleashing weapons of mass destruction – and there are good grounds for wondering whether our greed and our capacity for violence will combine to destroy our species. The desire to belong can certainly bring out the worst in us, creating in-groups and out-groups that might grow, like a cancer, into cultural, religious or ethnic enmity.

But even more powerful than our desire to oppose is our desire to align ourselves with groups that offer us the comfort of affinity. It's this desire that can save us from becoming too self-centred, ruthless and destructive. We are unlike most other animals in our capacity to maim and kill members of our own species, but we are like most other animals in our desire to 'flock together'.

◆

Not everyone wants to belong. There are people who go through life feeling like rank outsiders and preferring that. There are hermits, and isolates who seem to prefer their own company to anyone else's. In the present era, many apparent outsiders have come in from the cold via the internet: virtual communities may be far removed from what we have traditionally recognised as 'real' communities, but they provide a form of network – a version of belonging – for people who prefer to avoid face-to-face contact.

Yet even among those of us who think of ourselves as loners, you can find vestiges of the need to belong. At a conference of school principals discussing the problem of outsiders – non-joiners, the children who seemed not to belong – one principal said that in his school, with the encouragement of an alert and sympathetic teacher, several loners had collected themselves into an ironic little herd – part parody of the cool crowd and part protection against it. Whatever the motivation, the loners' group had developed some cohesiveness, doing for its members what herds always do: supplying a kind of 'minimum daily allowance' of social contact, a sense of identity and emotional support.

Here's a classic cry from an infamous outsider, Alexander Trocchi, whose autobiographical novel of drug addiction, *Cain's Book*, appears to document a particularly virulent strain of anti-social detachment. He writes of 'gaining in intensity at each new impertinence of the external world with which I signed no contract when I was ejected bloodily from my mother's warm womb'.

> I developed early a horror of all groups, particularly those which without further ado claimed the right to subsume all my acts under certain normative designations in terms of which they would reward or punish me . . . What shocked me most as I grew up was not the fact that things were as they were, and with a tendency to petrify, but that others had the impertinence to assume that I would forbear to react violently against them.[2]

While railing against a society that rendered him, by an accident of birth, 'shockingly underprivileged', and professing 'a horror of all groups', the narrator of *Cain's Book* nevertheless reveals his own profound desire to belong – not to the normative social groups he despises, but to an equally tight-knit, equally normative group comprising fellow addicts, prostitutes, petty criminals. In this milieu, he feels accepted precisely because he and his associates share a set of values, an identity, that gives them some measure of emotional security or, at least, emotional co-dependency. Their common refusal to 'join' became the very thread that bound them together.

OUR IDENTITY IS GROUP-BASED: SOMETIMES THE HERD, SOMETIMES THE TRIBE

The desire to belong drives our attachment to two kinds of group: we are both herd animals and tribal creatures. For instance, our workgroup is a herd; the organisation or professional group or trade union we belong to is a tribe. The sense of belonging at both levels is strong and satisfying, but the emotional dimensions are quite different.

The herd – typically comprising seven or eight people linked by friendship, a common interest or purpose – nurtures our confidence and self-respect, and wraps us in the kind of security blanket only membership of a small group can provide. The tribe gives us a larger-scaled, more corporate, more public – and sometimes noisier and more passionate – sense of identity and belonging.

We wear tribal badges with pride and sometimes with arrogance and defiance, but the herd is a quieter, less overt phenomenon. Herds are nurtured by personal contact; tribes engender a sense of belonging to an enterprise, an organisation or, sometimes, more amorphous linkages based on a idea, an ideal or a mission: International Socialism, 'the sisterhood', free marketeers.

Like most other animals, we tend to behave better in herds than tribes. Mob rule and the violence of crowds are tribal phenomena. Tribes are often at loggerheads with other tribes; herds rarely so. Tribes go to war; herds might create a bit of local mischief, but they are usually quite benign social networks that nurture the identity and emotional security of their members.

Political, religious, cultural and ethnic tribes are typically committed to set-in-stone dogma. They are sustained by their myths and legends. Tribes thrive on closed minds: the seeds of radical political and cultural change are less likely to be sown in tribes than herds. As the anthropologist Margaret Mead said: 'Never doubt that a small group of thoughtful, committed citizens can change the world. Indeed, it's the only thing that ever has.'[3] Perhaps it's a group of writers and academics meeting regularly for coffee and hatching a new political philosophy, a group of friends who play tennis together once a week deciding to mount an assault on youth homelessness in their city, or a few colleagues lunching together every day and gradually working out how their organisation could be revitalised. These are the ways herds can germinate fresh ideas.

But not always, of course. Many herds don't have a clear focus, let alone a revolutionary intent. They exist simply to maintain friendships, to reinforce their common values and prejudices, to observe the rituals of the group (often laughing at the same in-jokes, year after year) and to satisfy the desire to belong. Mead's point was simply that small groups are *potentially* more conducive to original thought and more likely to foster the kind of freedom that, anchored in the security of the group, encourages the examination of new ideas. Tribal talkfests and grand occasions are usually straitjacketed by their procedures, programs and rituals: they are good places for rousing renditions of the national anthem, but not for stimulating creative interaction between open minds.

Most organisations recognise the power of the herd. A workgroup of six or eight people will be more cohesive and generally more productive than a larger group, and that's usually the most effective span of management control, as well. (It's also the perfect size for a dinner party: if you exceed that number, the group is likely to break down into smaller herds.)

In case you hadn't guessed, I'm a herd man myself. I'm deeply wary of most tribes – especially the religious, political, commercial and sporting variety. I'm sceptical of a rowdy, hearts-on-our-sleeves tribalism because it can too easily lurch into triumphalism. Tribes tend to become self-obsessed, arrogant, powerful and therefore vulnerable to the corruption that flows from all that. (Herds are more transparent: there's nowhere to hide in a herd.)

Still, tribes are here to stay – ethnic and religious groups, monarchists and republicans, liberals and conservatives in politics, protectionists and free-traders, all the way down to the ferociously competitive tribes based on the 'school spirit' so energetically fostered by private schools, in particular.

◆

It's impossible to be precise about the size of tribes. While herds typically range from about five to seven or eight people, tribes can be of almost any size – into the dozens, hundreds, thousands or even millions. And the distinction between them isn't always precise, either: intermediate-sized groups of, say, fifteen or twenty people can sometimes work like a herd and sometimes like a tribe, but will usually break down informally into herd-sized factions – like the forwards and backs in a Rugby team, or the brass, wind and string sections of an orchestra.

Whatever the size and structure of our social groups and networks, they make an important contribution to our understanding of who we are and where we fit most comfortably. The process of working that out begins in childhood. Regardless of their emotional health or genetic complexity, our families supply the bedrock for our sense of belonging. We identify with our parents and siblings, and start to grasp the idea of belonging to *this* family, not *that* family. Then our nuclear family attends an event – a Christmas dinner, a wedding, a birthday celebration – where we merge with the extended family and we begin to grasp the difference between a herd and a tribe.

In the past, our desire to belong to a herd was most readily satisfied by the domestic herd – the household we belonged to. Today, in most Western societies, the institution of the family is undergoing revolutionary change, and the size of the average household has been steadily shrinking. Many factors have contributed to this trend, including high rates of marriage breakdown, falling birthrates, and more people now living alone, either voluntarily or involuntarily, for some period of their adult lives.

There has been a dramatic rise in the number of single-person households, especially in Europe and North America: one-third of all new households created in the USA during the 1990s were single-person households. In most developed countries, one- and two-person households already account for more than half of all households, and the single-person household is the fastest-growing household type. In Australia, single-person households are projected to account for over thirty percent of all households within the next twenty years: that level has already been reached in Quebec, Canada, and exceeded in Norway, Denmark, Germany and Belgium.

The growth in solo households doesn't mean there are more hermits than previously: it simply means that, in the context of our increasingly dynamic living arrangements, more of us than ever before are 'episodic soloists': people who move in and out of solo households as our circumstances change.

If a comfortable human herd typically comprises five to eight people, then it's obvious most of our households are already too small to count as herds. Shrinking households don't quench our desire to belong to a herd; they simply encourage us to look elsewhere for herds to join – which may be good news for the development and revitalisation of local neighbourhoods and communities.

Many parents of today's teenagers report that teen herds are even more close-knit than in the past, often operating as surrogate families, and the explosion in the number of book clubs, bush-walking clubs, community choirs, adult education groups, and formal and informal sporting groups are all signs of the growing demand for non-domestic herds to belong to. The development of food courts and gastro-pubs, and the proliferation of coffee shops on every suburban high street are, similarly, a direct response to the shrinking household: 'grazing with the herd' is an easy way for people who live alone, or in two-person households, to feel part of a herd. Many restaurants now provide a common table for individual diners who regard social interaction as part of the pleasure of eating.

Tribes and herds make such a rich contribution to our identities, it's not surprising that almost as soon as we meet someone for the first time, we start casting around for clues that might suggest a tribal connection or an overlap between the groups we each belong to. In places like Northern Ireland you simply ask, 'What school did you go to?' and an entire tribal identity, based on religion, is implied by the answer. In some other places, the key question is, 'What's your team?'

'Where do you live?' or 'What kind of work do you do?' or 'Are you related to the Mackays from Hamilton?' might offer hints about cultural identity, or socioeconomic status, or family background. The answers might lead to unfair and prejudiced assumptions, but these are the tribal signals we typically send each other when we are looking for short cuts in the process of getting to know someone. Friends in common, family links, schools, universities or churches attended, to say nothing of accents and dress, all suggest tribal associations that give us a hint about 'who this person is' and whether we might belong to the same or similar tribes.

RELIGION: THE STRONGEST AND MOST PERSISTENT BASIS FOR TRIBALISM

In his novel *Wobegon Boy*, Garrison Keillor describes the phenomenon of religious tribalism as succinctly as any solemn work of theology or sociology could:

A chasm separated the Hauge Synod, or Dark Lutherans, who believed in the utter depravity of man and separation from worldly things and strict adherence to the literal truth of Scripture, and the Old Synod, or Happy Lutherans, who believed in splashing some water on babies and confirming the little kids and then not worrying about it, just come every Sunday and bring a hot dish.[4]

With deadly accuracy, Keillor goes on to demonstrate how tribal divisions, once established, become entrenched and reinforced through prejudice and the erosion of mutual respect. These two factions of Lutheranism, he writes, 'were divided over the role of women and the colour of the sky and how to make coleslaw', but they were most bitterly divided over the question of whether believers would recognise each other when they got to heaven.

The very fact that they were all Lutherans made the tribal divisions between them even more intense than between more obvious rivals – theists and atheists, say, or Christians and Muslims.

The most vicious tribal wars are often like that. When fighting breaks out between groups who, on the face of it, seem like two chips off the same block, more logical, predictable rivalries are forgotten: all the tribes' energies are focused on the task of expanding a wafer-thin difference over dogma (religious, political or cultural) into an unbridgeable, institutionalised chasm.

The Roman Catholics currently have a leader who understands tribalism as well as anyone: in 2008, Pope Benedict XVI declared that only Roman Catholics are entitled to call themselves a 'church'. If they had been bothering to pay attention, the millions of members of other Christian churches would have found this proposition both offensive and absurd. (The Roman church has tried to claim pre-eminence from the beginning of Christianity, finally declaring itself the one true church in 1070 when the wildly ambitious Pope Gregory VII made a bid for monopolistic control of bishops and clergy throughout Europe. Plenty of people – William the Conqueror notable among them – rejected that claim, but its echoes can still be heard in the modern Roman Catholic tribe.[5])

Fighting over essentially the same piece of turf – whether geographical, cultural, political or theological – is always going to involve tense, sweaty, hand-to-hand combat. When the differences between tribes are so vast that they seem almost to inhabit different worlds, they tend to lose interest in each other. Most of the time, Christians would rarely waste a hostile thought on atheists, Hindus or Muslims, but when a group of Muslims wants to build an Islamic school in a nominally Christian neighbourhood, watch the tribal feathers fly. Or let political and military rhetoric conflate 'Christian' and 'the West', as in 'the struggle between Islam and the West' – as if Europe, in particular, isn't increasingly Islamic – and suddenly we are enemies again, facing each other across the vast battlefields of ancient hatreds. Perhaps there's even some comfort to be drawn from these grand enmities because they so richly fuel our desire to belong.

It can be a relief to be distracted by such titanic struggles from the internecine rivalries that preoccupy us when we are left to squabble over more petty divisions *within* our own tribes – fierce conflicts over whether women should be allowed to become priests, for example, or whether saintly figures need two or more 'proven' miracles to qualify for official beatification, or whether we will recognise each other in our 'resurrection bodies', or whether this or that scriptural text (in this or that translation from the Hebrew or Greek) might be taken to be literally true or, perhaps, *more* literally true than some other, less doctrinally convenient text.

AS FOR RELIGION, SO FOR SPORT

Most of the behaviour of religious tribes can be observed in sporting tribes as well.

Think of the conflicts between those who believe that any game called 'football' should only be played with a round ball that is only ever kicked, and those who believe that American Football, Rugby, Gaelic Football or Australian Rules are not only authentic versions of 'football', but are the only football games worthy of serious attention, whatever you may choose to call them. The focus of these rivalries might seem more trivial than the things religious groups fight over, but the passions are hardly less intense.

But there are far more bitter divisions between those who support different teams in the same code. Catholics and Protestants have nothing on that – except in parts of the world like Scotland, where football teams are defined in precisely those terms: in Edinburgh, Catholics support Hibs (Hibernian) and Protestants support Hearts (Heart of Midlothian), and anyone who crosses that line is either brave or foolhardy. In Glasgow, if you support Celtic, you're Catholic; Rangers, you're Protestant. When Mark Scott, a sixteen-year-old Celtic fan, was stabbed to death in 1995 by a Rangers fan, no one thought that was good, but neither was it altogether surprising, rampant tribalism being what it is. There was sufficient national outrage and shame, however, to stimulate the establishment of the Mark Scott Foundation, which has since offered leadership training to over a thousand young people through its Leadership for Life program.

In politics, similarly, the most bitter hatreds are reserved for the in-fighting between factions of the one party. Such factions typically behave like rival teams within the same sporting code, generating mutual distrust and even contempt among people who are supposed to be ideological colleagues.

The desire to belong is so powerful that it casts a particularly murky shadow across those who are thought to have 'deserted the cause'; 'crossed the floor' of the parliamentary chamber; left the church; decided to support another team. Indeed, hatred of 'the others' is the ugliest of all the characteristics of tribal behaviour, and you can see it in the arrogant, supremacist attitudes of many sporting fans, just as clearly as in religious bigotry and in the bitterness of political faction fighting.

I wouldn't seriously suggest (though many have) that sport is a religion, but I suspect Karl Marx, were he alive today, might well describe professional sport as the 'opium of the people'. Think of religion's arcane blending of history, myth and legend, its liturgical forms and its reverence for 'saints' – you can find close equivalents in sporting legends, in the heroes elevated to the sporting pantheon, and in the rituals, creeds, songs and 'liturgy' of the game.

Tribal influences on our behaviour are remarkably consistent, even in fields as apparently disparate as religion, sport and politics. In each case, the sense of belonging transcends all doubt, all disappointment and all disputes: come what may, I know where my loyalties lie and where I belong. Very occasionally, a supporter of the losing team in a well-played game will concede that 'Rugby was the winner' – just as Christians who become disenchanted with their own local church may take refuge in the sense of belonging, still, to the larger tribe called 'Christian'.

TRIBES BEGET MORE TRIBES

Don't talk about the left wing of the Party. It's which one of the four Left factions you belong to.

Conservatives and liberals within political and religious groups have been at each other's throats for centuries, though the focus of their disputes changes with the seasons. Currently, among worldwide Anglicans it's the question of whether a homosexual person should be ordained as a priest. And if a priest, what about a bishop? Such a prospect seemed to some conservatives in the Anglican Church to be so utterly repugnant, so unacceptable, and so symbolic of a general theological and moral decline among liberals that they broke away from the Lambeth Conference – the traditional gathering of Anglican bishops from all over the world – and established a rival conference.

The breakaway group, consisting of almost three hundred bishops, first met in Jerusalem in 2008 and called themselves GAFCON (the Global Anglican Future Conference). They seem likely to remain a separate group, tribalism being what it is, and the Archbishop of Canterbury, traditional leader of the world's Anglicans, has conceded the possibility of a split in the Anglican Church. Ere long, the precipitating issues will have merged into a more general separatist mentality. Hearts will be broken. Families will be divided. Church traditions and structures will be jeopardised. Bitter disputes will rage over who owns what property.

But the tribes will grow strong under the pressure of attack and defence, and life will go on.

Meanwhile, over in the Roman Catholic camp, all this is watched with the astonishment of a tribe that would never countenance such divisions – though the Jesuits might say they have long since operated as a tribe within a tribe. From time to time, fringe groups with names like 'Catalyst for Renewal' spring up, inspired by the idea of changing the culture of the institution from within, but generally evolving into self-perpetuating tribes. They are typically treated with disdain by the hierarchy of the church, who understand that to take them seriously – let alone persecute them – would be to legitimise them and reinforce their zeal.

The history of religion and politics is riddled with examples of old tribes spawning new tribes. The British Labour Party shocked its old guard when it reinvented itself under Tony Blair as 'New Labour', and it was only the heady electoral success of the Blairites that kept the dissidents reasonably quiet and 'united' – publicly, at least – under the Labour banner. In Australia, political and religious tribalism merged in spectacular fashion when the Democratic Labor Party (DLP) was formed in 1955. Closely associated with the Roman Catholic Church and committed to a passionate anti-Communist ideology, the DLP split the Labor vote and effectively kept the Australian Labor Party (ALP) out of power, federally, for twenty years. Tensions and hatreds between the DLP and the ALP exceeded any animosity either party might have felt for the conservative Liberals.

But what about tribal groups that aren't riven by the notoriously tectonic tensions of religion and politics?

Economists? Hold on, was that Post-Keynesian or Neo-Keynesian? Or Friedman-style monetarist? These are tribes like any other, and even the global financial crisis of 2008–09 saw very little movement between them, though Alan Greenspan, long-term head of the US Federal Reserve, shocked the monetarists by acknowledging that his policies may have contributed to the disaster. (A bit like US evangelist Pat Robertson admitting the Muslims might have a point.)

Geologists? They and other scientists caught up in the climate change debate have formed tribes – the committed, the deniers, the sceptics – that leave most of us deeply confused. The committed are at war with the deniers almost as much as with global warming itself, and these are no longer mere differences of opinion within a profession; they are combatants engaged in tribal warfare – just as, from 1973–2000, the University of Sydney had to maintain two quite separate departments of philosophy, to accommodate bitter tribal divisions among the academic staff.

I once belonged to a garden club. You'd think that would be a fairly benign group, but the politics were horrendous. The inevitable happened – one faction went off and started a rival club.

Try asking a yoga teacher about Pilates, or the Alexander Technique, Feldenkrais or Rolfing – or any of them about the others. Watch the glint of tribalism in their eyes, though the naive outsider might have assumed they were all in roughly the same business.

And don't for a moment imagine there's a single trible called 'clinical psychologist'. The various schools of psychotherapy have sparked intense rivalries – especially between the psychoanalysts and the cognitive behavioural therapists (CBTs). Psychoanalysts like to deal in myth and mystery, and are prepared to devote long years to trawling through the past, probing the possible origins of a neurosis – ranging, perhaps, from the repression of early sexual yearnings to the unconscious envy of a father's sexual access to the mother. The CBTs, on the other hand, favour a plainer, more direct attack on the symptoms: they believe we can solve our problems by thinking differently about them and learning new ways to behave that will break old patterns, regardless of where those patterns originally came from. For psychoanalysis, the deep wells of childhood are a rich source of material; for CBT, such wells are better left untapped.

Therapists on both sides of this divide can cite articles in the literature that support their views, and they bristle in the face of scepticism from the other side. They tend to organise and attend tribal conferences designed to reinforce their own dogma, and confine their professional reading to journals that reflect their own proclivities. In this, they are almost indistinguishable from religious groups who wouldn't dream of attending each other's conferences or reading each other's literature.

The desire to belong exerts such power over us that it would be hard for rival tribes to acknowledge that their differences may well be more a function of temperament and preference than science or 'truth'. Your faith sustains you in just the same way as our faith sustains us. Your satisfied clients are just as happy as our satisfied clients. We've helped in the healing process, our way; you've helped in the same process, your way. (You might think we have much to learn from each other, but that's not the way tribes operate.)

Scratch the surface: this isn't really about the efficacy of one technique over another, any more than Protestant/Roman Catholic conflicts are really about papal infallibility or the mystical properties of bread blessed by an ordained priest or the role of women in the church. If counsellors were less tribal, they'd be trying a little of this, a little of that, and determinedly resisting the dogma of any one school. They'd be urging 'horses for courses', and trying to find the best possible therapeutic approach for each individual client. Some enlightened individuals are like that but, more generally, tribalism exerts its powerful tug on psychotherapists as much as anyone else. Underneath all the professional disputes, this is about the desire to belong, and dogma – in religion, politics or professional life – is like a membership badge.

LANGUAGES ARE THE REPOSITORIES OF TRIBAL CULTURE AND IDENTITY

In *After Babel*,[6] George Steiner makes the compelling point that language is as much about keeping other people out of our tribe as about facilitating communication within our tribe. The French speak French to communicate with each other, obviously, but also to exclude Italian, German and English speakers. Doctors, lawyers, accountants, bankers, IT specialists, priests, economists and engineers all converse in the technical jargon of their trades, so those who don't belong to the club won't know what they're talking about. (A legal researcher once told me that when people who had appeared before a particular magistrate left the court, the most common question they asked their lawyer was: 'What happened?') Each group will argue, quite correctly, that this makes communication within the group more efficient – rather like professional shorthand. But that is only half the story.

Languages are the codes of belonging. We reveal our tribal identity by the language – the accent, the slang, the technical terms – we use. In societies with rigid class distinctions, accents and dialects locate us very precisely in the system and help us recognise other members of our class. As Steiner says, 'accents are worn like a coat of arms': no one knows this better than the alumni of the English public school system.

The more pressure other Canadians put on Quebeckers (or perhaps I should say Québécois) to become more integrated into the 'mainstream' of Canadian culture and politics, the more aggressively they will defend their distinctive position and, especially, their language. Language is, after all, our most obvious repository of culture, which is why indigenous peoples so deeply mourn the loss of their language as the process of assimilation into settler cultures occurs.

The different languages used by children and teenagers in the classroom, in the playground, on the street, on the internet or with their parents show how language declares our membership of particular groups. Many people have different vocabularies or different tones of voice to facilitate communication within the various groups they belong to, and to make it harder for the members of other groups to grasp what's being said – or what's really meant by what's being said. If we can't understand what our children are saying to their friends, that's probably because they don't want us to. 'LOL' in sms text messages is a classic case of a code that means different things to different generational tribes: parents use LOL as an abbreviation for 'lots of love'; for their children, it stands for 'laugh out loud' – or, at least, it did when this book went to press.

Learning any language is really about becoming acculturated – becoming immersed in the culture of the society or group who use that language. That's why translation is such a difficult process. The Argentinean writer Jorge Luis Borges expressed it like this: 'We do not consider English and Spanish as compounded of sets of easily interchangeable synonyms; they are two quite different ways of looking at the world, each with a nature of its own.'[7]

When our desire to belong is focused on a new group – perhaps a whole new society – the primary challenge is to learn the language. We don't 'get it' for a while, and then it is gradually revealed to us as the code that unlocks previously hidden nuances of culture.

Why do we need so many languages, so many dialects, so many code words? Because the desire to belong demands a strong sense of cultural identity, and the smaller the cultural group, the more deeply our desire to belong will be satisfied.

CONSUMER TRIBALISM

The same products and brands that sometimes act as personal 'status symbols' can also be used to identify us as members of tribes that stand for particular values, preferences, styles and ways of life.

The grandson of a friend caught onto this at an early age. 'I wouldn't trust any driver of a BMW – they'd be smokers and drinkers and gamblers,' he declared, brimming with a nine-year-old's confidence. This was reported to me, *sotto voce*, when I turned up at my friend's house in a rather elderly BMW. I could see the boy struggling to reconcile his grandfather's friend with the tribe he'd assigned me to.

You can have fun with this sort of stuff and none of it matters, except as a symptom of just how far the influence of tribalism can reach: 'If you drive this car, it says something about *you*. It puts you in a category.' I wouldn't take this too seriously if I were you (unless you're a Prius driver, perhaps).

> *I bought myself a Harley-Davidson – classic midlife crisis stuff, I know. But what I found was that any other Harley rider I passed acknowledged me. Very subtle, it was – just a raised finger. It was like a salute to another member of the tribe – a bit like the Masonic handshake.*

Fashion labels have moved to the outside of garments precisely because the marketers of those labels know they work like badges of tribal identity. Handbags, scarves, pants, tops, belts and dresses are increasingly designed to announce your tribe in no uncertain terms. Brands once regarded as discreet now emblazon their wares with logos, as anxious as any football franchise to identify their supporters.

Advertising campaigns are sometimes quite explicit in their attempt to recruit members to the tribe or to reinforce the tribal identity of existing users. ('Join the Golf club,' said Volkswagen, not very subtly, a few years ago.) From Coca-Cola's recurring gangs of exuberant youths leaping about in ever-more exotic aquatic settings to Citroën's once-famous borrowing of the song 'Fifty million Frenchmen can't be wrong', the so-called bandwagon effect has inherent commercial power. Popularity generates its own momentum, and this works as well for marketers as for politicians: popularity is generally perceived by the mass market as a sign of quality or value or, at the very least, social acceptability.

Even if the tribe on offer is as ephemeral as people who drink the same soft drink or beer, drive the same car, read the same magazine or wear the same brand of jeans, our sense of 'belonging' to (or eschewing) a commercial tribe is one of the consequences of the skilful marketing of brands as both personalities and tribal totems.

THE DARK SIDE OF BELONGING: MINDLESS COMPLIANCE AND CONFORMITY

One of history's most appalling examples of the consequences of an unrestrained desire to belong was the case of the Reverend Jim Jones and his People's Temple religious sect. In 1977, Jones moved most of the members of the sect from San Francisco to a new settlement, Jonestown, in the jungle of Guyana. A year later, four men visited the site on a fact-finding mission and were murdered as they tried to leave. Convinced that he would be implicated in the murders and afraid the People's Temple would be discredited and disbanded, Jones decided to pre-empt this possibility by terminating the project himself. Under his instructions, and as a symbol of their loyalty and devotion, about nine hundred members of the sect voluntarily drank strawberry Kool-Aid laced with cyanide in an astonishing mass suicide. Very few chose to escape.

Why? Most of the members of the People's Temple were poor, marginalised people who were so disorientated by the move to Jonestown that they had no other points of reference beyond their desire to belong, conform and comply. Whatever everyone else did – especially if they were told to do it by their leader – was accepted as what they should do too.

We're all familiar with the phenomenon of group pressure in far less bizarre settings than Jonestown. Any group might exert pressure on us because of our desire to belong to it or our attachment to it: this is what the group is doing; I want to be part of this group; I'd better do it too. Mostly, group pressure works in benign and even beneficial ways: we may be inspired and encouraged by a group to act more benevolently than we might otherwise have done or to be caught up in a community project we wouldn't have been able to mount on our own.

But it also works destructively. Gangs sometimes go on a rampage because the judgement of individuals who might have behaved more responsibly on their own is overwhelmed by their desire to go along with the group as a sign of their commitment to it. From the hooded extremists of America's Ku Klux Klan to the terrorists of al-Qaeda – not forgetting the obedient members of conventional armies – the world is full of salutary examples of how dramatically individuals' behaviour can be shaped under the influence of *belonging*. Perhaps suicide bombers are the ultimate demonstration of how virtues like loyalty and commitment can be perverted by pathological tribalism.

The desire to belong leads us into some of life's richest pleasures – circles of friendship, the feeling of being part of a neighbourhood, the excitement of being caught up in grand tribal occasions, the comfort and reassurance of knowing that we belong *here*, with these people, and that we are among kindred spirits. This is the desire that drives the formation of communities, encourages sociability and a harmonious way of life.

So it is sobering to realise it can cast a shadow dark enough to obscure our sense of right and wrong. To find that our own judgement is being impaired by our desperate desire to cling to membership of a group, or that we are participating in decisions or activities we would normally resist, is to realise that even this most civilising of desires must sometimes be restrained.

THE DESIRE FOR MORE

Betcha can't eat just one
Lay's US advertising slogan for potato chips

Hey! There were ten bananas in this bowl when I left for work this morning – I counted them. Who's been grossing out on bananas? Sometimes I think you kids just eat stuff because it's there.

We went for a holiday to the South Coast and it was so gorgeous we didn't want it to end. We even thought of moving there and buying a little business. A fortnight is never enough.

Shoes are my downfall. I know I don't need sixty pairs, but I love buying them and I love having them. I got booked for speeding last week and I thought, 'Damn! That's the price of a nice pair of shoes.'

When I'm reading a book I love, I don't want it to end. I slow down, just to spin it out.

There's no mystery about the desire for more: when you do something you enjoy, you want to do it again, and again. When you have something you like, you want more of it. The human appetite for whatever feels good seems insatiable: sex, money, food, power, books, laughter, music, clothes, cars, travel, education ('knowledge is power'), legal and illegal drugs – stimulations, distractions and comforters of every kind.

We don't confine this desire to things we think are good for us, or that make sense in the cold light of day. Sometimes we just want more of the things that give us a kick, even if we know they are likely to be physically, financially, reputationally or emotionally harmful, like philandering, smoking, drinking, gambling, speeding or reckless spending. The desire for more leads some of us to eschew committed relationships in favour of a series of ever-new affairs – we so enjoy the experience of falling in love that we want more and more of it. The same desire leads some of us to desert a long-term partner in search of more attention, more affection, more *edge*.

It's not always a matter of desiring more pleasure: sometimes we want to prolong a situation that seems manageable and comfortable; content with the status quo, we want more of it.

'What are you going to do today?' a man in a cartoon asks his companion on a park bench.
    'Nothing,' replies the other man.
    'You did that yesterday.'
    'I didn't finish.'

The desire for more can make competitors of us all. Parents are often gripped by child-centred versions of the desire for more: they want their children to have more marks, to be invited to more parties, to be more 'gifted', and even to be taller (obeying the evolutionary imperative that still drives us to regard height as an advantage).

We often treat intelligence rather like height, desiring more of it for our children and assuming that more is better than less. In fact, there is no evidence to suggest that more intelligent people lead more satisfying lives than less intelligent people, contribute more kindness or grace to the communities they inhabit, or are more likely to engage in altruistic rather than self-serving pursuits. Yet we talk as if high intelligence is to be admired as an achievement rather than simply acknowledged as a genetic accident.

◆

From an economic point of view, this is the desire that makes the world go round: strategies for economic growth always come down to finding ways of stimulating the consumer's desire for more – more houses, clothes, cars, gadgets, holidays . . . more of everything we associate with progress and success in capitalist economies.

The desire for more can also encourage higher levels of achievement in work, creativity and play. It's the series of small, incremental gratifications that whet our appetite for more, and keep driving us towards the greater satisfaction we assume will come from greater effort. The desire to extract more enjoyment out of life also encourages some of us to develop strategies for staying fit and healthy and for enhancing our wellbeing. And because love and friendship are such positive experiences, we desire more of them too, with benefits to society at large.

Yet it can all turn ugly so easily. The desire for more has an inherently dark side – greed – that can tip the balance towards excess, addiction and even mania, because there's no compensating desire to stop doing something we're enjoying, even if we know it might cause harm to us and others. This is one desire that regularly gets us into trouble unless it is balanced by moderation and self-control . . . and who, on a roll, wants to hear about moderation and self-control?

The desire for more is dangerous not only because it tempts us into excess, but also because it encourages feelings of entitlement and heightens our frustration: 'Why *can't* I have more?' It tempts us to distort our perspective, our values and our priorities. Even activities that seem harmless or virtuous in themselves can become damaging when we abandon ourselves to the surge of desire for more of them.

My husband was a religious nut-case. He used to go to church every day, pray for hours every night, and he never read anything but the Bible or religious tracts. He was like an addict. Then he announced he was going to live in a monastery in India for a year, to get closer to God and find his true vocation. So off he went. Needless to say, it destroyed our marriage.

WHEN OTHER DESIRES ARE FRUSTRATED, WE COMPENSATE BY INDULGING THIS ONE

Why do we so readily slip the knot of restraint – eat too much, buy too much stuff, drink too much, watch too much television or yield too easily to every urge and passion, even including an exaggerated religious impulse? Usually, we're trying to compensate for the disappointment that flows from the frustration of some other desires. We might not be aware of this compensatory process, but it's the most likely explanation for unbalanced, repetitive behaviour that involves an obsessive focus on just one outcome. People who feel they are not being taken seriously enough, for instance, might react by excessive attention-seeking behaviour – too much alcohol, too much ambition, too much criticism of others, too much reckless driving or spending, or too much sexual pressure on a partner.

Perhaps the excessively zealous husband described by that ex-wife was disappointed in his marriage and took refuge in his piety. Perhaps he was feeling unloved or unappreciated. Perhaps, in spite of his frequent church attendance, he lacked the sense of connection with a close circle of friends or an extended family. Perhaps his workplace was neither congenial nor satisfying. Perhaps he lacked a creative outlet.

We need to attend to all the strands of the web of desire if we are to lead a balanced, satisfying life. When we are not receiving the recognition we crave, don't feel 'connected', lack a framework of beliefs that helps us make sense of the world, don't feel useful or valued, or feel as if 'nothing is happening', the desire for more of something we like emerges from the shadows of our psyche, offering to console us in our disappointment.

And here's the easiest consolation of all . . .

MORE EATING AND DRINKING

The Western world is facing a significant health issue: the rising incidence of obesity. If unchecked, this will have serious consequences for the health of populations via an increased risk of heart disease, type 2 diabetes, and osteoarthritis.

We know this is the result of many factors. Yes, we're eating more fatty food, more processed and less fresh food. Yes, we're not exercising enough, and we spend too much time slouched on the couch in front of TV or hunched over a computer.

But another factor is that we're simply eating too much. Our portions are becoming too big. We're not just refuelling ourselves, we're stuffing ourselves.

Why? Simple, really: eating is one of the great sensuous pleasures of life and when we eat or drink something we like, we want more of it. Common sense and our own experience tell us there's a law of diminishing returns operating here: when it comes to the pleasure of eating and drinking, the more you have, the less you enjoy each additional increment. The first cup of coffee is great, so you decide to have another one, but the second never tastes as good as the first. Yet we manage to overlook that small piece of wisdom in the rush of desire for more.

It would be going too far to say we don't know when to stop, but sometimes it looks like that. When things get really out of hand, we call it an addiction. But even when it's not a pathological problem, our desire for more can get us into trouble.

Cravings are familiar to all of us, and certain foods are notorious for stimulating the desire for more: chocolate, ice-cream, cola drinks and alcohol are hard for many of us to resist, and hamburgers, fried chicken and pizza have become the staples of the fast-food industry precisely because they taste so good, are so readily available, so easy to eat and so relatively cheap – making them soft targets for the desire for more.

The fashionable term 'comfort food' is a tacit acknowledgement that food and drink are often used as compensation for stress, disappointment, loneliness and anxiety. The more more destabilised we are by the pace of change, and the more fragmented our communities and families become, the more likely we are to indulge our compensatory desire to eat and drink – more beer or wine, more Coke, more pizza, more McDonald's – more of whatever makes me feel better *now*. And the longer-term consequences for our health and wellbeing? Well, the desire for more of *this* is powerful enough to drive such questions out of our minds.

MORE SPENDING, MORE 'STUFF'

'Nothing happens until someone sells something' said a plaque on the desk of a marketing executive I once knew and, of course, no one can sell something until someone buys it. So in economic terms it's true to say nothing happens until someone buys something, since money needs to keep moving if the system is to be stimulated and lubricated. Abstruse and stratospheric financial transactions are all very well – and they make a few people very rich indeed – but, as they say in the trade, consumer spending is where the rubber hits the road.

This is why citizens in Western capitalist democracies are expected to behave like reliable consumers, toiling away on the treadmill of endless consumption. Australians caught a glimpse of the official attitude to their responsibility to spend when their federal government devised a 'stimulus package' to avert recession in the wake of the global financial crisis of 2008–09.

A key component of the Australian package was a handout of borrowed cash in which millions of families and individuals received payments of $900, to spend as they wished. The clear implication was that this money was to be spent, not saved or invested, and that the spending should be in the retail market-place. 'Your country needs you to go out and buy stuff' was the essential message.

When the point was made that many people struggling under a heavy burden of debt might be better advised to use the handout to reduce their debt, Australia's Treasurer conceded the point, then went on to explain that debt reduction was a good idea because it would enable people to return to their role as consumers more quickly. Since we had all been led to believe that the financial crisis was itself driven by the greed of operators in financial markets, this puzzled many people: 'If greed is bad, how can greed also be good?' That was a reasonable question, if you regarded the encouragement to spend as a stimulus to greed.

Consumers dutifully set about spending their handouts, and a recession was indeed averted – primarily because of a boost to Australia's economy from increased resources exports to China, but the consumer 'cash splash', along with a number of other measures including a government infrastructure spending program, was generally acknowledged to have been a contributing factor.

So can greed be a virtue? Or is it still a vice (as we used to think), or merely the morally neutral engine of capitalism? It looks as if the answer might be 'all of the above', or 'it all depends on your point of view'. In rather the same way as we now prefer to call debt 'credit', we appear to be in the process of rebadging greed.

We've also rebadged spending. We now talk about 'retail therapy', a term that adds a new dimension of respectability to the desire for more: 'I'm not just spending; I'm indulging in a little retail therapy,' and so the desire for more is transferred from the purchase of particular things to the experience of buying itself.

Does anyone else feel powerful when they shop? Say you buy something good for yourself, or something big, you do get a high. I think that's why some people get addicted to it, because they feel so good about themselves.

When I was living overseas for a year, I kept upping my credit card limit every month or so. Hey, it was Paris, what was I supposed to do?

I go into a kind of trance in a shopping mall. I suppose it's dangerous, but I love it. I have to limit myself, otherwise the place works like a magnet on me. We used to go shopping and buy what we wanted and then come home. Now it's more of an event.

There's a hazard in our desire to acquire ever more 'stuff', but there's not much sign of our giving it up any time soon, in spite of the dire warnings from environmentalists about an unsustainably profligate way of life in the West that is fast catching on in China, India and Brazil.

We might as well admit that we live in a materialistic society where spending is part of a day's work, the constant acquisition of more possessions is regarded as normal and proper, and those who resist the lure of materialism are regarded as eccentric if not actually weird. No car? No plasma TV? No mortgage? No credit card? No mobile phone plan? Aren't you rather letting the side down?

The lure of materialism is powerful because its 'buy more' messages are so simple and seductive: buy more stuff and you'll feel better, you'll help to reduce unemployment, people will see how successful you are. In the West, that's all true, up to a point, which is why capitalism survives: if we stop spending, the system freezes. The hazard is in letting our desire for more reduce us to people who think our value can be measured in material terms.

MORE MONEY

When it is directly put to them, few people would claim to believe that wealth is a measure of a person's worth. Yet we consistently behave as if it's true. This is one of the most insidious and destructive of all the myths that weaken our lives by offering us hollow goals. Beyond a certain point, no one accumulates wealth because they need the money: wealth becomes symbolic of something else – power, status, influence, 'success', an excuse for flagrant disregard of social convention . . . or even 'worth'.

Many years ago I was involved in an informal discussion about an appointment to the board of a private school. I suggested a distinguished academic lawyer who was also a prominent 'public intellectual'. My suggestion was dismissed as bluntly as this: 'He hasn't made any money.'

If we were to regard money as the index of a person's worth, where would that leave schoolteachers (including the teachers at the very school then under discussion)? Or counsellors? Or police, fire and ambulance officers? Or nurses? Or people who perform essential services in any society – garbage collectors, electricity linesmen, road workers, street cleaners, hospital orderlies? None of them is associated with wealth, yet all of them have worth, and their great value to our society is not reflected in the income they receive. We know that, but we don't always act as if we know it.

If it is true that, beyond a certain point, no one accumulates wealth because they need the money, then where is that point? It varies, of course, from society to society and person to person, according to the socioeconomic and cultural factors that have shaped our attitudes and expectations. Even within one street in one suburb, there's likely to be a wide range of opinions about that elusive concept. But it's reasonable to suggest that the 'certain point' is at the level of wealth where we can avoid the discomfort or inconvenience of not being able to lead a fulfilling life. It's a point above which you can afford occasional luxuries but below which even necessities are a struggle.

Scholars in the field of poverty research would say that poverty, in any social context, means the inability of people to participate 'normally' in the life of their community: feed and clothe themselves and their children to a conventional standard, have secure and comfortable accommodation, be able to afford the costs of education, transport, regular holidays, recreational activities and occasional treats such as going to the movies or eating out.

Beyond that point, there's plenty of materialistic pleasure associated with higher incomes: bigger houses, flasher cars, a more extensive wardrobe, more exotic holidays, smarter schools for the children, cosmetic surgery, and so on. The desire for more propels many of us up the ladder of affluence, perhaps in search of greater financial security, or higher 'status', or a more self-indulgent lifestyle. (In my experience, not many people say they are striving for higher incomes so they can contribute more to the relief of poverty, homelessness, misery or disadvantage in their societies, though some do precisely that after they've made their pile.)

Conventional wisdom says that beyond that 'certain point', more money doesn't produce a corresponding increase in your personal wellbeing, but it's very hard to know where to draw that line or even to know how to measure such things with any degree of precision. A respondent in one of my research projects insisted that 'anyone who says money doesn't bring happiness doesn't know where to shop'. It's quite apparent that for most people – leaving aside the extremely wealthy – more money does indeed seem to make life easier, more comfortable, more stimulating and potentially more satisfying (possibly more stressful, too, though the stress of 'keeping up with the Joneses' is quite different from the survival stress experienced by the poor). People who are materially well off tend to enjoy better health – perhaps because of a combination of better diet, better healthcare and the sense of being more in control of their lives – and they typically secure better schooling for their children than poorer families do. On the other hand, we all know people on low incomes who live deeply satisfying and productive lives, who give their children a secure and loving home and provide a good education for them, and who make a valuable contribution to the communities in which they live.

So let's not fall for glib generalisations, except perhaps this one: it's almost certainly true that when 'making money' becomes the all-consuming goal, we're likely to become emotionally crippled by the paucity and vacuity of that goal. If we achieve our goal and become very wealthy indeed, it will be hard to keep our non-material values intact; hard to maintain our level of compassion for the disadvantaged and marginalised in our society; hard to resist the sense of entitlement that afflicts most wealthy people. The desire for more money – like the desire for more stuff – can be a trap from which it is almost impossible to escape.

We don't have to dismantle capitalism or abolish money or return to an agrarian society to reject the myth that money equates to worth: all we need to do is live as if we *know* that money is not the measure of anyone's worth or success (except in the narrowest, most materialistic, most trivial sense). While we're at it, we might also try to establish whether there are any alternative, more authentic measures of a person's worth. My guess is that such a quest will always be futile: in the end, it will lead us to the conclusion that the whole idea of 'measuring a person's worth' is simply ludicrous.

Here's a useful test: when you feel the desire for more money welling up inside you, ask yourself, 'What's this really about? What do I need this *for?*' There might be a perfectly reasonable answer, but the question is still worth asking.

THE DARK SIDE: LESS FOR OTHERS

Addiction, greed and rampant materialism are three of the more obvious shadows cast by our desire for more, but the desire for another person to be diminished in some way – to be less successful than we are, to have less – is the ugliest. Darkened by this shadow, the desire for more can generate mean-spiritedness, a lack of compassion, a tendency to withhold charity: 'I haven't got enough myself – why should I give you any?'

Many people who prosper, in material terms, are cheerful and generous in their prosperity; pleased to see others do well; keen to offer encouragement and advice. It's as though they have been pleasantly surprised by their success, and grateful for it, and so they look for ways – via charitable giving or mentoring, for instance – to share their good fortune.

But others fall victim to that nasty trait the Germans call *Schadenfreude* – taking pleasure in another's misfortune. Such people live with a picture of a pie in their heads, and they worry about who might be getting a bigger slice than theirs. This is what drives anxiety about 'status' and the crazy idea that we should be valued according to how much wealth we've accumulated. If the desire for more is given free rein, it will lead us into some of the emotional dead-ends described in this chapter: a sense of entitlement; envy of others' success; anxiety about how we're faring in the race to be rich, famous or 'successful'.

At its worst, it will lead us to *want* others to stumble, to fail, to have less.

MORE GROWTH

In the early weeks of 2010, the continuing debate about Australia's optimum population size entered a new phase. Responding to estimates that Australia's population would grow from twenty-one million in 2009 to about thirty-five million by 2050, the then Prime Minister Kevin Rudd announced that he was very comfortable with such growth projections and, in one of his favourite turns of phrase, declared that he 'made no apology' for embracing the idea of Australia as 'a big country'.

Environmentalists and many other people, conscious of Australia's water and infrastructure problems, were aghast. With drought putting recurrent stress on Australia's rivers and dams, and most cities and towns experiencing regular water shortages – some of them dire – it seemed an odd thing to hope that the population would grow sharply in the absence of radically new water conservation and management strategies. (It also seemed odd to be enthusing about growth in the absence of equally radical strategies to provide adequate services for these additional millions.)

Australia might have particular difficulties with its water supply, and with congestion in its major cities, but it is far from being alone in embracing the idea of population growth. Most of the low-birthrate countries of the West are looking to immigration to boost their population, because there's a general assumption that population growth is fundamental to that universal political goal of economic growth.

Clive Hamilton, an Australian economist and environmentalist, has questioned the automatic assumption that economic growth is fundamental to economic survival or, indeed, to the wellbeing of the population. His book *Growth Fetish*[1] was pilloried by believers in the dogma of economic growth, but enthusiastically endorsed by many humanitarians and environmentalists, and by the economics editor of the *Sydney Morning Herald*, Ross Gittins. In a column supporting many of Hamilton's arguments, Gittins wrote: 'The one thing people like me aren't allowed to do is question economic growth. To almost all economists, business people and politicians, the need to maximise the growth of the economy is a self-evident truth.'[2]

Indeed, when a thousand of Australia's so-called 'brightest and best' participated in a weekend talkfest called the *2020 Summit,* one of their key recommendations (described ironically by Hamilton as 'one of their exciting new ideas') was to try harder to maximise economic growth.

In the same article, Gittins quoted British Prime Minister David Cameron, then leader of the Opposition, describing him as 'probably the only leading politician to question the primacy of economic growth':

> It's time we admitted that there's more to life than money, and it's time we focused not just on GDP, but on GWB – general wellbeing. Wellbeing can't be measured by money or traded in markets. It can't be required by law or delivered by government. It's about the beauty of our surroundings, the quality of our culture, and above all the strength of our relationships.

That sounded like an echo of a famous speech made by the US Attorney General, Robert F. Kennedy, at the University of Kansas in 1967, just months before he was assassinated:

> Gross national product counts air pollution, and cigarette advertising, and ambulances to clear our highways of carnage. It counts special locks for our doors and the jails for the people who break them . . . Yet, the gross national product does not allow for the health of our children, the quality of their education, or the joy of their play; it does not include the beauty of our poetry or the strength of our marriages, the intelligence of our public debate or the integrity of our public officials. It measures neither our

wit nor our courage, neither our wisdom nor our learning, neither our compassion nor our devotion to our country. It measures everything, in short, except that which makes life worthwhile.

This is not an argument against growth, per se, but the core of Kennedy's and Cameron's message is that economic growth guarantees nothing about the wellbeing of a society. Yet growth continues to be the economic mantra of our era, and most of us chant it cheerfully because it meshes so neatly with our own desire for more of whatever seems desirable. Prosperity is good; more must be better. Rarely do we stop and ask Hamilton's question: 'Towards what are we striving to grow?'

I'm no economist, but I must say the widely accepted business proposition that 'if you're not growing, you're dying' never rang true in the case of my own small research and consulting business. Twice in its thirty-five-year history, I responded to pressure to 'grow the business' by increasing the size of the staff and expanding the services we offered our clients. Both times I regretted it, because I didn't want to be a manager; I wanted to be a researcher. I didn't want to build a bigger business; I wanted to be able to support my family, serve my clients' needs, do interesting work, and enjoy myself. And I could do that best, it turned out, if I kept the business small. Growth is not the only acceptable goal in business.

MORE MEDIA STIMULATION

It starts in the preschool, or even earlier. Media-saturated Western societies offer their young a diet of constant audiovisual stimulation, complemented by highly charged preschool activities. Early childhood education is in a bind: increasingly, it has to compete with sophisticated online material for the children's attention and interest. The temptation to 'throw the switch to vaudeville' must be very strong; after all, children accustomed to constant stimulation are bound to want more.

> *We look after our grand-daughter two days a week. As soon as she arrives, it's 'What project are we going to do today, Gran?' She's so used to constant activity at the after-school care she goes to the other three days, she wears us out. I could sit her in front of the TV but then I'd feel guilty and, in any case, she'd want me to sit with her. She's no good at amusing herself. Never has been – not since preschool.*

It's not just children, of course. Why do so many of us find it hard to turn off the TV, or disconnect from the internet? Because the easy pleasure of media stimulation leads us to want more of it.

> *Even if we go out to a movie, I find I still go to the computer when we get home – I need that fix before bed. But you do get hooked – it can go on for hours, not just minutes, and then you wonder why you bothered.*

Some of us turn on the TV to watch a single program, and then turn it off again, but we're in the minority. More typical are the households where the television set is constantly on – or where there are several sets scattered around the house, tuned to different programs. The desire for more, if unchecked, can lead not only to saturation but also to addiction – in the case of the media, the addiction is often to the sound and movement, rather than program content.

If we turn the TV off, the place feels like a morgue.

I always turn the TV on before I go out – I hate the feeling of coming home to an empty house.

We are similarly at risk of addiction to mobile phones as a source of constant stimulation. The term 'phone', of course, is already rather inappropriate for an instrument crammed with so much brilliant technology. It gives us access to the internet, is just as likely to be used for text messaging as for voice calls, acts as a camera, a satellite navigation device and a lively little thing in your hand that offers endless distraction from the tedium of waiting for a bus, the nagging of parents (or children) or the boredom of a date that's going nowhere: 'Excuse me, I just have to check my messages.'

The desire for more stimulation via the gadgets of the information technology revolution is changing the way we live. In the dizzy IT world of the future, with data cascading all around us, it's hard to imagine there being a desire for more content, more convenience or more channels. Perhaps the new desire will be for more time with each other, or for more silence.

In the meantime, the IT revolution has thrown up yet another sign of the desire for more: when it comes to the consumption of new media, the demand for a continuous stream of content is so strong that the technical quality of the audio and video content has become almost irrelevant. At the very time when the quality of audio and video reproduction and transmission via traditional media – cinema, TV, radio, DVDs, CDs – has reached unprecedented levels of fidelity, young consumers, in particular, are cramming their MP3 players with music of such low fidelity it would make sound buffs cringe. And as huge, high-definition TV receivers dominate the market and 3D movies begin to join the cultural mainstream, avid mobile phone users enthusiastically receive visual material on tiny screens that offer picture and sound quality far inferior to what's available on the 'old' media.

In a similar irony, the desire to create instant (still and moving) pictures has led to the popularity of in-phone cameras whose picture quality can't match the technical standard now being offered by the new generation of digital cameras. (As the National Portrait Gallery of Australia noted in its 2010 exhibition, Present Tense: 'Lo-fi is the new black'.) In these early stages of the new technology, quality simply isn't the issue: the desire is for more convenience, more data, and more functions attached to one piece of equipment.

MORE VIOLENCE, MORE WAR

You might assume that the futility, the obscenity and the destructive evil of war – or of violence of any kind – would be so self-evident that we'd have long since abandoned it as a strategy for achieving anything. But no: futile, obscene and destructive as it is, we continue to act like the belligerent species we've always been. Our propensity for more violence (I hesitate to call it our 'desire'), including more war, contradicts all our rhetoric on the subject, but it persists.

Take a look at the video games that attract most attention from young males, especially, and ask yourself why violence is in such heavy demand as a spectacle, even among those of us who are never likely to raise a fist – let alone a gun – in anger. Some regard boxing as a barbaric sport, but it continues to pull the crowds and boxing champions continue to be granted celebrity status.

Why is on-screen violence, including the graphic simulation of actual killing, widely regarded as more acceptable than on-screen sex? Why are the most popular portrayals of conflict those that resort to violent solutions? Why do TV channels choose to replay close-ups of the moment when a football match erupted in a brawl? Why do war movies – and news footage of real wars – retain their magical power to entertain?

> *When the invasion of Iraq first happened, it was terrific to watch on TV – all those rockets and bombs. And then it got kind of boring and I stopped watching, until the ground war started and it became interesting again.*

> *There's too much sex and bad language in modern movies. I prefer to watch old war movies.*

When Barack Obama received the Nobel Peace Prize in 2009, he asserted that because 'evil does exist in the world . . . war is sometimes necessary'. He went on to say: 'We can understand that there will be war and still strive for peace.'

Why will there be war? Is it enough to say 'because there is evil in the world'? Or are we forced to say something even less palatable: that we are a warlike species and we want more of this abomination, just as we want more of everything else that lights up our imaginations, fuels our prejudices (including our hatreds), feeds our visions of our own greatness, boosts our patriotism, and gives us a thrill. Yes, a thrill – not for those staring death in the face, of course, but for the patriots beating their drums and waving their flags, and the leaders declaring war. Their faces might be grave, but I suspect that if we took their pulses we'd see how excited they are; how rich and all-consuming the experience of warmongering is. Not many of them admit it, although Margaret Thatcher did.

Look how eagerly George W. Bush and Tony Blair, along with a few others, rushed their armies into the invasion of Iraq, well before they had irrefutable evidence that would convince the United Nations that an unprovoked, 'pre-emptive' invasion was justified. (What unprovoked invasion was *ever* justified?) Throughout history, leaders have willingly committed their young men and women to horror and death on a grand scale, and expected credit for what they've done.

We dress war up in stirring, inspiring stories of heroism and sacrifice, but there's a nasty story we don't often tell: we go to war because that's one of the things we want more of – why else do we maintain the world's armies and arsenals? Our desire for war is bound up with patriotic greed, economic greed, religious greed, territorial greed, delusions of grandeur, paranoia, insecurity, cultural identity and values, and with the dark, ignoble side of human nature – the side that wants to crush opponents rather than deal with them.

But come closer to home. Which of us has never felt a surge of rage so strong we were tempted to strike out and hit something or someone? (Even my mild-mannered mother sometimes said she felt 'mad enough to spit'.) Road rage and supermarket-trolley rage are well-documented phenomena in Western societies: we all get angry, and sometimes we express it in violent ways.

A famously heated exchange between two philosophers at the University of Sydney collapsed into farce when one of them said, 'Your arguments won't look so pretty when I smash your face in.' Most of us resist that urge most of the time. We prefer to channel our aggression into angry words or smouldering thoughts of revenge, or to discharge our violent impulses by watching other people be violent – in the street or the school playground, on the sporting field, on the screen – or by reading crime novels laced with violence. Many of us relish stories of gangland killings, turf wars between drug lords or extortionists . . . even stories about people in wealthy neighbourhoods who poison each other's trees to protect an expensive view. Moves to clean up violence in various codes of football have not been greeted with universal approval among the fans: 'Bring back the biff' is the cry of those who love a bit of on-field mayhem.

Some of us – especially young male adults who drink too much – can't resist the urge to lash out physically, and those who strike others sometimes find that they enjoy it. They enjoy the adrenalin rush; they enjoy the sight of an opponent in pain; they enjoy the sense of power. Then they want more of the peculiarly uninhibited pleasure violence bestows on its perpetrators – hence punch-ups in the pub, stoushes between football louts, gang warfare, racial and religious taunts that escalate into the fire-bombing of churches, the torture of enemies, the lynch mobs . . . all the way to international terrorism and war. Bill Clinton once remarked that 'Israeli elections always close in the last few days towards the war party',[3] and the Israelis are not alone in that.

History, right up to the present day, says we can't help ourselves. Conflict brings out the worst in us, and conflict will always be with us. That's why there will always be violence. That's why there will always be war. War is the ultimate expression of our desire to come out on top, and to resolve conflicts in our favour without the tedium of argument, negotiation or diplomacy. 'Shoot first, ask questions later' is no joke. In *An Intimate History of Humanity*, Theodore Zeldin drew this gloomy conclusion: 'Will people stop irritating, hating or fighting each other when the spirit of racial, political, religious toleration gradually spreads over the world? Only those with short memories can believe it.'[4]

When you see how easily the desire for more can produce a deadly combination of greed and violence, and you add the ecological fragility of an overpopulated planet, it's hard to see how our species will survive, long-term. I hope I'm wrong about that.

THE ADDICT'S DESPERATE CRY FOR MORE

John Veals, one of the leading characters in Sebastian Faulks's novel, *A Week in December*,[5] is an investment banker plotting one of the most vicious and lucrative takeovers in financial history. Veals is utterly committed to his work, ruthless in the development of strategies that will further increase his already fabulous wealth, and apparently indifferent to the effects of his deals on the lives of other people. This will be the biggest deal of his life, involving the calculated destruction of a bank through manipulation of the share market, and the effects on thousands of age pensioners and shareholders will be catastrophic.

Veals is effectively estranged from his wife and family, though he appears blithely unaware of this: his desire for more wealth is so powerful and all-consuming that it filters out such inconvenient distractions as his drug-addicted son, his wandering daughter and his frustrated wife, Vanessa. To quote Faulks: 'What Vanessa hadn't foreseen was either the narrowness of her husband's life or the peripheral sliver of it that would be set aside to her.'

That complaint would be familiar to anyone who has lived with an addict of any kind: a gambler, a drug-abuser, a heavy drinker, a compulsive philanderer, a person gripped by obsessive ambition for power or status, or a workaholic who has lost contact with the world beyond the narrow focus of their work.

Faulks portrays Veals as a man whose only interest lies in the acquisition of money; a man who is prepared to go through the motions of social life only to the extent that his social contacts might be useful to his commercial aspirations. At one point in the book, a friend asks Vanessa whether she still loves her husband, 'but it was not a question Vanessa felt she could answer. How could you "love" such a man? What makes him tick? What does he enjoy?' Such questions strike Vanessa as incapable of answers, 'because her husband had long since migrated to a place where such matters had no meaning'.

In that description of a man who has migrated to a place where matters like love and personal relationships hold no meaning, Faulks has captured not only the dehumanising effect of a life lived only for material gain but, more generally, the isolating effect of addiction.

In the case of the fictional John Veals, the desire for more had found its sole expression in a world dominated by dreams of the next deal. In the case of a drug addict, the desire for more becomes ruthlessly focused on the next fix. In his chilling novel of drug addiction, *Cain's Book*, Alexander Trocchi describes the relentlessness of the quest for drugs to satisfy the addict's craving, and the irrelevance of those not directly involved in the chain of supply:

> There are moments when I despair of others, give them up, let them stray out of the circle of light and definition, and they are free to come and go, bringing panic, or chaos, or joy, depending on my own mood, my state of readiness.[6]

Like the narcissist, the addict cares little for anything that lies beyond the periphery of the addictive process; attaches little or no value to anything except the object of his or her addictive lust; lives in a world dominated by thoughts of the next drink, the next sexual conquest, the next fix, or the next business deal. A friend whose husband – a doctor – was helplessly addicted to prescription drugs spoke to his therapist and was told that her husband's addiction was so powerful, 'he would sell his grandmother to get the drugs'. And that wasn't meant as hyperbole.

The more fixated, obsessive and narrow our desire for more becomes, the more treacherous will be its effect on our lives.

MORE OF 'THE GOOD OLD DAYS'

There's nothing very complicated about nostalgia: it's the desire to recapture some of the dreamy pleasures we associate with times and places in our past. Memory is selective, of course, and the bits of the past we try to reclaim are usually those that reinforce our rosy conviction that back then, life was simpler and more undemanding – or simply more fun – than it is now. One of the most common remarks among today's grandparents is that 'I wouldn't like to be a young person growing up today', though today will soon become the focus of the rising generation's own nostalgia.

Nostalgia doesn't only express the desire for more; it also overlaps with the desire for control. For many people, the past is absolutely 'controllable', because we've long since mastered it; we survived it; we coped with it, and now we can safely embrace it. The past is a comfortable place in our imagination, because it keeps on being the same thing; it doesn't unleash any nasty shocks (unless we suddenly remember something we'd prefer to have left forgotten).

Some nostalgists love to dream about their childhood and adolescence, when they were on a journey of endless discovery, when everything seemed fresh and new (especially their hormones), anything seemed possible, they had no idea what lay ahead of them, and wouldn't have believed anyone who told them.

It's hardly surprising that the best bits of the distant past, selectively recalled and burnished, would seem more attractive to us than the totality of the present or the recent past, with its still-raw disappointments and tribulations, and its reminders of the slog of the long haul. It's no wonder some of us like to cling to the symbols of those earlier, more innocent and perhaps more carefree times: old photos, old toys, old sports equipment, old audio tapes and LP records – even if you can't play them on your new equipment, the covers are still evocative – and all the other mementos of that fondly recalled time when we were bursting with potential. Some of us like to present those days to our children as tough, demanding, austere and even grim, but that's not the usual focus of our nostalgia: most of us don't want to relive grim.

There's always a market for nostalgia, and not only in junk shops. The reincarnations of the VW Beetle, the Mini and the Fiat 500 might look cute and sexy to young buyers, but they carry rich emotional connotations for the over-sixties. Greeting cards that recapture the style of the forties and fifties, compilations of the recording hits of past decades, 'easy listening' radio stations, 'farewell tours' of singers and bands you'd thought long gone, the revivals of plays and movies – even radio serials – that recall the past, all figure prominently in the nostalgia market. Music has special magic because we recall it as the soundtrack of our young lives.

Know what I recall most vividly about National Service training? Johnny Mathis singing 'The Twelfth of Never'. It was played endlessly on the radio in our hut.

Listen! They're playing our song.

I can tell you one thing – there hasn't been any decent pop music since the Beatles.

Nostalgia comes in waves, according to our feelings of security in the present and our confidence in the future. Some older people take refuge in nostalgia because the current scene seems too daunting or challenging to them, and they feel more comfortable and secure with mental re-runs of the past. (Not all older people: many of our tribal elders are still in the vanguard of change, still thriving on the present and excited about a future they are helping to shape.)

Rationally, we know the past is beyond our reach if only because we are no longer the people we were back then. Of course we can learn from the mistakes of the past and our nostalgic musings might remind us that we still need to forgive some of the wrongs of the past (our own and others'). Wistful backward glances can be harmless, even instructive, but we weaken our grip on the present and sap our confidence in the future in direct proportion to our nostalgic clinging to the idea that the past was better.

No matter how much we might yearn for more of it, or how much we might enjoy an occasional re-run of the highlights, the past is not only, in English novelist L.P. Hartley's famous words, 'a foreign country'; it's a country that no longer exists. To imagine we can still live there, that we can have more of it or that it was 'better', is to delude ourselves, which is fine – plenty of us draw comfort from our delusions – except that we might be blinding ourselves to all the worthwhile things on offer in the here and now.

MORE *LIFE!*

The thing we want above all is more life.

When our lives are threatened by serious illness, most of us are reluctant to let go, grabbing at any available medical intervention rather than letting nature take its course. Although Western societies are becoming more enlightened about euthanasia, most of us would want to be sure that the decision to terminate our lives was made by us, not someone else – and certainly not by some remote bureaucrat, tucked away in a Department of Lifespan Planning somewhere.

People in their middle years, watching their ageing parents' decline into poor health, are inclined to say to their own children, 'Bop me on the head when the time comes, will you? I don't want to go through this,' or, more charitably, 'I don't want to put you through this.' But when the time comes, most of us seem determined to tough it out: we say we'll settle for less – especially if our quality of life deteriorates – but end up wanting more of whatever is available.

We know we're mortal; we know there's a finite lifespan available to each of us. At a rational level, we know the world got along perfectly well before we arrived and will continue to do so after we've gone. We recognise that although this feels like 'my world', it isn't. Each of us is merely one of billions who've spent some fleeting time here.

Yet the desire for more life is so powerful as to seem unquench-able in many of us. Life is one thing we are unashamedly greedy for. There's even a kind of cosmic greed that helps to explain the appeal of the many religions that offer the prospect of yet more life after death. Whether the offer is in the form of reincarnation or an eternal existence in a paradise beyond space and time, the life-after-death proposition is irresistible to those who can't imagine – or can't face – the prospect of their lives coming to a dead end.

Does the belief in an afterlife affect our attitude to death or the attitudes of the dying? Many devoutly religious people find themselves seeking ways to prolong life on earth, as if their fear of death – or their reluctance to die – is as strong as any non-believer's. Others, though, seem to embrace their approaching death as a transition into a confidently expected afterlife. According to family folklore, my maternal great-grandfather sat up suddenly on his death-bed, arms outstretched, and said, 'Lord, receive me,' then lay back on his pillow and expired. 'Going through the Great Door' is how one of my closest friends calmly described it to me on the day before his death. A Christian believer, he saw it as the next great adventure.

Another close friend, a defiant atheist, was equally calm when I visited him in hospital the week he died, to discuss what I would say at his funeral. 'If I hadn't done everything I wanted to do, this would be a tragedy,' he said of his looming death. 'But I have, so this is fine.' He was sixty-two, and, having declined any further treatment for the cancer that was killing him, he was ready to go.

Another friend, another atheist also facing premature death from cancer, had found no peace at all. On my final visit to his hospital bed, he gripped my arm and said, 'Get me out of here. I'm scared if I fall asleep I won't wake up.'

A Buddhist friend, confident of her reincarnation, says she doesn't fear death; she only fears not being conscious at the time of her death. For her, it's a fascinating prospect and she doesn't want to miss the moment of transition.

Based on my own experience of the death of my parents and seven of my closest friends, all I can say is that some believers are calm in the face of death and some are not. Some non-believers in an afterlife feel panic as their death approaches, others don't. The picture is confused, but my general impression from listening to many families' stories is that when people are conscious of the approach of their own death, even a premature death, most face it with equanimity. Religious faith or the lack of it seems to be an unreliable predictor of how people will deal with the process of dying. Another general observation is that the people surrounding a dying person are usually more distressed than the one who is passing away.

As a species, though, it's clear that our most persistent desire is the lust for life. Unless it has been swamped by a destructive addiction that we know might actually shorten our lives, this is a desire that holds most of us in its grip until we reach the end of the road. By then, most of the other things we lusted after – power, possessions, money, status, sex – strike us as faintly ridiculous. A common deathbed experience is to wish we had desired less and loved more. Perhaps we should be learning that lesson from the death of others, rather than waiting for a wake-up call that comes, uselessly, on the very threshold of our own big sleep.

THE DESIRE FOR CONTROL

Accidents will occur in the best-regulated families.

Charles Dickens, *David Copperfield*

Of all the desires that drive us, the desire for control is the one most likely to disappoint and frustrate us. It's the one we seem to understand least and the one we most frequently try to satisfy in inappropriate ways.

Symbolically, we're suckers for the illusion of control. We never feel quite so comfortable as when we are in the driver's seat of a car. We become addicted to video games and mobile phones that make us feel like masters of the universe. We clutch the TV remote as if it's an instrument of power. We fondly recall a childhood where we controlled model trains and cars, and dolls stayed where we put them.

Most of us hate being put in situations where we feel we have no control at all. Fear of flying is usually about loss of control, as are many other phobias: fear of open spaces, crowds, riding in lifts, thunderstorms, being on a boat far from shore, sitting too far from the exit in a theatre, being intoxicated.

We mock as 'control freaks' those we judge to be obsessive about control, but this is an area where few of us are free from some obsession. We might place things carefully at right angles on our desk, set the table or make the bed *just so*, or go quietly crazy if the car keys are not where they are supposed to be.

How much energy have we wasted fretting about our lack of control over other people's behaviour or events that are beyond our control? How much wiser, how much healthier we would be if we were able to lower, just a little, our expectation that the world should conform to our wishes.

Here are some announcements that will be familiar to you:

Your flight has been cancelled due to circumstances beyond our control.

This store will be closed until further notice due to circumstances beyond our control.

Unemployment is rising due to circumstances beyond our control.

Question: Which circumstances are *not* beyond our control? Isn't it the very nature of circumstances – favourable and unfavourable – to be beyond our control? Surely circumstances are things that shape us, things we react to, rather than things we can control?

The global financial crisis of 2008–09 reminded us yet again how many things are beyond our control: the greed of the already wealthy; the fluctuation in patterns of world demand for everything from iron ore and gas to cars, houses and credit; the recklessness of some mortgage brokers and money-market traders; the fickleness of shareholders who treat the market like a casino rather than as a means of investing in the work of companies they believe in; the fragility of under-regulated capitalism.

Ever since primitive man was struck by lightning or buried in an avalanche, or the village women were stolen by a horde of invaders, we've known that life is unpredictable and events are frequently beyond our control. A train is blown up by terrorists; our water supply is threatened by prolonged drought; unemployment, inflation and interest rates rise and fall, but we keep imagining that, one day, we'll have all these things under control.

Even if you don't think on so grand a scale, nothing in human history encourages the idea that the important things in our lives – especially our relationships – are ever under control or that 'getting my life under control' has ever been a realistic goal.

Yet the desire not only persists but seems to be increasing in its intensity. The yearning for control has become a modern Western madness. Stressed and destabilised by the rate of change, we have been looking in the wrong place for a solution to our anxieties and insecurities: the desire for control may be perfectly natural and even healthy, up to a point, but it depends what – and who – we're trying to control.

WHAT KIND OF CONTROL DO WE DESIRE?

At its simplest and most childish, the desire for control is about wanting our own way. Early on, it looked as if we might get away with it: we demanded food and were fed; we cried and were comforted; we lay in a dirty nappy and were cleaned up. As we grew beyond infancy, we made the painful discovery that that kind of control wouldn't last. If our parents were smart, tantrums soon lost their power to influence anyone to do anything. We began to adapt to the idea that we were part of a community – a family, a school, a neighbourhood – in which many people with many different and often competing demands were learning how to coexist. Cooperation (the very opposite of control) looked like a lesson we'd better learn if we were ever going to find a manageable way of getting along with all these other people while getting at least some of our own needs and wants met.

Maturation, in other words, is mainly about learning to accept that we can have much less control than we might wish over events in our lives, especially those involving other people. The learning takes place, the adaptations are made, but the desire for control doesn't leave us. We learn how to cooperate, collaborate, compromise and even capitulate, but we secretly keep wishing it were otherwise.

Some of us refuse to learn these lessons, and find ways to disguise our unhealthy attachment to an unrestrained desire for control. At its most dangerous, the desire for control creates an all-consuming ambition to perpetuate the centre-of-the-universe illusion of childhood. I once worked on a committee with a man who made no secret of his ambition to become its chairman – not because he thought he would do a better job than the incumbent, but simply because, as he once remarked, 'It's no fun being anything but chairman.' Over the years, I watched him accumulate chairmanships of one organisation after another. His desire for control appeared both desperate and boundless. Eventually, as he achieved more and more of the appointments he coveted, and abandoned the quest for the few that were denied him, he appeared to relax into the role of *eminence gris* and I then wondered whether the motivation for such obsessive behaviour was as much about the desire to be taken seriously as about the desire for control. (We need to keep saying it: there's rarely a single, or simple, explanation for human behaviour.)

Some politicians enter politics for a similar combination of reasons – not because they are passionate about the idea of conscientiously representing their constituents, but because they perceive politics as a 'power profession' and they want to taste that power. Of course many politicians enter politics for noble reasons and devote themselves to a lifetime of selfless public service with the quite unambiguous aim of making the world a better place. I have personally known several politicians who are just like that, but it tends to be the power-seekers who grab the limelight.

For most of us, 'control' has rather more modest connotations. We want to get the household budget, the garden shed, the CD collection or sock drawer under control. Sometimes, we wistfully dream of 'getting my *life* under control' but most of us wisely abandon that grandiose goal in favour of attempting to win small victories over some more immediate sources of chaos, irritation or disappointment.

You can't control the traffic when you're running late for an appointment, but you can control your own reaction to it. Yet very few of us, when we complain of a loss of control, are thinking of our ability to control ourselves. More commonly, we fantasise about controlling external events, controlling our environment, controlling our workload, controlling our children, controlling troublemakers in society.

One of the most dramatic moments I've ever witnessed in a research project occurred when a woman participating in a group discussion about the impact of change on women's lives suddenly jumped out of her chair and exclaimed: 'I feel as if I'm on a runaway train!' She rushed from the room with her hands over her face and was quickly consoled by one of her friends in the group. When she returned to the discussion a few minutes later, it emerged that she and her husband were in the throes of a separation, their house was on the market and their unmarried daughter was unexpectedly pregnant.

As the conversation proceeded, it became clear that her reference to the 'runaway train' had struck a responsive chord in the group. The malaise reported by these women was far less specific than hers: it was a more general sense that life itself was speeding out of control; that everything was changing too quickly; that the old rules and conventions were being swept away; that new technology was frightening in its potential impact on our lives, and especially on the lives of our children; that society itself seemed to be undergoing changes for the worse: poorer manners, rougher language, more crime and violence, declining morality, people not acknowledging each other as they once did, more stress . . . always more stress.

A closely associated complaint was that the institutions we used to respect – the church, in particular – were no longer worthy of that respect. Declining esteem for politicians, the media, big business, trade unions and even sport (now seen to have been irredeemably tarnished by its commercialisation) added to the general air of woe.

In ninety minutes of conversation, those women had managed to capture the essence of one of the most widely held beliefs in

Western society: the belief that the rate of change has not only destabilised us, as predicted by Alvin Toffler more than forty years ago in *Future Shock*,[1] but that it also involves a 'dumbing down' – a deterioration of previously recognised standards of decency and civilised behaviour which, in its own way, feels like a loss of control.

Rather than accepting such beliefs at face value, we need to explore where they have come from, and whether they might be justified. But first, let's ask ourselves this: how much control might an individual realistically expect to have over the processes of social change, economic upheaval and technological revolution – let alone the natural world? Life is not like a train or a plane, where someone is in charge and the destination is clearly defined. We live in a world where volcanoes erupt, both literally and metaphorically; a world of tsunamis, cyclones, floods and droughts; a world where, patently, no one is in charge or, if they are, they are massively incompetent, and have no regard for the scale of human suffering and havoc created by such disasters.

And that's just the natural phenomena. Wherever humans gather, chaos and unpredictability are never far away. Relationships are risky. We talk as if humans are rational creatures, but the evidence is overwhelmingly to the contrary. We often act from the heart rather than from the head; we are impulsive, emotional, reckless. Our ambition gets in the way of our good sense; our competitive urges sometimes swamp our compassion; our prejudices blind us to truth. We are driven by primitive instincts and passions that seem at odds with our sophisticated way of life and our towering accomplishments – from space travel to genome mapping, organ transplants and all the other advances in modern medical science, to say nothing of the miracles of modern communications technology.

We know far more than humans have ever known, but we still kill and maim each other by the million – in wars, road accidents, murders and other varieties of mayhem.

Control? On the evidence, you'd have to say an individual's span of control could only ever be narrow. But in contemporary Western society, our increasing preoccupation with the idea of control may be a natural consequence of the remarkable changes in our way of life. The greater the rate of change, and the greater the scope of the changes, the more likely we are to feel that things are 'out of control' and therefore, as a form of compensation, to become obsessed with the idea of control.

ANXIETY: A NATURAL RESPONSE TO A LOSS OF CONTROL

The various phobias referred to at the beginning of the chapter are extreme versions of the vague sense of stress and anxiety most of us experience when we are plunged into unfamiliar circumstances – whether it's entering a room full of strangers, making an offer on a house for the first time, learning how to conduct online banking transactions, mastering a new mobile phone, turning up for work on the first day of a new job, or finding ourselves just a few days out from our wedding.

But what happens when whole societies are plunged into unfamiliar circumstances, and their citizens feel as if the pace of social, cultural, technological and economic change has become too swift? The answer is there for all to see: most Western societies are suffering epidemics of anxiety and depression, and an increased risk of cardiovascular disease associated with 'perceived stress and lack of situational control'.[2]

And why not? Everywhere we look, change is in the air and much of it is happening too quickly for comfort or on too grand a scale to be easily absorbed.

Take the Australian case. In the past thirty-five years, Australians have reinvented the institution of marriage (and abandoned it in droves), transformed the nature of family life (almost twenty-five percent of Australian families with dependent children are now single-parent families), sent the birthrate tumbling to an all-time low, shrunk our households, felt the tremors of a restructured economy, widened the gulf between wealth and poverty, and rewritten our labour market statistics (especially those involving female participation and part-time work). We have redefined the very meaning of 'Australian' in the context of new regional alliances, and the emergence of a truly multicultural society with greater ethnic diversity than any society in human history. Like every other Western society, Australia has also been swept up in the information and communication technology revolution that has transformed the way we live and work and redefined notions of privacy and identity, especially among the young.

Many Western societies can tell even more dramatic stories. In the same thirty-five year period, Spain has transformed itself from a military dictatorship to a constitutional monarchy, broken the stranglehold of Roman Catholicism on its politics and culture, experienced a dramatic rise in its standard of living and absorbed more than five million immigrants into a total population of only sixty million, while watching its birthrate, at 1.1 babies per woman, fall to the lowest level in Europe (though Greece, Germany and Italy are not far behind).

Ireland is emerging from centuries of domination by the Roman Catholic church, and sectarian violence has finally receded. Ireland has revolutionised its education system, been transformed from the economic 'basket case' of Europe to one of its tiger economies – now slumping again in the wake of the global financial crisis – and found itself, after being an exporter of its people for centuries, playing host to thousands of immigrants, mainly from Eastern Europe.

Canada has experienced many of the same upheavals as Australia. Its birthrate is not quite as low as in Western Europe, but at 1.6 babies per woman, it has fallen way below replacement level. Like so many other Western countries, Canada is now relying on immigration to maintain population growth, and that involves all the usual challenges of cultural and economic integration, with the added ingredient of a strong Muslim presence among current immigrants helping to make Islam Canada's fastest-growing religion.

While New Zealand has been dealing with the cultural, economic and technological upheavals typical of Western societies during this time of revolutionary change, it has also overhauled its voting system, with far-reaching implications for political party structures and alliances, and entered into new arrangements for a deepened 'mutuality of respect' between Maori and Pakeha (European settlement) people based on greater recognition of the spirit, as well as the letter, of the Treaty of Waitangi. New Zealand, like many other countries, is also facing the challenge of more ethnically diverse immigration. According to New Zealand historian Michael King, the anti-Asian prejudice of a hundred years ago is showing signs of re-emerging, following a surge in numbers of immigrants from China, Hong Kong, Taiwan and Korea and the prospect of the Asian proportion of the New Zealand population reaching thirteen percent by 2021.[3]

Reeling from the effects of its 2009 recession, the UK is still wondering how some of its most trusted financial institutions could have gone to the brink of extinction, how jewels of the British car industry such as Rolls Royce, Land Rover and Jaguar could now be in the hands of the Germans and Indians, or how the term 'British manufacturing' could already seem archaic. Culturally, Britain has experienced such a sustained influx of immigrants from the Indian sub-continent, the Caribbean and Africa over the past thirty years that white-skinned Anglo-Saxons may well be a minority of the British population by the end of this century.

According to the US's Pew Research Centre, almost twenty-five percent of the world's population is now Muslim, and the growing influence of Islam in European culture is reflected in the numbers: in the past thirty years, the UK's Muslim population has grown from eighty thousand to about two million; between five and ten percent of the populations of France and Germany are now Muslim, with a steady rise anticipated; some projections suggest that one-third of all European newborns will be Muslim by 2025. None of this matters, unless you're a European Christian who wants to resist both the resurgence of Islam and the tug of history: in Switzerland, the 2009 plebiscite that banned the building of minarets on Muslim mosques was a symptom of just such unease. Yet it is easy to forget that while many English churches are now being turned into mosques, many Catholic churches in Spain still show signs of their Islamic origins, or the Islamic phases of their architectural evolution. Even the Parthenon in Greece was, for part of its history, a mosque.

Challenging times for many Western societies, to say nothing of the challenges of fast-paced change now enveloping economies like China, India and Brazil. Perhaps we shouldn't be surprised that some people feel as if they're trapped on a runaway train, or that 'stress' is the most common complaint about life in contemporary Western society.

NARROWING THE FOCUS OF CONTROL

Faced with all this rapid and unpredictable change – whether resulting from technology, threats to the global financial system, the mass movement of people across national borders, or the changing character of our economies (for example, the massive shift of manufacturing out of Western countries and into the developing economies of Asia) – a popular response has been to narrow the focus of our desire for control. We turn away from a big picture that looks too dark and daunting and devote ourselves to the minutiae of our personal and domestic lives.

Rather than engaging with such huge problems as the plight of refugees and asylum-seekers, or the health and welfare of indigenous populations, or trade imbalances and tariffs – to say nothing of terrorism or climate change – we turn the focus inwards. We distract ourselves from the world's bad news by concentrating on the size and shape of our bodies, the whiteness and straightness of our teeth, the removal of wrinkles that previous generations regarded as 'war wounds' to be worn with pride. We embrace Botox, cosmetic surgery, tattoos and body-piercing in a big way, as if to say, 'The big picture is beyond me, but I can create my own little picture right here on my own body.' We throw ourselves into home renovations, cooking and gardening – on TV as well as in reality: 'Here's a way to take control of my own little world. I don't know what to do about America's national debt or China's level of carbon emissions, but at least I can choose the perfect tile to top off our bathroom renovations.' Using self-indulgence as a form of insulation from our anxieties, we increase our levels of debt to finance our materialist binge.

We hunt for schools that will 'control' our children and, in some countries, become increasingly willing to pay big fees to send them there.

Our social attitudes harden. We welcome legislation that we hope might get 'things' (i.e. other people's behaviour) back under control. We urge judges to be tougher on criminals, and governments to introduce more mandatory sentencing. We entertain the idea of harsher censorship of the media. We become less compassionate, less tolerant, more prejudiced.

Some of us resort to a dogmatic, hardline fundamentalism, whether in religion, economics, environmentalism or, indeed, medicine and psychology. We welcome the sense of control that certainty brings – the comfort of black-and-white simplicity – no matter how delusional it might be.

Whether it happens to show up as gung-ho materialism, social conservatism or religious fundamentalism, the underlying motivation is the same: it's all about control.

INTERPRETATION AS A FORM OF CONTROL

Who doesn't want to feel empowered by cracking the code? Who wouldn't love to get their minds around a Theory of

Everything? Who doesn't try to make sense of things as a way of controlling them?

We are born interpreters. Making our own sense of whatever is happening is how we put ourselves in the picture. It's how we relieve ourselves of that awful sense of uncertainty, that ambiguity, that lack of clarity that so unnerves us. We mine our experience to come up with 'meanings' to explain what's going on.

In 1926, Virginia Woolf wrote an essay called 'The Cinema' in which she described the experience of watching a film called *The Cabinet of Dr Caligari*. She observed a dark shadow that appeared 'like a tadpole' in one corner of the screen and then 'swelled to an immense size, quivered, bulged, and sank back again into nonentity'. Woolf's interpretation of that bulbous shape was that it was a representation of fear itself, and she was impressed that film could make emotions visible in such a graphic way. In fact, the shape was not part of the film at all: it was the result of a malfunctioning projector.[4] But once you've attached meaning to a shape, a word, a movie or an event, that becomes its meaning for you; that's how you have, conceptually speaking, taken control of it.

I once offended someone by dismissing the film *Four Weddings and a Funeral* as an entertaining romantic comedy, but hardly meaning-of-life material. He begged to differ: for him there was indeed a meaning-of-life moment in the film. He described it to me, and I couldn't even recall it. He'd made his own sense of the movie; I'd made mine. When it comes to movies or TV programs – or novels or poems or plays – the audience has the upper hand: we are the ones in control because our own needs, our own predispositions, our own attitudes are like templates of meaning we lay over the material we're watching or reading.

A colleague once attended a psychology conference at which, he assured me, one of Mahler's symphonies had been 'explained' in psychoanalytic terms. Uh-huh, I thought; I wonder what Mahler himself would have made of that so-called explanation. I was reminded of another colleague who once won a competition run by a poetry magazine. The meaning of her poem was analysed by the judges who complimented her on her subtle use of the image of the phoenix rising from the ashes. 'What's a phoenix?' she asked me, mystified.

Ah, the cognoscenti might respond, she was unconsciously drawing on the legend of the phoenix, even though she'd never heard of it: the image might even be buried in our 'collective unconscious'. Maybe; maybe not. What's significant is how we relish the sense of control we obtain from feeling that we have interpreted something – understood it – in our own way, whether or not the person whose behaviour we are interpreting would agree.

We do it all the time. We 'know' what's upsetting someone who is behaving badly: we attribute it to his parents' appalling example, his unhappy love life, his uncontrollable hormones, his lack (or his excess) of religious faith. There's power in the knowledge (or, more likely, the belief) that reveals hidden meanings to us. We love secrets, gossip, the inside story.

As long as we can keep the upper hand by making judgements about other people's 'bad behaviour', we feel in control: to admit the presence of those same shortcomings in ourselves would be to concede too much. Humility is about shedding the desire for control; pride and prejudice allow us to cling to a warped sense of our own mastery.

DIALLING UP OUR DESIRE FOR CONTROL: THE MAD PURSUIT OF PERFECTION

Our obsession with control makes us vulnerable to the blandishments of those twin seducers, 'excellence' and 'happiness' – magic code words (like the word 'control' itself) favoured by the swelling ranks of perfectionists.

In response to a growing sense of chaos and uncertainty, many of us are drawn to the idea that it doesn't have to be like this; that there is a 'better way' and that if only we could lift our game – in our relationships, our parenting, our work, our level of fitness, our 'lifestyle' – we could be floating on a cloud of excellence, high above the hoi polloi, sharing the rarefied upper air with the fabled bluebird of happiness. What we're forgetting is that if we let the inherently imperfect state of the world induce stress in us, then the pursuit of perfection will only increase it.

What parents, in the current climate, would send their child to a school that wasn't a centre of excellence for something? What organisation – from an international mining company to your local gym – would not claim to pursue excellence? 'Excellence in aged care' I recently saw on the side of a bus, and I idly wondered if anyone would dare admit they were simply doing their best.

How many marriages, how many romances, have foundered because one partner was seduced by the mad cult of perfectionism into believing that relationships should be without blemish, flaw or disappointment?

Perfectionism both feeds and feeds off the culture of control. There's no one as cranky as a fitness fanatic with a cold: 'If I'm perfectly fit and healthy, why do I still get sick?' We fantasise about a perfection that's just beyond our reach: 'If I could just control my wife's spending, we'd have the perfect marriage.' 'Why can't we find the perfect teacher at the perfect school', or the perfect holiday, the perfect latte, the perfect job (the perfect nose-job)? Inspired by the notion of 'the perfect storm', some finance journalists even referred to the 2008–09 global financial crisis as its economic equivalent, as if the perfection of the disaster might be some kind of consolation.

Those involved in the so-called helping professions, along with the authors of many of the self-help tomes lining our bookshelves, are at risk of encouraging this utopian madness. 'I wish I could get my life under control' might be a popular cry, but it's a symptom of a misunderstanding of what life is about. How easily we forget that life is for living, not for controlling – except in trivial ways, like that sock drawer, or those car keys . . .

Human relationships are inherently messy because they are driven more by emotional than rational factors – and thank goodness for that. Because relationships are unpredictable and ultimately impossible to control, so are families, communities and organisations. Control, like perfection, is simply the wrong goal.

◆

Why did we ever think a period of sustained social and cultural dislocation and economic upheaval would not take its toll? Have we exacerbated the problem by putting too much emphasis on 'positive outcomes' like excellence and happiness, and not enough on the process of living courageously, kindly, even nobly?

Thinking positively is all very well – better than thinking negatively, no doubt. But thinking realistically has even more to commend it: to be realistic is to acknowledge that the richness of life lies in its contrasts, its light and shade, and in our capacity to experience and deal with the full spectrum of human emotions and responses.

Like the relentless quest for excellence, the pursuit of happiness seems to have been hijacked by the prophets of perfection. The word 'happiness' has come to us via a much-diminished translation of the Greek word *eudaimonia*. The early usage of that word itself passed through several transitions from its original connotation of being blessed by divine powers, with implications of prosperity. Over time, the Greeks broadened their interpretation of *eudaimonia* to embrace the idea of living virtuously, fulfilling one's need for a sense of purpose, doing one's civic duty, living in accordance with reason, being fully engaged with the world and, in particular, experiencing the richness of human love and friendship – in other words, something that comes closer to our current use of the word 'wholeness' than to 'happiness'.

Today, we talk about happiness as if it consists of little more than sensory pleasure, or a burst of bliss, or the mere absence of pain or sadness. In fact, if we were to enlarge the concept to come closer to its original meaning – incorporating ideas such as wellbeing, fulfillment, contentment or wholeness – even some forms of pain, sacrifice and disappointment could, paradoxically, squeeze in under its umbrella. Aren't those things, after all, part of a complete, rich, fulfilling life? Isn't there a kind of sweetness about some of the many varieties of sadness?

If this is what we mean when we urge each other to 'be happy', I'm all for it. But I fear that happiness has taken on a rather narrower, more vacuous and vapid meaning that has confused it with the desire for control. Happiness means you're 'in control' and that's to be contrasted with sadness, which presumably means you're not in control – as if you can choose to be either happy or sad. Sadness is getting a bad press at the hands of the merchants of happiness: in fact, you can't have one without the other and the absence of the contrast would lead to an emotionally monochromatic existence. 'Be happy' implies that you must not be sad, but how else could you know happiness? 'Be whole' might be a better injunction.

When I hear parents say they only want their children to be happy, I'm tempted to ask: 'What, exactly, do you mean by "happy"?' If, as I suspect, they are thinking of the modern (absence-of-sadness) kind of happiness, rather than the ancient kind (living virtuous and fully engaged lives), I'd then want to ask: 'Is that *all* you want for them? Do you really want them to be as emotionally deprived as that? Don't you want them to learn how to cope with disappointment, failure and even unfairness? Don't you want them to be *whole?*'

In the next breath, those same parents will assert that 'we grow through pain'. Yet they'll go to extreme lengths to minimise their children's risk of pain, let alone pain itself. And when sadness comes to them or their children, in the form of loss or disappointment, they'll be more intent on taking control (perhaps by swallowing a pill) and 'moving on' than on growing through it, blithely unaware of Proust's wisdom on the subject – 'We are healed of a suffering only by experiencing it to the full'[5] – or of F. Scott Fitzgerald's: 'The redeeming things are not "happiness and pleasure" but the deeper satisfactions that come out of struggle.'[6]

Don't we owe it to our children – and to each other – to avoid making false promises about what life has to offer? Shouldn't we be more open about what's involved in a healthy, balanced existence?

Illness is a dramatic example of the kind of struggle that shapes us, without our having a skerrick of control over where and when it might strike. No one wishes illness on themselves – well, some textbook hypochondriacs might, or those looking for an escape from difficult circumstances via the passive surrender to illness. Yet when serious illness happens, most people who recover regard it as having been a chastening, life-changing experience that was more blessing than curse. Charles Darwin, prodigiously productive, wrote that 'ill-health, though it has annihilated several years of my life, has saved me from the distractions of society and amusement'.

> *I wouldn't wish a stroke on anyone, but it certainly caused me to rethink my priorities. I was one of the lucky ones – now I'm getting on with all the things I always said I wanted to do.*

> *Cancer was a helluva way to discover what's really important in life – and it isn't about making more money. That experience taught me that our families and friends are all we've got.*

Failure is another reliable sign that life is *not* under control. We know failure is a more effective teacher than success when it comes to learning what it means to be human, so why don't we value it more highly when it happens? Why do we interpret failure as a sign of inadequacy when it's such a crucial part of the process of maturation, right through life? Winners might be grinners, but losers are learners.

Optimism is a great trait to possess, but only if it can be kept in its place when the circumstances call for a different perspective, a different expectation. (Ask a dying person how they feel about visitors trying to sound up-beat.) In many ways, unbridled optimism is as unrealistic – and as prejudicial to a balanced assessment of our situation – as unbridled pessimism. But we continue to dwell on the positive as though 'a positive outcome' will be the sign that we have life under control.

The one thing we can guarantee is that the quest for perfection sows its own seeds of disappointment. Perfection is not available; excellence is, by definition, exceptional; happiness is, of its essence, fleeting.

THE ILLUSION OF CONTROL: EXCESSIVE SURVEILLANCE AND REGULATION

CCTV cameras are everywhere in our cities; draconian anti-terror legislation has been enacted in many countries; state-sponsored torture and child abuse has occurred in countries where people have previously prided themselves on resisting such things (the USA's Guantanamo Bay prison in Cuba, Australia's refugee deten-tion centres). Many countries, renowned as liberal democracies, have sacrificed some of their civil liberties in favour of massive security crackdowns. Such things might once have scandalised us, but our yearning to 'get things under control' makes us remarkably acquiescent in the face of galloping over-regulation.

The question is: do increased regulation and surveillance give us a greater sense of control? Does installing more security systems in our homes – bars on windows, motion-sensitive lights, electrically operated gates, flashing alarms – increase our sense of domestic peace and contentment? Quite the opposite. Such devices merely strengthen our conviction that there is a problem to be dealt with: the more we try to protect ourselves, the more conscious we are of the need for protection and the more our fears and insecurities are likely to increase.

The more we retreat from public transport, parks and other public spaces, or try to 'control' them with security devices, the less safe they will become. The safest public place is a well-populated area. We need more street life – not more CCTV cameras – to regain control of such places. In many Western societies, the fear of violent crime exceeds its incidence: perhaps an unrealistic and unhealthy obsession with control is driving our fear.

In the corporate world, does more legislation and regulation guarantee the elimination of bad corporate behaviour – slack lending practices by financial institutions, for instance, or misleading annual reporting, exploitative pricing, excessive salaries and bonuses, manipulative marketing or deceptive advertising? Of course some regulation is necessary, but corporate behaviour is human behaviour, and we know that human behaviour is not easily controlled through regulation. Give kids too many rules and they become loophole specialists, and it's precisely the same with tax lawyers. Excessive corporate regulation simply spawns new ways to hide the truth.

An increasingly enthusiastic attitude towards regulatory control is a direct reaction to our uneasiness about the erosion of values we imagine were once commonly accepted. If you feel you can't trust other people to live by the same set of values as your own, or if you believe there is generally less self-control in society than there was, it's a natural reaction to want to impose more external controls through more rules and regulations. We have even evolved the concept of 'educative laws' designed to make us act in ways that simulate moral sensitivity – Australia's racial vilification laws, for instance, or Canada's laws relating to so-called hate crimes, or the widespread laws now relating to sexual discrimination, all the way down to local council regulations about dog walking (plastic bags having become politically incorrect for every purpose except this one).

The motive of those who support such legislative programs is clear: let's force people, through legislation and regulation, to act *as if* they are responsible citizens with a well-developed sense of social and moral responsibility and then, in the process, they might learn to become that kind of person.

Heightened anxiety and a loss of control – whether real or imagined – drive voters all over the world to support governments' initiatives in the direction of increased regulation and surveillance. We think those things will make us feel more secure – more 'in control' – and so we encourage our legislators to go further, and further. One day, we may wonder where so many of our freedoms went.

There is a complicated relationship between external controls imposed on us and internal controls that flow from our own values and self-discipline. The more external controls are imposed on us, the less we feel the need for control from within, and that's the pathway to acquiescence and to social and political disengagement. Obedience is a very different thing from moral sensitivity.

DREAMING OF A MAGIC WAND

The desire for control is understandable and, when kept in proper perspective, it can be perfectly healthy and even productive. Control is the mother of efficiency, and the management of many aspects of our lives relies on maintaining some semblance of control: bills have to be paid on time, and appointments need to be kept, so a bit of administrative control is essential.

But the current obsession with control looks to me like a symptom of the soul's unease – a cry for help in learning how to cope with rapid change in our lives and in our societies. The most useful response to that cry, whenever we hear it, is not to say, 'Here's how to get your life under control,' but to explain that the deepest sense of wellbeing springs not from mastery of our circumstances – let alone mastery of others – but from mastery of ourselves and, most especially, of our emotions.

Some of us need guidance about how to manage our anger in the face of frustration, or to subdue our violence in the face of provocation, or to resolve our bitterness in the face of disappointment. What we don't need – and shouldn't expect – is a magic wand that will remove frustration, provocation or disappointment from our lives.

Our strong attachment to the 'magic wands' of the IT revolution – ranging from TV remote controls to iPhones and BlackBerrys – is symbolic of our deep desire to be in control of the world. These devices create the illusion of control because they so easily connect us to a vast web of information, entertainment and communication.

Such symbolism is harmless enough, unless it fuels a deeper, more reckless desire for control: if so much can be achieved with the pressure of a finger on a hand-held screen, or a voice command, why can't other things be so easily controlled? Why can't I control my kids, for instance, the way I can control the sat-nav system in my car? Why isn't dinner ready at the touch of a button?

To avoid falling into that kind of trap, we need to shift our focus from control to participation and engagement; from an unhealthy perfectionism to a more realistic acceptance of life's disorderliness, irrationalities, unpredictability and disenchantments, as well as its joys, gratifications and occasional small triumphs.

This is not to suggest for one moment that we should settle for lives of misery, frustration and disappointment, or that we shouldn't encourage our children to fulfill their potential (as long as we're realistic about what that means, and are not confusing it with our desire to control them, or to have them compensate us for our own unrealised potential). But it is to suggest that adapting to our circumstances – accepting that things are the way they are – is a good starting point for working out how best to respond to them.

An unrealistic dream of control has contributed to the distress of many people by promoting a utopian view of relationships, achievements, outcomes, and even possessions. Might it not be time to lower our expectations of how we should feel, what we can have, and what we can control?

CAN WE EVEN CONTROL THE CLIMATE?

The climate change debate – is global warming carbon-induced or not; brought on by human activity or not; reversible or not – has offered us the tantalising prospect of a measure of control we've never previously dreamed of: 'Control the climate? Wow! How can we do that?'

How, indeed? Nations' statements of intention to reduce carbon emissions may or may not be translated into reality: we will have to wait and see if the reversing of what looks like an irreversible – and possibly cyclical – process actually occurs. Whether or not that turns out to be possible, most of us agree that it would be sensible to concentrate on accelerating the development of clean and renewable energy, partly because the environmental effects seem self-evidently positive, and partly because that looks like the way to take control of our long-term energy needs.

In the meantime, while the experts thrash out their strategies, we can observe how the culture of control has been further fuelled by this issue. Mike Hulme, professor of climate change at the University of East Anglia, argues that climate change has moved from being a predominantly physical phenomenon to being a social and cultural one as well, 'reshaping the way we think about ourselves, our societies and humanity's place on Earth'.[7]

Hulme regards current talk about climate control as an echo of the ancient Greek myth of Prometheus, the god who stole fire from Zeus and gave it to the mortals. It reveals 'our desire for dominance and mastery over nature but also that we lack the wisdom and humility to exercise it'. Hulme interprets the climate change debate as a modern version of three other myths as well: the Garden of Eden myth that reveals our desire to return to a simpler, more innocent 'nature'; the Apocalypse myth that talks about climate change in the language of fear and disaster; the Themisian myth, named after the Greek goddess of law and order, that puts climate change in the context of a debate about justice and equity.

His point is that climate change has now become a psychological construct as well as a topic of scientific debate, and that we have drawn on the themes of mythology to articulate our fears and our dreams of control.

When it comes to converting those dreams into practical measures for taking control of the climate, the strategies being proposed by governments for tackling climate change (such as emissions trading schemes) seem remote or confusing to most lay people, and certainly beyond the control of individuals. Fearing that climate change is a reality – and quite possibly a cataclysmic reality – individual citizens are asking how we ourselves might be recruited into the war on warming. Should we be driving our cars less? Turning off more lights in our houses, saving our air-conditioners for truly extreme heat and cranking our heaters down a notch or two? Insulating our homes more effectively? Paying more attention to the clothing we wear and relying less on artificially controlled environments to keep us warm or cool? Should we be deliberately trying to cut down on all non-essential travel, especially by air – in spite of the marketing initiatives of the airlines urging us to do the opposite?

That all sounds sensible but, as usual, most of us tend to wait for instructions – or regulations – before we put such ideas into practice. Perhaps our leaders have not yet understood that we are more likely to support big-picture strategies if we are also encouraged to implement miniature strategies of our own. If there's no call for individual, personal action, individuals tend to lose interest.

THE DARK SIDE 1: THE ABUSE OF POWER

One of the most frightening experiments in the history of psychology was carried out by Stanley Milgram at Yale University between 1960 and 1963. It was such an illuminating study that Milgram was awarded the Socio-Psychological Prize of the American Association for the Advancement of Science in 1964.

In essence, the experiment went like this. Pairs of volunteers were introduced to each other and briefed on an experiment in learning and memory in which one of them was to be the 'learner' and the other the 'teacher'. An 'experimenter' was also present – a rather stern-looking, aloof character who was in charge of proceedings.

The three people go into a room where there is an apparatus that looks a bit like an electric chair, with wires connected to it. The 'learner' is strapped into the chair, with the 'teacher' watching, and an electrode is attached to his wrist. Paste is applied by the experimenter, to avoid 'blisters and burns'. The experimenter explains that the electrode is connected to a shock generator unit in the next room.

The experimenter then takes the 'teacher' into the adjacent room where there is indeed an electric shock generator. (Put yourself in this position: seeing what was involved, would you now be prepared to go ahead with the experiment or would you decide to pull out, before it even starts?)

The shock generator has an array of thirty switches, labelled with voltages ranging from 14 to 450 volts. The voltage figures are accompanied by descriptive words, ranging from 'slight shock' up to 'extreme intensity shock'. The highest two voltage switches are simply marked 'xxx'.

Here's a brief description of what typically happened, from the 'teacher's' point of view:

You are told to administer a shock to the learner every time he gives a wrong answer on the learning task, and you are instructed to 'move one level higher on the shock generator each time the learner flashes a wrong answer'. You are also told that although the shocks can be extremely painful, they cause no permanent tissue damage . . . The learner makes a number of errors and is given progressively more intense shocks. After receiving shocks of 75, 90 and 105 volts, he merely grunts. At 120 volts he shouts to the experimenter [through the wall between the two rooms] that the shocks are becoming painful. At 150 volts, he shouts, 'Experimenter, get me out of here! I won't be in the experiment any more! I refuse to go on!' At 180 volts, he yells, 'I can't stand the pain', and by 270 volts his response becomes an agonised scream. Thereafter there are shrieks of agony, and vehement refusals to go on with the experiment or provide answers to the learning task. When the 300-volt shock is reached, he pounds on the wall. If you, the 'teacher', say at any point that you don't want to continue the experiment, the experimenter tells you that you must.[8]

And here's the result: sixty-two percent of the people acting as 'teachers' continued to obey the experimenter, all the way up to the 450-volt level.

Before your stomach churns too much, you need to be reassured of one thing (though it hardly affects the scariness of the findings): the experiment did not involve the use of actual electric shocks; the 'learner' was an accomplice who was not being harmed at all, and was simply acting in a pre-arranged way – shouting, screaming, thumping on the wall, etc.

Needless to say, the impact of that experiment was profound: no one liked the findings, and there was something of a hue and cry over the ethics of an experiment that relied on deception. But sixty-two percent compliance? What should we make of that?

There are many ways of interpreting those findings, especially as they fly in the face of common sense: who in their right mind would go on hurting someone for the sake of an experiment, even if the experimenter seemed like a tough cookie? Milgram himself was focused on the question of obedience to authority, and was inclined to interpret these findings as saying something very nasty about the human tendency to obey orders, even when the orders are clearly appalling. (It didn't require much imagination to see how this research could help explain the behaviour of many Nazis who defended their war crimes on the grounds that they were only obeying orders.)

But perhaps there's another contributing factor here. Might Milgram's work also shed some light on the desire for control? Might such blind obedience to the experimenter (or to a superior officer) be only partly about acquiescence, and partly about our response to the apparently hard-to-resist offer of absolute control over another person?

It's a disturbing thought, but one that is rather confirmed by our observations of everyday life: put some of us in a position of authority and we seem to relish it too much; to become arrogant or even 'drunk with power'; to enjoy the sense of control over others in a way that goes beyond mere obedience to our superiors. Some of us react like that to being put in a uniform; some to being promoted in the workplace; some to the sense of power we appear to have, as parents, over our own children. Stories of abuse of children in orphanages, schools and hostels – or of prisoners in jail, or refugees in detention centres – suggest that being handed unfettered control over others can bring out the worst in us.

There's no doubt the desire for control has a dark side: perhaps this is what Lord Acton was referring to when he famously observed that 'all power tends to corrupt; absolute power corrupts absolutely'. Power corrupts precisely because it gives free rein to the dark and dangerous aspects of our desire for control. When bullies are allowed to win, their desire for control can become insatiable.

These worrying facts about us also relate to our desire to be taken seriously: If you take me *too* seriously, the normal restraints on my desire for control may be loosened.

THE DARK SIDE 2: REVENGE

A thirst for revenge is natural, normal, and difficult to ignore. But ignore it we must if we are ever to evolve into a more civilised species. Revenge represents the unleashing of one of our most primitive expressions of the desire for control: he hit me (= loss of control), so I must hit him back (= regaining of control). And because I am now in control, I will hit him harder than he hit me.

It happens in the playground. It happens in the boardroom. It happens in international relations, all the way to war. And religion has a case to answer here: the idea of a god who exerts control over the world by taking terrible revenge on the enemies of his people and inflicting dreadful damage on those who don't toe his prescribed line is deeply embedded in most religious cultures. If you grow up with that kind of material being presented to you as an example of what is just and right, it wouldn't be surprising if you incorporated it into your personal view of the world.

For Christians, it's even tougher than for Jews. Jews at least have one consistent storyline, but Christians must deal with the contrast between the vengeful God presented in the Old Testament and Christ's messages of loving-kindness and forgiveness presented in the New. Being human, most Christians find it a struggle to reconcile these competing claims of forgiveness and vengeance, partly because the urge for revenge is a natural part of the desire for control: to forgive is to relinquish all thoughts of control.

A Christian once told me that one of the reasons she needs to believe in an afterlife is that she wants the evildoers who got away with it in this life to be punished in the next. She wants to feel her God is in control of the universe, and revenge on such a grand scale would be a sign to her that this was so.

For all of us – those with religious faith and those with none – this struggle is between the dark and noble sides of our nature. Our noble selves recognise that forgiveness is a healing, therapeutic process that does indeed involve relinquishing control and abandoning the comfort-zone of self-righteousness. Our dark selves want to yield to the powerful tug of that old Law of Reciprocity – an eye for an eye – and to use revenge as an instrument of control over the person who has wronged us. ('An eye for an eye and a tooth for a tooth' is itself often misunderstood as a proposition. In context, it was intended to convey the idea that the punishment for a crime should be appropriate to the offence: an eye, and no more than an eye, for an eye; a tooth, and no more than a tooth, for a tooth.)

Justice and revenge are very different things – one civilised and measured; the other brutish and primitive. Most Western societies frown on those who take the law into their own hands; we frown also on those who regard the justice system as being primarily about revenge, rather than an institution committed to meting out humane punishment and, where possible, creating opportunities for restitution and rehabilitation.

Calls for revenge reduce us to the level of those who have wronged us. We can't criticise the way someone behaves and then behave in the same way without corrupting our own values. We can't claim to be civilised if, somewhere in our breast, we harbour the hope that wrongdoers will be cast into eternal flames. That's the desire for control gone mad.

Forgiveness is hard. Leaving punishment to the legal system is hard. But if we try to take matters into our own hands, we too become offenders.

THE ONLY LIFE YOU CAN CONTROL IS YOUR OWN

The desire for control is in all of us; it can easily get out of hand; it can become an obsession; it can bring out the worst in us – and yet it persists and must be understood.

It persists for the very good reason that, when properly channelled, it can help us order and direct our lives in ways that will increase our sense of satisfaction and fulfillment. The key to living with this desire is to recognise that the only life we can control is our own.

If you like tidiness, be tidy, but don't expect everyone else to be as tidy as you are. If you want a beautiful garden, create one, but don't expect all your neighbours to do likewise. If you choose to believe that there never was a moon landing, go ahead, but don't try to change *my* mind. If you think people should control the amount of time they spend in front of television or a computer, control the amount of time *you* spend in front of television or a computer. This desire only causes trouble when you try to extend your range to include the control of others.

What about children?

If you're a parent, it's tempting to think that control of your children is your responsibility, but control is simply the wrong word. Love them, advise them, nurture them, discipline them, train them by example, socialise them, support them, listen to them . . . and then let them become themselves. They are not your robots.

If you're a teacher, you might think you need to control the class but, again, 'control' is a word that can lead you into error. Yes, you need to impose some discipline on the children in your care, so they are able to function cooperatively and remain open to the possibility of learning. You need to discourage bullying, disruptive behaviour and intimidation. But you are an educator – your main job is to evoke responses from the children, not impose things on them. Make sure you're getting the balance right; make sure you're listening; make sure you're responding to them too, so the Law of Reciprocity can operate in a positive way. Take an iron-fisted approach and you'll lose them: silence in a classroom isn't a sign of control, but of mere obedience and quite possibly discomfort, or even fear – none of which is conducive to exploring ideas, thinking about problems or learning how to find answers to important questions.

If you're an employer, or a manager, you might be tempted to think 'control' is part of your responsibility. It never is. Management doesn't work that way unless you're attracted to the idea of blind obedience – as in the Milgram experiments – where the result will be your employees' abdication of responsibility rather than their acceptance of it. Management is the art of bringing out the best in people so that they willingly contribute their knowledge and skill to the task at hand. That's never a matter of control, but of consultation, collaboration, cooperation and occasionally inspiration.

You can bully people into submission; you can cajole them into unwilling compliance; you can outmanoeuvre and undermine them. If you have the power, you can even force them to do what you want them to do. But all of that is likely to backfire over time. You'll breed resentment; you'll lose the respect of those you have unduly influenced; some of them might even burn with thoughts of sabotage or revenge.

Ultimately, the only thing we can control is our own behaviour. Our example can be luminous; our style can be engaging; our way of handling situations can be impressive. But, in the end, people (including our partners and children) are free to follow our example, or not.

It's one thing to recognise that we are unlikely to be able to control other people. The real breakthrough comes when we accept that we have no right to do so.

THE DESIRE FOR SOMETHING TO HAPPEN

At last! Something is happening to me!

An existential philosopher,
after being knocked down by a car in a Paris street

For most people in affluent Western democracies, life meanders along pleasantly enough, punctuated by occasional highlights, crises and tragedies. Most pleasures are minor rather than intense, and all are fleeting; most lives give quiet satisfaction, interspersed with moments of despair; most families and friends offer us a bittersweet mixture of affection and irritation, comfort and anxiety, joy and pain. There's a heroism in people's dogged persistence over the long haul; in their ability to pick themselves up from disappointment, failure or tragedy and start again; in their determination to be good parents, good neighbours, good citizens, responsible workers.

'You can't escape the tedium of life,' a teacher at my school was fond of saying.

But we know the treadmill is not for us: we are not lab rats. We need breaks, breakouts, breakaways. The desire for something to happen nags at us, a persistent voice in the back of the mind that's intent on rescuing us from intellectual and emotional atrophy: *Act! Move! Create! Change! Make yourself uncomfortable! Do something different!* It's good advice: this desire has surged powerfully through our brains from birth but is vulnerable to complacency and apathy as we age – and who wants to be driven by apathy?

◆

What's the statement that exasperates parents more than anything else they hear from their offspring? *I'm bored.* What's our most lethal judgement of a film, a play, a book, a lecture, a party or, indeed, a person? *Boring.* While it's tempting to respond that you can't possibly be bored by anything if your mind is still active, we recognise this as the ultimate put-down because we know that when we are not being stimulated, we don't feel fully alive. We need something to react to.

On Friday nights, we go into town and just drive around, waiting for something to happen.

I once attended a church service where the minister made an impassioned appeal to his congregation to play a more active part in the ritual of communion: 'If you don't respond with an audible "amen", the act is not complete,' he said.

'Rubbish!' called a woman from the back of the church, and a brief but heated exchange followed.

I've forgotten most of the church services I ever attended. They followed their inexorable pattern, the comforting predictability of the order of service seeming to be the main point of the exercise. But I'll never forget that moment when it felt as if *something happened* simply because it wasn't what normally happened.

Attending my first Anzac Day ceremony in our local park, I was struck by the number of people who said afterwards, 'You should have been here last year – the horse bolted.'

Action, events, things that provoke us; this is the stuff of life. We are defined by how we react to the unusual, the disruptive, the unexpected. It is our behaviour at such moments that reveals us, rather than our thoughts or our dreams or the resolutions we make about our future behaviour. All the smart talk about attitudes evaporates: this is a time to act, and actions *always* speak louder than words. 'My life is my message,' said M.K. Gandhi.

WE ARE WHAT WE DO

One of my professional mentors, Dr Peter Kenny, head of audience research at the Australian Broadcasting Commission (now Corporation) in the early 1960s, caused something of a flurry in the ranks of senior management when he produced a paper that deflated a lot of the nonsense then being talked about program policy. He had analysed the programs the ABC was actually running at the time, and insisted that 'our policy is what we do'.

Corporate types love forming committees to devise 'policy', or to construct 'mission statements' or 'codes of ethics', but Kenny's argument went to the heart of the matter: employees and customers – or audiences, in the case of the media – will draw their own conclusions from their direct experience of how the organisation actually treats them. Nothing clarifies a policy like being on the receiving end of it.

Politicians can pontificate all they like, but we finally vote them in or out of office on the basis of what they've done, not what they've said they would do. And they know it: 'The time for talking is over' may be a great political cliché, but it's always said with relish, as if to say, 'Here's the challenge I've been waiting for – the challenge to *do* something – preferably something that will render my opponents irrelevant and demonstrate my strength as a leader.' Margaret Thatcher, the UK prime minister who waged war against Argentina over the disputed control of the Falkland Islands, told a Scottish Conservative Party conference in 1982 that 'it is exciting to have a real crisis on your hands, when you have spent half your political life dealing with humdrum issues like the environment'.

George W. Bush and Tony Blair knew what she meant. Along with a handful of allies, they rushed into the 2003 invasion of Iraq, responding to a manufactured crisis they hoped would position them as strong and decisive leaders. (How ironic that each of their premierships was fatally wounded by the opprobrium surrounding that invasion and its aftermath.)

No political leader would wish an economic recession on their nation, but some leaders were buoyed by the global financial crisis of 2009 that gave them something tangible to respond to. When *something happens* that demands a response, the character of politics suddenly changes.

Most of us know, deep within ourselves, that we are mere bags of wind until we act. Actions are us in a way that our thoughts and fantasies, our Facebook messages, are not. Even the opinions we express are not us until they are tested by the need to act, when they are either confirmed or exposed as hypocrisy. 'What we do' trumps 'what we think' every time.

How often have you exaggerated your description of a minor event to make it sound more significant, or to add a touch of drama in the retelling? We like to make it sound as if something worth recounting has happened to us – even if something *almost* happened to us, it can give us a buzz: 'A woman in our office would have been on that plane that crashed if she'd gone on the Thursday instead of the Tuesday.' A sniffle attracts more attention if we call it the 'flu; a minor traffic delay needs to be an 'unbelievable traffic jam'; a rainstorm sounds better if it's torrential; and what parent with teenage kids wants to tell you they are just acting like normal teenagers? There has to be *drama*; something has to be *happening*.

Sitting in the dining car on a long-distance train in Australia, travelling through an arid wilderness, I observed how agitated my fellow passengers became when the train manager announced that we were about to 'cross' our sister train travelling in the opposite direction. People jumped out of their seats, cameras at the ready, as the other train raced past us.

When the fuss had died down, a man at my table remarked, 'Well, at least something happened.' Then we all went back to staring out the window at the desert, rather like hospital patients whose world shrinks to the routines of the institution and who start to engage with the minutiae of hospital life – the food, the nurses' roster, the ethnic origin of the doctor on the last shift.

In one of literature's nastier insults, Somerset Maugham said of Henry James: 'He did not live, he observed life from a window, and too often was inclined to content himself with no more than what his friends told him they saw when they looked out of a window. But what can you know of life unless you have lived it?'[1]

WILL ONLINE ACTIVITY SUFFICE?

Maugham's question crosses the minds of many parents who worry about the time their offspring spend in front of a computer screen. 'Why don't they go outside and kick a football, or ride their bikes?' Of course, playing computer games is a form of activity – quite different from, say, lying on a bed and gazing at the ceiling – and many young people are no more devoted to their computers, mobile phones and MP3 players than their parents were to television and transistor radios, and for precisely the same reason: ready access to a media world where *something is always happening*. But many parents believe engagement with the virtual world to be qualitatively different from – and perhaps to fall short of – engagement with what they call the 'real' world and their offspring may simply call 'offline'.

There's nothing inherently virtuous about kicking a ball or riding a bike or, indeed, reading a book, rather than watching TV or playing a computer game, logging on to a social network such as Facebook or sending and receiving Twitter messages. The question in parents' minds is whether some of these activities are healthier than others – intellectually, socially and emotionally as well as physically; whether some of the time spent glued to a screen might be better spent socialising face-to-face or engaged in physical exertion.

Their concern seems well founded. UCLA neuroscientist Gary Small has shown that face-to-face conversation provides greater stimulation of our 'neural circuitry' than more passive activities, even mentally stimulating ones such as reading or online interaction.[2]

Some parents are concerned about whether their children's heavy consumption of electronic data will turn them into media addicts or couch potatoes, but others have a more sophisticated worry: if children are only learning how to react to events on the screen, how will they cope when called on to act in real life? Will they transfer what they've learned from one setting to the other? And if they do, will they be as violent, or as vulgar, in real life as they often seem to be on the screen?

In fact, most children have no trouble distinguishing between real and virtual worlds, online and offline communication, and there's no evidence to support the view that even quite heavy exposure to media depictions of violence will automatically cause a child to become violent. Any child's situation will be too complex for such simplistic causal analysis.

But there's another concern: will the rapid-fire stimulation available in cyberspace make us impatient with slower, potentially less stimulating encounters like dinner-table conversation, classroom teaching, books or speeches? Will we demand that everything be entertaining? Perhaps the answer is already clear, and that's why parents and teachers are so worried: after all, former US President Ronald Reagan declared, as long ago as 1966, the year before he was elected Governor of California, that 'politics is show business'.

A related worry is that too much risk and danger has been written out of the script for today's children: 'If everything is so controlled and supervised, and everything must be "fun", how will kids ever learn to deal with challenges or take necessary risks?'

The point is illustrated in some gently ironic prose from P.G. Wodehouse:

> When some outstanding disaster happens to the ordinary man, it finds him prepared. Years of missing the eight-forty-five, taking the dog for a run on rainy nights, endeavouring to abate smoky chimneys, and coming down to breakfast and discovering they have burned the bacon again, have given his soul a protective hardness, so that by the time his wife's relations arrive for a long visit he is ready for them.[3]

UNCERTAINTY IS GOOD FOR US

From our earliest years, it's the changes, the surprises, the discrepancies and uncertainties that stimulate the leaps in our cognitive development and produce the most significant effects on our personality. We remember rare events – whether pleasant or unpleasant – for far longer than ordinary, routine events. We note exceptions. We focus on the unusual.

This helps to explain why, in adulthood, we can travel a familiar route from home to work and be unable to remember anything about the trip, unless something unusual occurs. It's also why nagging is ineffective as a persuasion strategy: endlessly repeated messages soon lose their sting because there's no uncertainty or element of surprise.

Jerome Kagan, a professor of psychology at Harvard, believes we have underrated the power of unfamiliarity in cognitive and social development, and that 'nodes of uncertainty' are even more influential than the libidinous factors described by Freud in shaping our personalities. Children, he says, are most powerfully influenced by the puzzles that confront them, demanding to be solved.[4]

Kagan's views are supported by new work being done in the field of neuroscience, where brain functions can be directly observed in ways that were previously impossible. Mark Johnson, director of the Centre for Brain and Cognitive Development at Birbeck College in the University of London and winner of the British Psychological Society President's Award in 2008, describes the new research like this:

> These methods . . . reveal that postnatal brain development is a dynamic, plastic process in which many emerging functions are shaped by the physical and social environment of the developing child. Indeed, the child helps to further her own subsequent brain development by actively seeking out novel and important types of information from her environment.[5]

We've all observed how babies constantly shift their gaze to new and unfamiliar objects and people. Young children quickly become bored by the familiar and seek new domains to conquer: like other young animals, such as puppies and monkeys, they are continually exposing their brains to new sources of information that will contribute to their own brain development.

While emotional security is an important source of comfort, identity and reassurance in a child's development, parents who worry about the need to create and maintain a stable environment for their children might be missing the point.

> *When I was growing up, I went to ten different schools in twelve years, because my father's work kept us on the move. So I was determined to give my own kids the stability I never had. But now I look at them and wonder if they might have benefited from a bit more upheaval in their lives. They're very, very comfortable, and is that a good thing? They seem a bit too conservative to me, even a bit complacent. I wonder if stability is a bit overrated.*

It's not just children, of course. Recent research suggests that the brain retains far more plasticity than previously believed and that stimulation is the key to maintaining cognitive function into old age.[6] For people wanting to keep dementia at bay, crosswords and other mind games have become a popular form of stimulation, but they are unlikely to be as effective as activities that demand social interaction, especially those that also involve some physical exertion. (The real value of games such as crosswords is in the learning. Once you've mastered the strategy for solving them, it's time to move on to some fresh challenge.)

We have long known that cardiovascular exercise strengthens the heart and the blood vessels that supply the brain and helps people who engage in those activities feel mentally sharper. But it's now clear that activities like walking and cycling have an additional advantage beyond the benefits of exercise: they expose us to new situations, to the possibility of unexpected events and unplanned conversations. Personal encounters – talking, interacting, engaging – are a crucial source of brain stimulation, which gives card games like bridge or board games like Scrabble an advantage over solitary Sudoku or crosswords.

To stay sharp, we need things to happen. We need unexpected events to crash into our lives and disturb our complacency; we need surprises; we even need emergencies if we are to be fully functioning, mature and balanced adults. Learning to deal with the hard stuff – illness, failure, bereavement, retrenchment, disappointment, disaster – teaches us far more about ourselves than we can ever learn from breezing through the easy stuff. Why else do people who suffer traumatic upheavals in their lives so often recount those events as if they were highlights?

In *Surviving Mumbai*, Victoria Midwinter Pitt's TV documentary about the 2008 terrorist attack in Mumbai, survivors who had endured the terror of being held as hostages or hunted by gunmen spoke of their lack of anger towards the terrorists. Some of them felt rather sorry for the gunmen, seeing them as naive pawns in a deadly game being masterminded by others. Their experience of terror, surrounded by violence and death, had allowed them to discover extraordinary depths of courage and compassion they might otherwise not have known lay within them.

THE PUSH–PULL OF CHANGE

Here's one of the great contradictions of human nature. On the one hand, we seem to crave stability, ritual, repetition and the comfort of the familiar and the predictable. We place a high value on constancy in our lives – especially the emotional constancy of knowing we are securely loved – and we strongly resist changes that come too quickly, or those that come all at once, or those that threaten our very way of life.

On the other hand, we seem to be constantly yearning for things to be different; for a change in our circumstances; for a break in the pattern of our normal routines. We *seek* change, and have done so from the very beginning of our lives.

Perhaps our problem is that we haven't fully understood the difference between the changes that stimulate and energise us and those that are more likely to debilitate or distress us. Emotional upheavals can be shattering:

> *I thought it was the end of the world when my wife left me. I could never imagine recovering from it, but eventually I did. We usually do, don't we? In the middle of all that, my neighbour's son was killed in a car accident at twenty-two – that helped me put things into perspective.*

But upheavals in our circumstances, or the upheavals that flow from intellectual challenges, can be a source of fresh energy and enthusiasm:

> *I was quite good at my job, but I just felt I needed a change. So I'm on secondment to another department for six months, just to see how it goes.*

> *I took the plunge – resigned from my job, took the kids out of school and we all took off in a caravan for a year. You don't want to die wondering.*

Midlife crisis? Of course. And why not? The urge to do something different is one of the most common experiences among people approaching middle-age in relatively prosperous, stable Western societies. When the trajectory of life seems predictable, our progress steady and our situation stable, that's the very time when feelings of restlessness emerge and we're likely to ask ourselves one of the oldest questions in the world: *Is this all there is?*

Having achieved what we thought we wanted, we want something else – perhaps something a bit wild and reckless, but certainly something capable of dragging us out of the rut we perceive ourselves to be in, even if life in the rut is comfortable.

The US psychiatrist Gordon Livingston describes the many patients he sees who are going through the 'traditional identity crises that have men of a certain age pursuing affairs and buying sports cars. Often they'll tell stories of inhibited adolescences, early marriages, unsatisfying work, and a longing for excitement . . . much of what they aspired to now seems like a burden. They are preoccupied with what they might have missed.'[7]

The midlife crisis is by no means confined to men. Many middle-aged women who have chosen to be full-time mothers return to the workforce precisely because they crave more stimulation, as well as more independence. Since the gender revolution has made it less likely that young women, including young mothers, will leave the workforce for more than a short time, the traditional midlife quest for distraction and relief will become as common among women as men.

Sometimes we merely dream of change, perhaps fuelling our fantasies by identifying with a movie character who is doing what we wish we were doing, or reading the kind of books that transport us into an exotic world or, at least, a different kind of existence from our own. Sometimes we travel. Sometimes we do something uncharacteristically dramatic, something that's clearly going to create chaos and upheaval in our lives, even if we don't want to admit that was our motivation.

> *I came home and said to my wife, 'I've resigned.' She said, 'You've what?' I said, 'I've resigned – I can't stand another day at that place.' She said, 'So how are we going to eat?' and I just shrugged: 'We'll think of something.' It seemed impulsive at the time, but it was the best thing I ever did – it forced us to rethink our lives and we needed to do that. Everything's worked out okay, after a few hiccups.*

The purchase of lottery tickets and participation in other small-outlay gambling, like poker machines, is sometimes driven by desperation – *My luck must change soon, and then I'll be out of this financial mess I'm in* – but it's sometimes driven by those same dreams of a breakout, a radical rearrangement, a twist of life's kaleidoscope. Such dreams lurk just below the calm surface of many comfortable middle-class lives.

The question is: why? Is it that we know, deep within us, that if we don't change we will wither and die, intellectually and emotionally, if not actually? Or is it that we crave change more than we care to admit; that we love surprises and challenges because they bring us to life and force a reaction from us?

Yet the very notion of upheaval is at war with our apparently sincere wish for stability and stasis. Just as the homeostatic mechanisms of the body automatically adjust for tilt or for temperature change (making us shiver to warm up or sweat to cool down), we imagine that we automatically seek that kind of emotional stability, too. Who wants to be shocked by an unwelcome turn of events? Who wants to be obliged to change their minds?

Perhaps this tension between our intellectual need for surprise and uncertainty and our emotional need for security and stability accounts for the restlessness of the human spirit documented by poets, philosophers, theologians and psychologists. It often feels as if we desire one thing *and* we desire its opposite.

Theologians speak of 'a divine discontent'. St Augustine wrote: 'Our heart is restless until it rests in you.' The Australian priest and writer Richard Stamp describes 'an urge to jostle and push at boundaries, a dissatisfaction with things as they are and a desire to shape and change things. In humans this shows itself in the reach for exploration, the need to invent a better mousetrap, the desire to improve things. Without this inbuilt discontent we would never have achieved anything . . .'[8]

Some will go for a theological, some for a psychological explanation of our restlessness. Some will be content to observe it without trying to explain it at all. What is inarguable is that the desire for something to happen is an integral part of our nature, and 'happen' usually means change. When we try to deny the desire for action, stimulation or provocation, we may find ourselves sinking into a torpor of contentment and complacency. A cocoon of security and order – spun from our routines, our rituals, our familiar trappings and our comfortable old prejudices – rarely brings much satisfaction, and may even produce a kind of self-loathing that reveals itself as cynicism. *Nothing ever happens to me* is rarely a boast.

Perhaps it's time to abandon the pretence that we resist change and don't welcome it when it comes. Of course we don't like tragedies casting their shadows across our well-planned lives; we don't like shocks that frighten us; we don't like to think our world is falling apart emotionally or financially. But the deeper truth seems to be that we need change in our lives because we thrive on it.

At last! Something is happening to me! Whether or not that was ever actually said by a philosopher lying bleeding in a Paris street, it is not as silly as it sounds.

WE NEED SOMETHING TO LOOK FORWARD TO

What gets you out of bed in the morning? For many of us, it's the prospect of the good things – the potential gratifications – the day holds. I'll meet a friend for lunch. I'll finish writing that report. I'll book my holiday. I'll ask the boss for a raise. I'll go to a movie after work. I'll get out into the garden.

In spite of all the injunctions to live in the present, not to 'wish your life away' nor focus too much on what lies in store, most of us are powerfully driven by a sense of anticipation. Indeed, you could argue that one of the identifying characteristics of humans is their capacity to take the future into account; to look forward to things; to maintain hope in the future.

My younger sister turns eighty next year and we're all [four sisters] going on a cruise. You need something to look forward to.

When the Austrian neurologist and psychiatrist Viktor Frankl tried to make sense of his experiences in a German concentration camp during World War II, one of his conclusions was that faith in the future – even the ability to look to the future – often explained the difference between prisoners likely to survive and those likely to perish.[9] Hope, vision, faith and an *interest* in the future seem to sustain us and drive us.

Even the prospect of getting chores done – getting unpleasant things off the agenda – can be a great motivator.

I get myself through an exam by thinking about what I'm going to do afterwards.

On a grander scale, this is the appeal of a paradise in the afterlife. When the African-American slaves consoled themselves by singing their 'spirituals', the recurring theme was that there was something to look forward to. This life might have been oppressive, unfair and barely tolerable, but another life lay 'over Jordan', in a home waiting for them beyond the grave: 'Swing low, sweet chariot, Comin' for to carry me home.'

Throughout history, many people of religious faith who have found themselves in far less appalling circumstances than slavery have consoled themselves in the same way: I can tolerate anything in this life, because of the promise of a blissful life to come, in which my virtue will be rewarded (and, perhaps less charitably, the bad guys won't get away with it any more). Even suicide bombers are presumably propelled in part by the desire to have something to look forward to – a heavenly paradise that will transcend any pleasures of this earthly life and make their sacrifice worthwhile.

Adherents to the various branches of Buddhism are committed to the idea of living in the moment, focusing on the here and now, emptying the mind of any distractions through meditation

– especially those distractions that pull us into the future. Meditation, whether Buddhist or any other kind, is a hard discipline precisely because it has to compete with our inherent desire to have something to look forward to. Yet most Buddhists believe in reincarnation and have that to look forward to: their attempts to focus exclusively on the here and now are certainly not driven by the idea that this is all there is.

Like all the desires that drive us, the desire for something to look forward to is felt most keenly when it is being frustrated, as it is for people who feel trapped in a job they don't like or a marriage whose loving core has crumbled. It's often around middle age that it occurs to us that this is not what we want to be doing with our lives, that the prospect of spending year after year working at a job we dislike or maintaining a hollow marriage amounts to the very opposite of something to look forward to.

Our most common strategy for dealing with such frustrations is to concentrate on the satisfactions we obtain from things outside the job or the marriage: we distract or console ourselves through weekend activities with friends; we take up hobbies; we throw ourselves into sport and recreation; we lose ourselves in escapist media fare; we entertain the prospect of romance or immerse ourselves in elaborate plans for the next holiday.

But sometimes even these things are not enough to compensate us for the frustrations of being in the wrong job, or the wrong marriage. Every job entails tedium, discipline and occasional bursts of frustration or disappointment, but when we can't think of anything we really enjoy about what we're doing, it is probably time to look elsewhere. Once that decision is made, the escape from an unrewarding situation can become the thing we look forward to.

I remember the moment. I was getting ready for work one Monday morning and I thought, why am I doing this? I don't want to be doing this. Some people actually enjoy their jobs – why don't I find a job I enjoy? I liked the people at work well enough, but I didn't like the work itself, and I wasn't proud of the industry I was in. There was never anything to look forward to – no real sense of satisfaction. So I decided to set myself a time limit – six months. I decided I would have to be gone from that job in six months. I suddenly found a new burst of energy. I had a purpose in life. Even that job became more bearable because it had become a stepping-stone to the next thing, whatever that turned out to be.

For most of us, the tug of the future is irresistible. When we know something is planned, something is promised, something is going to happen that lies just ahead of us, we are energised, motivated, even excited. Yes, we need to focus on the present (if only to cross the road safely), and we might as well extract everything we can from each experience that comes to us. But where would we be if we didn't yield to the desire to play with the future in our minds; to imagine ourselves in an anticipated situation; to experience the special thrill of waiting for a thrill to come?

Half the fun of a holiday is in the planning and the imagining. And what young person in the first flush of a romance hasn't enjoyed floating through the week on a cloud of anticipation about what the weekend has in store for them? Overly intense anticipation can be a problem, not only because it might distract us from the sensations and experiences available to us in the present, but also because it increases the risk of disappointment when the anticipated event occurs. But when the stakes are high enough, most of us are prepared to take that risk: we enjoy the sense of abandonment to anticipation and recognise that anticipated pleasure is part of the pleasure of the event itself. Indeed, to resist the desire for something to look forward to would be to dull our senses and take the edge off our joy in approaching pleasures – especially future encounters with those we love and whose company we enjoy.

> *When I was sixteen, if a girl said she'd go out with me, I couldn't think about much else. It was like being swept along on a wave – in those days, you were just tingling at the prospect of holding hands.*

Why do people buy lottery tickets in their millions? Because of the desire for something to look forward to. Why do they read their 'stars'? Because they are hoping for something to fuel their faith in the future – if not the prospect of a dark stranger or a windfall, then perhaps the resolution of some long-running conflict or the offer of a new job.

'I NEED SOME EXCITEMENT IN MY LIFE!'

For most of us, the desire for *something* to happen occasionally swells into the wish for something *exciting* to happen.

We benefit from experiences that set our pulses racing, give us an adrenalin rush or add colour to lives quagmired in busyness or measured by the beat of a relentless tedium. (Who can resist slowing down as we pass a traffic accident? *Hey, we might see some blood.*)

Small children love being chased; they love being 'found' in a game of hide-and-seek; they love being tickled; they love the rush of excitement as they are pushed ever higher on a soaring swing. Fairground rides take them to the next level of excitement, providing an early taste of the thrill that danger – even mock danger – generates.

As we grow older, life itself provides more than enough excitement for many of us, but some highly charged individuals never lose that childlike attachment to thrills: from extreme sports to reckless love affairs, fast cars, edgy gambling or adrenalin-fuelled deals, their appetite for excitement seems insatiable. For them, unlike the rest of us, the desire can't be satisfied on the emotional roller-coaster of family life, or in even the most vigorous tussles on the tennis court or golf course, in the occasional thrills of workplace gratification, or by a conventional touristy holiday: they need to 'go to the edge'. Some do that literally, by climbing high and dangerous mountains, skydiving, heli-skiing, or sailing boats in open water, as if only by deliberately putting themselves in the path of danger can they generate the kind of excitement that makes them feel fully alive. Others use drugs to take them on a trip to a less literal inner 'edge'. In both cases, the goal is to achieve an altered state of consciousness via a heightened sense of excitement.

Some people get their kicks on the couch, playing video games, or watching endless TV footage of a plane crash or news of a serial killer, a pack rape, a race riot, a terrorist attack or a political crisis. While complaining about the media's emphasis on scandals and disasters, they soak it all up with zest. 'What must it have been like to be on that plane, knowing you were going to die?' 'Imagine being that girl.' 'How could anyone do that to another human being?'

Even news of environmental degradation, climate change or an economic meltdown generates a tingle of excitement: How bad is this? What will happen next? Will we survive? Our appetite for bad news is partly driven by an understandable curiosity about the limits of human experience, including the limits of bad behaviour, but it's also a form of surrogate thrill-seeking.

So is sport, of course. Every kind of sport exists to add excitement to our lives; to generate an exhilarating sense of tension; to create an artificial environment in which we can act out primitive rituals whose origins are buried deep in our culture. All games ultimately derive from the hunt or the battle – that's why so many of us take them so seriously and accord almost mythical status to the heroes of the sporting arena: they are the symbolic versions of the champion hunters and warriors of the remote past. That's also why fathers tend to be so emotional about their sons' sporting performances: at some primitive level, they feel their sons are being tested for their fitness for hunt or battle.

'Run, run,' I found myself calling enthusiastically when my eight-year-old son (who hated playing cricket) was hesitating at the crease, having surprised himself with a rather good shot. Anxious to please his over-excited parent, he made a brave but belated dash for the other end and was run out. The umpire – both charitable and perceptive – called 'not out' on the excellent grounds that the folly was the father's not the son's. At that point, I withdrew in embarrassment and reflected, yet again, on the large and small acts of madness we perform in the heat of the moment.

The watching of professional sport is a far different matter. The frenzy of loyal supporters is a sign of just how desperately we crave excitement. 'I live for football' – or hockey, or baseball, or the races – is hardly an exaggeration for spectators whose working lives seem drab by comparison with the thrill of the chase on the sporting field.

Spectators' enthusiasm sometimes gets out of hand: England's football hooligans are a recurring case in point. But every culture has its own variety of sports lust. Australians, Canadians and New Zealanders sometimes berate themselves for being sports mad – witness the outpouring of national pride at the 2000 Sydney Olympics, the 2010 Vancouver Winter Olympics and New Zealand's America's Cup yachting victories in 1995 and 2000. But they are amateurs compared with the passion of the Scots, the Spanish, the Brazilians, the French or the Italians. (The Italians have the painter Caravaggio to emulate: when defeated in a game of tennis, he shot his opponent dead.)

◆

Mating rituals, from flirting to marriage, are a popular source of excitement at any age, but the yearning for a fresh burst of sexual excitement becomes an obsession for many people, especially middle-aged men who fear a decline in their sexual prowess, or women who have had enough of being taken for granted. The midlife search for a last-ditch sexual adventure is sometimes conducted within the safe boundaries of a committed relation-ship where various strategies – from sexy lingerie or tantric sex workshops to exotic holidays or Botox – might be employed to 'spice up' a couple's sex life. But the game is often played in the minefield of extramarital affairs.

> *I put my hand there, she puts her hand there – same old thing, night after night, year after year. You don't like to admit it, but it can get boring and you are vulnerable if someone else shows a bit of interest in you.*

> *A mate once told me the time to start worrying is when your wife starts buying glamorous underwear and wearing it to work.*

The boss who falls in love with his young and attractive personal assistant, jeopardising a long-term marriage and a stable family life; the bored housewife who begins an affair with the pool cleaner; the husband who starts having 'coffee' with a recently divorced female colleague in need of consolation and advice; the neglected middle-aged wife who can scarcely suppress her sexual fantasies about her parish priest . . . such scenarios are all too predictable, but no less fraught, no less painful – and no less exciting – for being clichés. And, in another cliché, they are mostly destined to end in tears. So why do we do it? We are not mindless victims of such circumstances, but our judgement can easily be impaired by the tide of hormones (especially the ebb tide) promising to sweep us away to a more dangerous and potentially more thrilling place, shimmering with sexual heat.

Following such adventures, a sheepish return to the fold might lead to a blissful rekindling of a relationship that had previously been taken for granted, but the risk is considerable: the greater probability is that the return will be marked by a partner's grudging admission that 'these things happen' and the wary re-establishment of a relationship from which another kind of bliss – ultimate trust – has been lost.

Our desire for sexual excitement operates a bit like a heat-seeking missile. Perhaps if we understood its power, we might be more cautious in the selection of its target, though the history of the universe hardly encourages confidence in the likelihood of that.

◆

Marketing companies know the depth of our desire for excitement, and they also understand that, for most of us, the excitement needs to be safe: the thrill of being first with the latest – whether in chewing gum flavours or holiday destinations, a vibrant new colour that will transform your living area, or bouncy and shiny hair that will make you the centre of attention. 'The ultimate driving machine,' promises BMW, the implication being that a BMW driver will have access to the kind of excitement not available to dullards who've settled for the safety of a Volvo or the reliability of a Toyota. 'The excitement machine' is a marketing label now pinned on everything from sports cars to rock stars and movie directors who churn out reliable hits.

The rash of cities around the world mounting festivals designed to inject excitement into the lives of their citizens – and to attract excitement-hungry tourists – is another response to our need for more stimulation than is supplied by the routines of daily life. Even Edinburgh, a jewel among European cities, has felt the need to dub itself 'Festival City' and Sydney is said to 'come alive' during its annual arts festival. Car numberplates in the state of Western Australia come right out and say it: 'The state of excitement'.

Even if you're disappointed in some particular quest for excitement, *that* can be what happened.

> *We once took the kids to this disused mining town. I don't know what we were thinking of. You could see the foundations of the twenty-five pubs that used to be there, and there were various mine-shafts and things. Our youngest lost his football down a mine-shaft, so that provided a bit of excitement. The museum was the climax – dusty and untidy and only fascinating if you were an amateur geologist. The star turn was a fake gold nugget. We all spoke in whispers and I got the giggles. The kids are in their twenties now, but they still talk about that holiday, and of course they've embellished the story over the years. They'll never let us forget it – like the pizza we once bought that made the entire family sick.*

HOW SERIOUS ARE WE ABOUT 'PEACE OF MIND'?

It's one of the great paradoxes of the human psyche: we want to be left in our comfort zones and yet we thrive on the experience of being taken out of them. Our intuitive understanding of that is why, even among the most settled and comfortable of us, there's a lurking desire for something to *happen*.

Perhaps that helps explain a fundamental contradiction in our attitudes towards this thing called 'peace of mind'. We *claim* to be yearning for it, yet we often act as if that's a mere fantasy. We *say* we want to slow down, de-stress and learn how to relax. We pay a fortune to massage therapists, yoga teachers, acupuncturists and other practitioners of various kinds in our search for relief. We seek counselling; we attend meditation classes; we swallow tranquillisers; we drink too much; we cling desperately to 'the short break' as a kind of high-octane holiday, or the furious weekly work-out at the gym to compensate for the lack of gentler, more integrated exercise every day. We push ourselves to extremes, high on endorphins, mistaking exhaustion for contentment. The struggle to find ways of reducing our stress often looks stressful in itself.

Are we fooling ourselves with all this talk about de-stressing, simplifying and slowing down? While some people have found personal pathways to peace, many more act as if stillness is tantamount to death. Most of us seem addicted to stimulation and find silence hard to cope with, even in small doses – like a pause in the conversation. Yet even the most restless souls occasionally claim to hanker after 'peace of mind'.

Observing these swirling contradictions, I'm tempted to ask, is the buzz, the rush, the stimulation generated by our busyness something we crave – and perhaps even need – more than the stability and calm we often say we want? While most of us would say we should be trying to strike a balance between the two, why does the achievement of that balance seem so elusive? I suspect it's because many of us actually welcome distractions from questioning the meaning and purpose of our lives. We half-know th
examined in a contemplative moment, such qu
us to a radical rethink about the way we live.

No doubt there are personality differences at work here: some of us are naturally inclined towards introspection and contemplation; others are more extraverted and action-oriented. If we were all preoccupied with the quest for personal peace, perhaps nothing would get done – too much *om* and not enough *oomph* doesn't sound like the right balance either. After all, it's the irritating grain of sand in the oyster that creates the pearl; it's the itch that gets the book written, or the picture painted, or the deal closed. The world needs souls to be restless sometimes.

A stillpoint at our 'centre' can be a precious place of refreshment where we nurture our sanity. Time regularly set aside for quiet meditation can help maintain our emotional stability and keep things in perspective: many people use yoga, music or religious practices for precisely this purpose. But for most of us, 'peace of mind' is a resource for living, not a way of life. It's the bracing sense of uncertainty that keeps us going.

THE DESIRE FOR
LOVE

One word frees us of all the weight and pain of life:
That word is love.

Sophocles, *Oedipus at Colonus*

'Love' must be the most flexible word in the English language. We bestow it with indiscriminate enthusiasm on dogs, children, cakes, friends, coffee, sexual partners, movies, music, books, clothes, jewellery, family members, houses, cars – to say nothing of all the paraphernalia of the IT revolution: 'I *love* my iPhone.'

So what kind of love do we desire? Romantic, erotic, altruistic, parental, sacrificial, familial, material, ethereal, companionate, divine? Those and more. Love, in all its varieties and manifestations, lights us up. Whatever emotions we care to label as love, they are overwhelmingly positive.

Love has the power to enlarge the spirit; to bring out the best in us; to encourage a greater openness to others and to inspire us to perform acts of kindness. Love comforts us, reassures us and boosts our confidence in ourselves.

Love can summon up our deepest reserves of passion and intensity and abandon us to bliss. It can bind us to our families and close friends throughout our lives. Even the pain of parting from a loved one, and the grief of bereavement, are exquisite reminders of the way loving relationships can enrich us and develop our capacity for empathy.

LEARNING TO LOVE

If we're lucky, it all begins in our mother's arms. We learn about love from the experience of being loved, nurtured and valued as babies and children. If we're unlucky, we'll miss out on that formative experience and might spend half a lifetime trying to work out what we've missed and how to compensate for it. We're not doomed if we missed out, though: there are many ways of compensating for the loss of early nurture. Being loved at any age is an education in love. But the lessons we learn about love in childhood will inevitably shape our attitude to and our capacity for love.

What do we learn, exactly? If we have devoted and caring parents in those formative years, we learn about a remarkable phenomenon called unconditional love: the idea that whatever we do, wherever we go, however much we might annoy or disappoint or offend them, our parents will still love us. This kind of love is based on a level of acceptance that doesn't depend on what we do, but only on who we are.

We learn that love is associated with intimacy – the intimacy of the mother's breast, the intimacy of being cradled in a parent's arms, the intimacy of bath-time, of bedtime stories, of cuddling up in our parents' bed, of being part of the physical closeness of a family.

As part of the lesson about intimacy, we learn about the magic of touch. In the nineteenth century, the Scottish philosopher and educationalist Alexander Bain came to the conclusion that soft, warm touch was the fundamental pleasure in all experiences of love. He called touch 'the alpha and omega of affection'.[1] Among human infants and the young of many other species, physical contact – being cuddled, held, stroked, embraced – is a powerful source of emotional comfort and security, and the need for affectionate touching never leaves most of us.

We learn from our childhood experience that a parent's love involves sacrifices made on our behalf; that love is a gift freely given and unearned. As we grow older, we might also learn that loving people (especially in the family) doesn't depend upon liking them as well.

We learn that love needs to be spoken. As children we begin to learn the language of love – the endearments, the sweet nothings that become as important to us as the actions that support them. By the very tenderness in the way these things are said, they enrich our sense of affection and reassurance.

We learn that faith is part of love. We discover that our parents believe in us; they encourage us (if we're lucky) to explore and fulfill our potential; they believe we can do more than we think we can. This kind of faith helps us grow in confidence and gives us an underpinning of emotional security, so we learn to expect that from love, too.

When we add all this up, it turns out we've learned to appreciate ourselves. We've learned about self-respect as well as love – that self-respect is love's conduit. We have to believe in ourselves – to value ourselves – if we are ever to feel worthy of another's love; and unless we feel worthy of it, we won't fully receive it. In the same way, we need a clear sense of our own value as a person if we are ever to find the courage to love.

◆

That's an idealised list of the lessons we might learn from our parents and families about love. Few of us will have been fortunate enough to have learned all of them. Some of us will have learned other lessons as well – bitter lessons, painful lessons about rejection, about our failure to meet our parents' expectations, about love being distributed in unequal proportions among us and our siblings. We might have encountered a highly conditional form of love that's dependent on how well we did at school, in sport or music, or in our conformity to the standards and conventions of the family. We might have learned that love can be given or withheld, like a reward or a punishment, or that love can be treated like a thing to be bought with gifts or other indulgences. We might have discovered a parent's capacity for jealousy of the love between the other parent and their child. We might even have sensed that a child's mere presence can be a nuisance or an inconvenience to a parent.

Whatever the lessons, they'll stick with us and shape the character of our desire for love. We might be unable to accept any love that falls short of a mother's unconditional love for her children – an unrealistic expectation in any adult relationship between independent and fair-minded equals. We might seek relationships that will compensate for the wounds we suffered in childhood, though no adult relationship – except perhaps with a counsellor – should be expected to do that, because there'll be too much taking and not enough giving.

Even if our childhood experiences of love have been exemplary, this is not an uncomplicated story. The very closeness and devotion of parents can create problems for us as we mature and start to recognise that we can't continue to have all our needs met by someone else. We come to realise – and it is an especially painful awakening for those of us who have had an indulged childhood – that there are reciprocal arrangements in families, at school and in the neighbourhood that call on us to make accommodations and adjustments in the light of other people's needs. We also have to deal with the discovery that parents have a special intimacy with each other to which we can never be admitted.

Not surprisingly, most marriage preparation classes and marriage guidance counsellors lay heavy emphasis on the kind of childhood we experienced and the dynamics of our early family life. These experiences illuminate our understanding of love, and influence our capacity to give and receive affection.

FALLING IN LOVE

This is what all the fuss is about. This is what inspires those endless love songs and poems. This is what the romantic comedies and the gauzy wedding photos celebrate.

Yet most of the love in our life is not romantic. Our desire for love is mostly satisfied through the love of friends, or family members, even the love of pets. The deep love between spouses in a long-established relationship might have begun with a high degree of romantic passion, and sex might remain central to the relationship, or it might not. It's impossible to generalise about that, or even about what people want as their relationship matures, and it would be presumptuous of any of us to assume that we can understand the trajectory of other people's intimate lives.

Still most of the talk about love is about romance and sex. In any intimate relationship, whether heterosexual, homosexual or companionate, 'falling in love' is the first of the three phases of love that typically occur in the evolution of an enduring relationship.[2]

Falling in love can be easily described. It's like a sickness, according to some physicians. Indeed, through the sixteenth and seventeenth centuries, medical treatises on 'lovesickness' were taken very seriously. The condition is characterised by high anxiety, a high level of agitation, loss of appetite and loss of concentration. (In my own case, as a young man, actual nausea as well.) One telling symptom is an obsessive focus on the person we love – always thinking about them, and manufacturing opportunities to talk about them.

It's a wild, erratic, volcanic time in anyone's life, usually accompanied by high sexual energy and intense sexual desire. There's an urgency about it; an impatience; a need to be with the other person as much as possible and a feeling of desolation when we are apart. Jealousy is often present because the intense feeling of devotion is accompanied by a corresponding sense of vulnerability: 'I couldn't bear to part with her. What if someone else tries to take her from me?' Such feelings are heightened by an exaggerated sense of the beauty, charm, wit and general desirability of the loved person. Since she is so obviously utterly enchanting, why wouldn't other people be just as enchanted as I am?

There are two decoys that can delude us into thinking we are experiencing the full passion of romantic love. 'Falling in lust' is almost indistinguishable from 'falling in love' in the early stages, because of the intensity of sexual desire in both cases. Yet the difference between them is clear: love is primarily a celebration of the inherent value of the person we admire – whether as a partner or a friend – whereas lust is primarily about our own need for sexual gratification (though it may sometimes be a dark expression of our desire for control).

The second decoy arises from the very intensity of our desire for love: we can fall in love with love – with the idea of love. We can inflate and over-interpret the small thrill of a flirtation, or the blindness of a fleeting infatuation, simply because we *want* to be swept away. In *Kissing Frogs*, Andee Jones describes her experience of seeking romantic love through internet dating and writes that 'internet-dating sites make it easy to construct our own ideal persona for another person to fall in love with',[3] and vice versa, of course. The desire for romance can easily fool us into a heightened expectation of love 'just around the corner'.

◆

Falling in love usually impairs our judgement, as many hormonal fluctuations do. Our value system can become unstable, especially if we are striving to fit in with the perceived values of the one we love. Anxious to please – to appear compatible – we find ourselves enthusing about movies or music or food we don't normally enjoy. The loved one's idiosyncratic habits, gestures and turns of phrase might ultimately come to seem irritating or even infuriating, but at this early stage they will be regarded as quaint or charming. We tend to overstate the worth of the other person, to overestimate the likelihood of this being an enduring relationship, and to make reckless declarations of love and devotion that will seem hollow if we 'wake up' from this state and lose the intensity of feeling that propelled us into it. Many aggrieved ex-lovers have complained that 'You said you would love me forever.' ('I meant it at the time' is a pretty lame defence.)

For some of us, this is a 'meaning-of-life' moment: it's as if we see things more clearly than before and believe we have discovered the only thing in the world that really matters: 'Imagine if I'd missed out on this!' Rationally, we might reject the notion that there's only one person in the world for us, but that's how it feels when we're falling in love: he or she is *the one*.

The human organism can only stand so much of all this intensity. While it is happening, we feel as if it will never fade; nor do we want it to. But time passes; either it evolves into the next, more constructive phase of *being* in love or the ardour begins to cool. Many lovers know that awful moment when it dawns on them that the passion has begun to seep out of the relationship; the desire has begun to ebb; the 'falling' stage was all there was ever going to be.

What brings it to an end? Often, it's the rapid plunge into a sexual relationship that robs the romance of its mystery and dispels what Bertrand Russell described as the 'glamorous mist'.[4] This is one reason why, before the sexual revolution, people tended to marry young and have children quickly: the intense sexual desire and joyful anticipation characteristic of the 'falling' phase propelled them into the 'being' phase before their enthusiasm could be threatened by the reality check of actually living together.

Today, when the vast majority of couples have begun a sexual relationship well before marriage, and when having multiple sexual partners is the norm rather than a stigmatised exception, it is perhaps not surprising that people's sexual passion might begin to fade well before a serious commitment is made.

'We're totally committed, for the time being' is a remark that sounds odd to members of older generations, but makes perfect sense to the rising generation of young Westerners for whom 'keeping your options open' is a way of life.

Does this mean that marriage will become a more stable institution when young people are not entering it in the first flush of passionate, romantic love? Do greater sexual experience and less sexual urgency mean couples will be more cautious and possibly more rational about the factors involved in making a 'good' marriage? That is what advocates of the sexual revolution have long argued, and there is evidence of a slight drop in the divorce rate in the USA and Australia as the marriage rates in those countries have fallen. But divorce rates are not necessarily a good guide to the state of marriage, and the picture is confused by young people's claim that because they set higher standards for their marriages than their parents did, they are likely to marry later and to divorce more easily than previous generations.[5]

Of course you want to marry for life, but only if the relationship is working.

Because falling in love is such a rich and intense experience, many people try to keep the flame alive either by setting themselves the goal of maintaining a wild sex life in their marriages – perhaps attending workshops to establish how this might be achieved – or by constantly falling in love with new people, or by trying to postpone the natural transition to the next phase of love. When Goethe believed he was falling in love with Charlotte Buff, the fiancée of a friend, 'he sought to make permanent the fleeting experience of falling in love' by attempting to foster an intense romantic friendship with her without any thought of sexual activity.[6]

Fleeting it is, and fleeting it will always be. We might prolong it by sexual abstinence, or by preserving the romantic state as if it is to be worshipped as 'sacred', but in the end, falling in love *is* a fall, and we have to land somewhere.

BEING IN LOVE

Some couples move straight from friendship to 'being in love' without ever going through the falling stage, but that's unusual. The more typical pathway to being in love is via the experience of falling in love leading to the realisation that this is serious, that we want it to lead somewhere and that we want to start work on the building of a long, stable and committed relationship.

But this is still a preparatory stage. It's not settled; not fully resolved. That's why some cultures place heavy emphasis on a formal 'engagement' where a couple announce to the world their intention of marrying and settling into a long-term relationship, while accepting that they might yet change their minds.

This is a time of radical readjustment of priorities and a refocusing of attention and energy. It is when we catch our first glimpse of the meaning of the term 'love's work' – the business of relationship building which many of us find the hardest yet most rewarding work of all. This is the phase in the evolution of love when we shift the focus from 'me' and 'you' to 'us' and the need to foster and nurture the relationship between us.

STAYING IN LOVE

This is not necessarily about marriage or even permanence. But it's a new phase of love where the focus shifts from the excitement of 'falling' and the radiant freshness of 'being' to something that feels more secure and more enduring. Now, we desire a different kind of love. We are no longer exploring and testing each other; we are ready for commitment, consolidation and the building of mutual trust.

A question that troubles many younger people contemplating a long-haul relationship is this one: 'Does commitment kill passion?' Will moving beyond the 'being in love' stage represent a transition into something duller and less energising? Will the thrill of romantic passion be lost to us? Will regular sex become too predictable? Will our partner become bored and look elsewhere for excitement? Will the experience of living together, year after year, perhaps raising children, extinguish the romantic spark?

There seems little doubt that an unrealistic attachment to the ideal of romantic love as the best or purest form of sexual love drives many partners into extramarital affairs and keeps the divorce rate high. Equally, there's no doubt that the nature of love – whether passionate or companionate – must inevitably change as we respond to the experience of being in a long-term relationship. But duller? Less energising? Predictable? *Worse?* It depends who you ask.

> *I don't want to rekindle romance in my marriage – it's far better and far stronger as it is, thanks very much. Of course we enjoyed romantic passion in the beginning. That's why we got married. But we've enjoyed married love much more, to be frank, because it isn't so fragile. It's built on commitment and trust. And I don't want some sex therapist telling me I'm missing something.*

If our desire for love becomes fixated on romantic love, then any relationship we enter will be lucky to survive beyond a few years. But if our desire is for a more mature and enduring kind of love – with a strong component of friendship, partnership and mutual support as well as sexual intimacy – then long-term loving relationships are not only possible, but sometimes turn out to be quite magical.

'Happily ever after'? That glib phrase doesn't deserve the currency it has enjoyed, but it doesn't deserve to be dismissed too lightly either. It depends on what we mean by happy. Many people in long-term relationships speak of a level of contentment, rooted in mutual trust, that exceeds their expectations, even though it might have been tinged with tragedy, disappointment, tension and occasional conflict. Their relationship mightn't be lit up by fireworks, but there's certainly a warm inner glow.

Not everyone is willing or able to adapt to the 'staying in love' phase. In the UK, Canada and Australia, about forty percent of contemporary marriages are expected to end in divorce; in the USA, the figure is closer to forty-five percent and in Scandinavia it is more than fifty percent. Those figures represent millions of personal stories too complicated to account for in a few glib generalisations, but they do suggest a widespread sense of disappointment that erodes many couples' initial enthusiasm for the journey. Many of those divorces are the end-point of a process of evolving incompatibility that took years to crystallise into impatience, indifference, hatred or simply a loss of love – even a loss of the desire for love.

◆

Much has been written about 'companionate love' as a long-term alternative to passionate love. In *A New Look at Love*, Elaine and G. William Walster describe companionate love as 'a lower-key emotion. It's friendly affection and deep attachment to someone . . . The only real difference between liking and [companionate] loving is the depth of our feelings and the degree of our involvement with the other person.'[7]

While that might be an accurate description of the kind of love that binds close friends and keeps many couples together in later life, it would sound to some loving couples a bit like cardigans and slippers at twenty paces. Yes, there might be trust, there might be a comfortable companionship, and there might even be an unswerving commitment. But isn't there also such a thing as *marital passion* that might be different from the passion of love's romantic phase, but no less satisfying?

Most loving couples who stay together for a long time will experience the full spectrum of human emotions in their dealings with each other, but their experience tells them that episodes are episodes, and that negative or hostile feelings are likely to be transient and not lethally damaging to the relationship. They may discover that the desire for love is as powerful as love itself because it can sustain a relationship through seasons of doubt or disharmony.

To young people in the full flush of romance, a love that offers more companionship than passion might seem like one step from death. And many couples come to the same conclusion as they age. Time spent together is not a reliable predictor of what might happen next.

> *Leaving him was the best thing I ever did, but I should have done it twenty years ago. When I finally took the plunge, the kids said, 'Why did you put up with it all these years?' and I said, 'Mainly for you, I suppose.' They said I shouldn't have bothered. But you do what you think is right at the time.*

> *People talk about working at your marriage. My mother is always going on about that. Well, I don't want a marriage you have to work at. I don't mind a few tiffs, but if it feels like hard work, why would you persist?*

There's no evidence to suggest that as we age and mature, the desire for love diminishes. We still need the affirmation of love, the comfort of love, the reassurance of love, the rich reward of having our offer of love accepted, the particular form of emotional security that only comes from being loved. We might obtain all those gratifications from close friends, from families and from transient intimacies, but those who are lucky enough to find they can maintain a loving relationship, year after year, into a shared old age, speak of the deep contentment that flows from still being together, and still wanting to be.

UNCONDITIONAL LOVE? THERE'S USUALLY ONE CONDITION ATTACHED

How often have you heard some version of this story:

> I've given up on men. Just hopeless. I thought we were happily married. I thought we were set for life. I was his second wife, which meant I had to get involved with the kids from his first marriage. We had them with us every weekend. I couldn't have children, but I treated those kids as if they were my own. I was as close to them as I was to him. I really loved them. And then he ran off with his secretary. I know I'm making it sound like a cliché, but it was a cliché. He went, and so did the kids. Now I never see them because of course I'm not their mother. Needless to say, it hasn't worked out with the secretary, but it's not my problem any longer. I'm over it. Now I have a lovely golden retriever – at last I have some unconditional love in my life.

Or this:

> The big difference between your mother and your wife is that your mother loves you no matter what, but your wife . . .

Earlier in the chapter, I suggested that unconditional love might be an unrealistic expectation in adult relationships. Yet we continue to hold it up as an ideal – and perhaps to desire it – because our early childhood experience of it is so powerfully formative and it's such a precious thing to experience.

Before the sexual revolution, there was an acceptance in many traditional Western marriages of a double standard. Wives, typically the submissive and dependent partners, would be expected to put up with almost anything because their property rights and earning potential were so limited compared with their husbands'. That kind of helpless dependency could easily be interpreted by a husband as a form of unconditional love, born of the wife's need for identity, shelter, security, a father for her children, and financial support. In fact, it was a situation that often burned with resentment, disappointment and barely suppressed rage. It suited men, because it fitted well with their male supremacist attitudes, but it was one of the key triggers for the revolution that was to come.

Now, in Western societies where genuine sexual partnerships are the ideal, if not always the reality, and where education levels and career prospects for women are generally equal to those of men, unconditional love (particularly of a woman for a man) is destined to become one of the rosy memories of childhood. Why should partners who exist as equals in a relationship be expected to offer each other a love that has no conditions, no standards, no expectations attached to it?

He expected me to give him the same unconditional love his mother had always given him. Well, she was totally unrealistic about him, and I wasn't going to fall into the same trap. I loved him alright, warts and all, but he didn't like me mentioning the warts. And I think he used to talk to his mother more than was healthy – I'm sure she was still telling him how wonderful he was, even when he was behaving like a complete prat. Eventually I said to him, 'If you want unconditional love, get a dog.'

When his mother died, I said to him, 'There goes your unconditional love.' He thought that was a bit heartless, but I meant it. As long as his mother was around, I think he clung to the idea that he deserved unconditional love from me, as well.

What's wrong with unconditional love? For young children, nothing. It's as vital to their emotional development as discipline is. Between adults, though, it is an unrealistic expectation. Most of us enter long-term relationships in a spirit of goodwill, but the reservation is always there, even if unspoken: if you disappoint me too bitterly, let me down too badly, deceive me or abuse my trust, I might not be able to go on loving you, even if I agree to stick with you.

People sometimes do stand by their partners – and their close friends – through all kinds of upheavals in their relationships, and who's to say whether it's unconditional love at work, a cold, loveless commitment or something in between? (Old joke: What's the four-letter word that keeps wealthy couples together? Answer: Half.)

Hillary Clinton shocked feminists around the world when she stuck by Bill: 'Did she not know what was going on?' they asked, as revelation after revelation about Bill Clinton's infidelities and indiscretions came to light. Some women took a cynical, pragmatic view: she's ambitious, and she doesn't want to destroy 'Clinton Inc.' while it serves her political purposes. Others assumed this was a fine example of unconditional love, and admired Hillary for that. 'Stand by your man [or woman], no matter what' is still considered a virtue in some quarters.

Most of us would scratch our heads at the prospect of a love that persists beyond the loss of a partner's love – the lack of mutuality would make that seem as absurd and unhealthy as unrequited love. We'll put up with a great deal and forgive a great deal as long as we keep hearing 'I still love you' (and believing it). A wise counsellor once told me that the 'left-over' partner in a disintegrating marriage can hardly be expected to hold fast to the promises made in the marriage ceremony, once the other partner's love has been withdrawn. 'If someone stops loving you,' he said, 'where's the reciprocity in that?'

'BEST FRIENDS'

Most of the non-sexual things we can say about love between partners in a romantic relationship can also be said about the love that binds close friends – especially those who regard each other as 'best friends'. Even the falling, being and staying in love stages of a sexual relationship have a kind of parallel in the stages of a blossoming friendship, beginning with a recognition of mutual attraction, the discovery of shared values and interests, and the evolution into an established relationship that might outlast the romances and even the marriages of the friends involved.

At its best, the love between close friends is based on respect for the inherent value of this person, rather than on their usefulness to us as an instrument to achieve some end of our own – an enhanced sense of our popularity or status, for instance, or a useful contact, or a good person to be seen with, or an entertaining source of gossip.

Though the conventional view is that women are generally better at intimate friendship with each other than men are with men, I'd dispute that. The bonds between men might be less explicitly acknowledged than those between women, but the rituals of male bonding – often involving drinking and playing or watching sport – are at least as powerful as those that bind women to each other.

Intimate non-sexual friendship across the gender divide has been problematical in modern Western societies. In some parts of eighteenth-century England and America, conventions such as 'bundling' (where an unmarried man and woman might lie in a bed together, with their clothes on) created circumstances regarded as perfectly respectable for the fostering of non-sexual intimacy between men and women, but today we are more wary. Even a man and woman seen dining together in public on multiple occasions will, in the absence of a 'reason' for them to be spending time together, be assumed to be having a flirtation, if not an affair.

Opportunities for non-sexual intimacy between men and women have, paradoxically, become more restricted since the sexual revolution because sexual access is now taken to be so easily achieved. In *An Intimate History of Humanity*, Theodore Zeldin refers to *amitié amoureuse* – loving friendship – as an idea as interesting as companionate marriage, and one worth exploring as 'a new form of art'.[8]

There is some anecdotal evidence to suggest that the rising generation of young adults might be challenging recent conventions and establishing new ways for men and women to develop close friendships based on non-sexual intimacy. This is a significant step in the right direction, opening up the possibility of rewarding friendships between the sexes in ways that have, for too long, been regarded as vaguely improper, unwise or risky.

THE END OF LOVE

A very close friend (I thought) once phoned me and said, 'Are you sitting down? I just want to tell you that our friendship is terminated.' Recalling it even now, I'm still shocked by the brutality and the formality of it and still unclear about his reasons for dumping me, though his wife later told me that this was a habit with him – dropping the friends from one phase of his life whenever he moved on to another. In this case, our friendship had sprung out of a working relationship, and he was moving to another job.

I know I'm not alone in experiencing the slap of rejection by a friend. I've heard many other people express their bewilderment over the end of a previously loving, apparently flourishing friendship – in or out of marriage.

Not all friendships survive, of course. Why should they? Friendship is often the result of a lucky accident of time and place, so it's not surprising that as life evolves and our situations change, friends sometimes lose contact with each other, physically or emotionally, perhaps only commemorating their previous closeness by the sending of greetings on birthdays or Christmas cards. Some friendships simply fizzle out; some crumple under the pressure of competitiveness, jealousy or a violent disagreement.

Most love affairs don't survive either – nor should they, since most of them are experiments in love. The passion of romantic love has to go somewhere – sometimes it matures into a loving long-term relationship, and sometimes it hits a wall of tough reality: 'We don't really have the heart for this, do we?'

Falling out of love is just as easy and almost as common as falling in love. Sometimes it's a gradual transition we scarcely notice until it occurs to us one day that we don't want to be together any more. Sometimes it's traumatic and hurtful, especially if one partner wants to go on and the other doesn't. Sometimes it's a blessed relief for all concerned.

If being in love were mainly about our hormonal drives and the mutual pleasure we obtain from sexual activity, we'd never fall out of love (though biologists tell us the 'falling in love' stage can be maintained for about two years – long enough for the pair to bond and produce their first offspring in the days before efficient contraception).

So why do so many couples drift apart? Why is falling out of love so easy? Why are so many marriages across Western society destined to end in divorce?

Sexual relationships end for all kinds of reasons, including some cases where the hormonal spark simply dies and there's nothing left in the way of companionship substantial enough to support a continuing relationship. But a prime contributor to the collapse of sexual relationships – in marriage or elsewhere – is the precise converse of the thing that brought the couple together in the first place. If the desire to be taken seriously is a major factor in bringing a couple together, then it remains a major factor in either keeping them together or driving them apart:

He doesn't take me seriously any more.

She doesn't understand me.

I just don't feel good about myself when I'm with him.

I used to feel like her hero – now I feel like the villain of the piece.

'I don't love you any more' is a hard declaration for anyone to make – far harder, for most of us, than a declaration of love. It's not likely to be a cry for help in the way that 'You don't love me any more' often is, so the question is: how should we respond when we find ourselves on the receiving end of a partner's withdrawal? Clearly, the contract is broken; the loss of even the desire for love has seen to that. The challenge, now, is to develop an exit strategy that preserves our respect for the love we once had.

People who have been in a loving relationship, or even a close friendship, know the line between love and hate is easily crossed: the very intimacy of the relationship means we know so much about each other that there's plenty of ammunition if we decide to wage war. Yet some separating couples recognise their parting as a test of the value, the authenticity and the seriousness of the love they previously felt for each other.

In divorce, there is some nobility in the idea that we should honour the time we spent together, acknowledging the love that drew us together in the first place and kept us together for as long as it did. That's a hard line to stick to if you feel like the aggrieved party, but the couples who manage it report a triple benefit: their own mental health is not put at risk by simmering hatreds or resentments, their circle of common friends is not broken, and they can maintain a respectful relationship when they need to see each other.

The end of a marriage – like the end of love in any setting – is best thought of as a transitional, evolutionary process. We are moving from one stage of our lives to the next, and the pain of the transition may be eased if we can acknowledge that, at least for a while, we satisfied each other's desire for love.

THE DARK SIDE: SAD, BAD, MAD LOVE

The lack of love in our lives can make us feel cold and empty; its loss – whether in romance or friendship – can create bitterness and resentment in us. When our desire for love is frustrated, we may react with anger, aggression, even violence; we may sublimate our frustration into a burst of creativity, religious fervour or reckless over-indulgence; we may withdraw into a cocoon of introspection; we may hunt for some version of love on the internet.

There are times when the desire for love is so overwhelming that we seek it in the most unlikely, irrational or desperate ways. A lonely man, bereft after a divorce, begins trawling internet dating sites, creating an idealised identity for himself that almost guarantees disappointment in the women who agree to meet him. A young woman, yearning for love that might compensate for a life of rejection, plunges into a defiant pregnancy in the hope of producing a baby who will love her when no one else does, who will be reliably there to hold and cuddle, who will never abandon her, and who will create a new identity for her: 'Now I'm a mother, and no one can take that away from me.'

Desperate, ill-judged declarations of love generally come across as an assault, an attack, or an affront.

He says he loves me and that's why he can't leave me alone. But if he really loved me, he'd respect the fact that I sometimes do need to be on my own.

When Mike realised I was seriously thinking of leaving, he wanted sex three times a day. He was desperate for it, as if he was trying to show me how much he loved me. But it didn't feel like love – it just felt like pressure. It was gross, actually.

She sends me these text messages that are just embarrassing. I've told her I'm not interested but she says she really loves me and I'll eventually realise what I'm missing.

The stalker, the jilted lover who won't let go, the possessive lover who can't bear his partner to spend time with anyone apart from him, the person who makes repeated phone calls and sends endless text messages in the absence of any encouragement or even in the face of explicit requests to desist – these are manifestations of a desire for love so seriously misdirected that no one but the person involved would attach the word 'love' to such behaviour.

And then there are those who seem destined to be disappointed in love, always choosing a potential lover who is incompatible or inappropriate, who seems attractive for reasons that scarcely qualify as love at all. The Italian poet and novelist Cesare Pavese, reflecting on his miserable love life, wrote in his diary:

Might it be true you only fall in love with women who are very popular . . . and what you like about them is that everybody desires them and you suffer because you want to be the only one to possess them.[9]

A common complaint among ex-partners is that even a reasonably amicable split can turn ugly if one of the partners meets someone new. 'I don't want her but I don't want anyone else to have her, either' might sound unreasonable and possessive – and might seem a million miles from what we would normally call love – but which of us is reasonable when it comes to the management of our emotional lives, especially after a marriage or love affair has ended?

After my husband left, it took me ages to find my self-confidence again, and I think he liked that. He would come around and offer to help with jobs around the house, or drive me places. It was as if he wouldn't let me go, even though he was the one who left the marriage. I think he had a girlfriend at first, but that didn't last. Then I started going out with someone, and he went ballistic. He would come knocking on my door quite late at night, or ring me at all odd hours. Eventually, I threatened to call the police if he wouldn't leave me alone. That shut him up.

My wife was determined to go, even though she could never really say why. She wanted to stay friends – she just didn't want to be married to me. After she left, we'd meet occasionally, all reasonably friendly, although it always got tense if I

was foolish enough to mention the 'r' word – reconciliation.
She wouldn't have a bar of that. It took me a while to accept
that she really didn't love me any more – she just wanted me
on a string. She was pretty chilly when I told her I was going
to remarry, but it was the baby that really turned her nasty.
She had never been interested in having children but when
she found out my new wife was pregnant, she started telling
our friends she'd always wanted kids and I was the one who
wouldn't have them. Now she's telling anyone who'll listen
that the split was all my idea in the first place.

One of the first lessons we ever learn about romantic love is
actually a lesson about love itself: if it's not reciprocal, it's not
love. Apart from the first rush of attraction, before anything
has been declared, you can't separate love from the idea of a
relationship. Unrequited love is a neurosis: if it persists, it needs
treatment. The lovesick swain is an appealing image, at least to
poets, but if there's no response from the loved one, the sickness
should not normally persist beyond a few weeks. Similarly, the
person who desperately wants to 'be friends' with someone, in the
absence of any encouragement, may be in the grip of a distorted
or unrealistic desire for a particularly intense or exclusive variety
of friendship.

Narcissistic self-love is another manifestation of a distorted
desire for love. Devoted admiration of the self is actually a barrier
both to giving love and to receiving it from others. The 'closed
system' of the self-absorbed narcissist is a pathetic, tragic distortion
of the very idea of love because of the absence of any relational
context for it. (Even those who resort to masturbation for sexual
relief generally incorporate the idea of connection with someone

else into their fantasies. The quaint idea that masturbation is a form of 'self-love' rather misses the point: in most cases, masturbation is precisely the opposite – it's a yearning for sexual union.)

The desire for love always turns dark when it is simplistically equated with sexual love, partly because sex is so famous for blurring the distinction between love and lust. Though sex is an important part of the relationship between many loving couples, love itself transcends the sexual urge. The lover who can only interpret a partner's lack of interest in sex, however temporary, as a withholding of love has foolishly narrowed the meaning and focus of love to one tiny fragment of all love's possibilities.

The desire for love is not a means to an end in the way sexual desire usually is. Sex is also rather less discriminating than love: many people can recall occasions when they were persuaded, for all kinds of reasons, to have sex with someone they didn't love, but who could ever be persuaded to *love*?

THE 'SPECTRUM OF LOVE'

If you've ever attended a Christian marriage ceremony, you will probably have heard someone read the thirteenth chapter of Paul's first letter to the church at Corinth (1 Corinthians 13) from the New Testament. Many couples choose to have that passage read because it strikes them as a stirring description of the gold standard of love.

Whether our love is in the context of a sexual relationship or a deep friendship, these words express what most of us aspire to in the love we give and receive. The essence of the chapter is contained in three short sentences:

Love is patient; love is kind and envies no one. Love is never boastful, nor conceited, nor rude; never selfish, not quick to take offence. Love keeps no score of wrongs; does not gloat over others' sins, but delights in the truth.

In the late nineteenth century, Henry Drummond, a Scottish clergyman, preached a sermon based on 1 Corinthians 13 that was later published as a book, *The Greatest Thing in the World*. It became an international publishing phenomenon, outsold only by the Bible. From his analysis of those three verses, Drummond distilled what he called the nine ingredients of the Spectrum of Love: patience, kindness, generosity, humility, courtesy, unselfishness, good temper, guilelessness, sincerity.[10]

Drummond's point was simple and direct: love is about action as much as feeling; goodness is as much about courtesy and kindness as anything grander; the person who truly loves seeks no recognition or reward for their acts of love. Love is inseparable from personal integrity.

Beyond the agonies and ecstasies of love, beyond the metaphors, beyond the intimations of bliss and the terminal misery of spurned lovers, the central idea of the literature of love is clear: true love is constant and faithful. Love perseveres (though not in the face of rejection: then it withdraws without rancour). Fickleness is love's antithesis and deceitfulness its undoing.

The desire for love is the deepest of all our desires because love is our richest source of emotional security, personal serenity and confidence. When freely given, love is also our most enduring contribution to a better world.

ENDNOTES

WHY DID I DO *THAT?*

1 Gordon Livingston, *Too Soon Old, Too Late Smart*, Hachette Australia, Sydney, 2005

THE DESIRE TO BE TAKEN SERIOUSLY

1 Helen Bamber, in an ABC TV interview with Andrew Denton as part of his 'Elders' series, 23 November 2009
2 Professor Bruce Robinson, talking on *Life Matters*, ABC Radio National, 7 January 2010
3 Dan Silkstone, 'Lightning Bolt in rush to achieve immortality', *Sydney Morning Herald*, 17 August 2009
4 John Marsden, 'The Arts and Sport', *Weekend of Ideas*, Manning Clark House, Canberra, 2008
5 Neil Simon, *Rewrites: A memoir*, Simon & Schuster, New York, 1996
6 Alfie Kohn, *Punished by Rewards*, Houghton Mifflin, New York, 1993

7 Dr David Delvin, *The Book of Love*, New English Library, London, 1974

THE DESIRE FOR 'MY PLACE'

1 'Australians at Home', *The Ipsos Mackay Report*, Ipsos Australia, No. 114, December 2004
2 Anthony King, *Housing assistance; the lifetime impact*, Australian Housing and Urban Research Institute, Report No. 20, July 2002

THE DESIRE FOR SOMETHING TO BELIEVE IN

1 Joseph Campbell, *The Hero with a Thousand Faces*, Fontana Books, London, 1993 (first published 1949)
2 Don Cupitt, in an interview on *Compass*, ABC TV, 23 March 2003
3 I am grateful to Dr Bruce Kaye for supplying the form of words to express this point
4 Clifford Geertz, *The Interpretation of Cultures*, Fontana, London, 1973
5 James Wood, 'God in the Quad' in *The New Yorker*, 31 August 2009
6 Richard Dawkins, *The God Delusion*, Houghton Mifflin, New York, 2006
7 Sam Harris, *Letter to a Christian Country*, Knopf, New York, 2006
8 Christopher Hitchens, *God is Not Great: How Religion Poisons Everything*, Twelve Books, New York, 2007
9 Richard Eckersley, *Ockham's Razor*, ABC Radio National, 2007
10 Hans Küng, *Theology for the Third Millennium: An Ecumenical View*, translated by Peter Heinegg, William Collins & Sons, London, 1988
11 Though generally attributed to this English essayist and novelist, the quote cannot actually be found in his work . . . so we *believe* Chesterton said it, or something like it, just as we *believe* Socrates rather superciliously declared 'The unexamined life is not worth living', though we only have a translation of Plato's account of Socrates's work to go by

12 Bertrand Russell, 'The Recrudescence of Puritanism' in *Sceptical Essays*, Unwin Books, London 1960 (first published 1935)

13 A.A. Mason, 'A Psychoanalyst Looks at a Hypnotist: A Study of Folie à Deux' in *Psychoanalytic Quarterly*, 63:641–679, 1994

14 Jonathan Miller, *The Body in Question*, BBC Television, 1978

15 William Barrett, *Irrational Man*, Heinemann, London, 1961

16 Sheila O'Neill, 'OK, so HRT is not the elixir of youth. Now what?' in *Osteoblast*, March 2006

17 Richard Eckersley, personal email to the author, January 2010

18 Diane Nash, quoted in David Remnick, 'The Promise' in *The New Yorker*, 15 & 22 February 2010

19 Ian Stevenson, *Twenty Cases Suggestive of Reincarnation*, University Press of Virginia, Charlottesville, 1974

THE DESIRE TO CONNECT

1 Carl Rogers, 'What it means to become a person' in *On Becoming a Person*, Constable, London, 1961

2 J.D. Salinger, quoted by Lillian Ross in *The New Yorker*, 8 February 2010

3 Lama Surya Das, *Awakening the Buddha Within*, Bantam Books, Sydney, 1997

4 Viktor Shklovsky, 'Art as Technique' in *Russian Formalist Criticism: Four Essays*, Lee T. Lemon and Marion Reiss (eds), University of Nebraska Press, Lincoln, 1965 (essay first published in 1917)

5 Pam Heaton, 'Music – shelter for the frazzled mind?' in *The Psychologist*, Vol 22 No. 12, December 2009

6 Richard Gill, 'The young person's guide to the orchestra . . . is lacking' in *The Sydney Morning Herald*, 2 September 2009

7 Richard Glover, 'The literary art of mud brick houses' in *The Sydney Morning Herald*, 30 January 2010

8 Carl Rogers, 'Dealing with breakdowns in communication' in *On Becoming a Person*, Constable, London, 1961

9 Meghan O'Rourke, 'Good Grief' in *The New Yorker*, 1 February 2010

10   Erich Fromm, *The Art of Loving*, Harper Colquhoun Books, New York, 1962

11   Martin Amis, *The Pregnant Widow*, Jonathan Cape, London, 2010

12   Richard Jefferies, *The Story of My Heart*, quoted in Victor Gollancz, *A Year of Grace*, Penguin, Harmondsworth, 1955

THE DESIRE TO BE USEFUL

1   Wendy Iredale and Mark Van Vugt, 'The peacock's tail of altruism' in *The Psychologist*, Vol 22 No. 11, November 2009

2   Robert Cialdini, *Influence: The Psychology of Persuasion*, William Morrow & Company, New York, 1983

3   Thomas à Kempis, *The Imitation of Christ*, translated by Betty I. Knott, Fontana Books, London, 1963

4   Bertrand Russell, 'In Praise of Idleness' in *In Praise of Idleness and Other Essays*, Unwin Books, London, 1960 (first published 1935)

THE DESIRE TO BELONG

1   Carl Rogers, 'Directions in Therapy' in *On Becoming a Person*, Constable, London, 1961

2   Alexander Trocchi, *Cain's Book*, Calder, London, 1992 (first published 1960)

3   Margaret Mead – a remark apparently made in an interview, widely quoted but not attributable to her written work

4   Garrison Keillor, *Wobegon Boy*, Viking Penguin, New York, 1997

5   Bruce N. Kaye, *Conflict and the Practice of Christian Faith*, Cascade Books, Eugene, Oregon, 2009

6   George Steiner, *After Babel*, Oxford University Press, London, 1975

7   Jorge Luis Borges, Introduction to *The Aleph and Other Stories*, Jonathan Cape, London, 1971

THE DESIRE FOR MORE

1   Clive Hamilton, *Growth Fetish*, Allen & Unwin, Sydney, 2003

2   Ross Gittins, 'When growth turns into a monster' in *The Sydney Morning Herald*, 7 May 2008

3 Taylor Branch, *The Clinton Tapes*, Simon & Schuster, New York, 2009

4 Theodore Zeldin, *An Intimate History of Humanity*, Sinclair-Stevenson, London, 1994

5 Sebastian Faulks, *A Week in December*, Hutchinson, London, 2009

6 Alexander Trocchi, *Cain's Book*, John Calder, London, 1992 (first published in 1960)

THE DESIRE FOR CONTROL

1 Alvin Toffler, *Future Shock*, Bantam, New York, 1971

2 S.N. Hayes and B.J. Gersh, 'Chronic stable angina' in P.S. Douglas (ed.), *Cardiovascular Health and Disease in Women* (2nd edition), W.B. Saunders, Philadelphia, 2002

3 Michael King, *The Penguin History of New Zealand*, Penguin Books, Auckland, 2003

4 Caroline Maclean, 'Gloomy Sunday Afternoons' in *London Review of Books*, 10 September 2009

5 Marcel Proust, *In Search of Lost Time*, Vol vi, 1925

6 F. Scott Fitzgerald, in an undated letter written to his daughter

7 Mike Hulme, 'The true meaning of climate change' in *New Scientist*, 5 September 2009

8 Hans and Michael Eysenck, *Mindwatching*, Michael Joseph, London, 1981

THE DESIRE FOR SOMETHING TO HAPPEN

1 Somerset Maugham, *A Writer's Notebook*, Heinemann, London, 1949

2 Gary Small & Gigi Vorgan, *iBrain: Surviving the Technological Alteration of the Modern Mind*, HarperCollins, New York, 2008

3 P.G. Wodehouse, *Summer Lightning*, Penguin, Mitcham, Vic, 1954 (first published 1929)

4 Jerome Kagan, *Surprise, Uncertainty and Mental Structures*, Harvard University Press, Cambridge, Mass, 2007

5 Mark Johnson, 'Developing human brain functions' in *The Psychologist*, Vol 22 No. 11, November 2009

6 Norman Doidge, *The Brain that Changes Itself*, Scribe, Melbourne, 2007

7 Gordon Livingston, *Too Soon Old, Too Late Smart*, Hachette Australia, Sydney, 2005

8 Richard Stamp, personal email to the author, 2009

9 Viktor Frankl, *Man's Search for Meaning*, Beacon Press, Boston, 1959 (first published 1946)

THE DESIRE FOR LOVE

1 Alexander Bain, quoted in Irving Singer, *The Nature of Love 3: The Modern World*, University of Chicago Press, Chicago, 1987, p 349

2 Irving Singer, *The Nature of Love 3: The Modern World*, University of Chicago Press, Chicago, 1987

3 Andee Jones, *Kissing Frogs*, Finch Publishing, Melbourne, 2010

4 Bertrand Russell, *Marriage and Morals*, Unwin Books, London, 1961 (first published 1929)

5 Rebecca Huntley, *The World According to Y*, Allen & Unwin, Sydney, 2006

6 John Armstrong, *Love, life, Goethe*, Penguin, London, 2007

7 Elaine and G. William Walster, *A New Look at Love*, Addison-Wesley, Reading, 1978

8 Theodore Zeldin, *An Intimate History of Humanity*, Sinclair-Stevenson, London, 1994

9 Cesare Pavese, *This Business of Living: Diaries 1935–50*, translated by A.E. Murch, quoted in Tim Parks, 'Stop it and Act', *London Review of Books*, Vol 32 No. 3, 11 February 2010

10 Henry Drummond, *The Greatest Thing in the World*, Hodder & Stoughton, London, 2009 (first published 1890)

ACKNOWLEDGEMENTS

The idea for this book has been with me for a long time, but the specific impetus for writing it came from my publisher at Hachette Australia, Bernadette Foley, who has been a continuing source of support and encouragement.

'The desire for "my place"' is a revised and extended version of my 2008 Annual Lecture for the National Trust of Australia (NSW Division).

'The desire for control' is based on my 2008 Annual Lecture for the Australian Psychological Society, later published as an essay, 'The culture of control', in the Spectrum section of the *Sydney Morning Herald*. It has been extensively revised and expanded here.

As mentioned in the Introduction, the italicised quotations that occur throughout the text are drawn from many sources, but primarily from participants in the long-term social research project, *The Ipsos Mackay Report* (previously *The Mackay Report*). My thanks to Hugh Amoyal, chief executive of Ipsos Australia, for permission to quote from these reports.

I am grateful to Bruce Kaye, Robert McLaughlin and David Mackay for their critical advice and guidance and for reading and responding to sections of an early draft of the manuscript. I have also received encouragement and advice, including specific suggestions about content, from David Dale, Virginia Henderson, Alanna Mackay, John Sheldon, Norman Swan, Julian Wood and my personal assistant, Stephanie Wells.

My wife, Sheila, has been unfailingly supportive, and her enthusiasm for the project has sustained me. She has read and commented on each draft of the manuscript and contributed several case studies and other insights from her field of medical research. I gratefully dedicate the book to her.

INDEX

Hugh Mackay is an Australian psychologist, social researcher and the author of thirteen books, including five novels. In recognition of his pioneering work in social research, he has been awarded honorary doctorates by Western Sydney, New South Wales, Macquarie and Charles Sturt universities. He was elected a Fellow of the Australian Psychological Society in 1984 and received the University of Sydney's Alumni Award for achievement in community service in 2004. He has been a newspaper columnist for more than twenty-five years, and is currently working on his sixth novel.